AF605912

ON AMISTÀ

Negotiating Friendship in Dante's Italy

On Amistà

Negotiating Friendship in Dante's Italy

ELIZABETH COGGESHALL

UNIVERSITY OF TORONTO PRESS
Toronto Buffalo London

Toronto Buffalo London
utorontopress.com
Printed in the U.S.A.

ISBN 978-1-4875-4817-9 (cloth)
ISBN 978-1-4875-4819-3 (EPUB)
ISBN 978-1-4875-4820-9 (PDF)

Library and Archives Canada Cataloguing in Publication

Title: On amistà : negotiating friendship in Dante's Italy / Elizabeth Coggeshall.
Names: Coggeshall, Elizabeth A., author.
Series: Toronto Italian studies.
Description: Series statement: Toronto Italian studies | Includes bibliographical references and index.
Identifiers: Canadiana (print) 20220396663 | Canadiana (ebook) 2022039671X | ISBN 9781487548179 (cloth) | ISBN 9781487548193 (EPUB) | ISBN 9781487548209 (PDF)
Subjects: LCSH: Dante Alighieri, 1265–1321 – Criticism and interpretation. | LCSH: Dante Alighieri, 1265–1321 – Friends and associates. | LCSH: Italian literature – To 1400 – History and criticism. | LCSH: Friendship in literature. | LCSH: Friendship – Italy, Northern – History – To 1500.
Classification: LCC PQ4432.F75 C64 2023 | DDC 851/.1–dc23

We wish to acknowledge the land on which the University of Toronto Press operates. This land is the traditional territory of the Wendat, the Anishnaabeg, the Haudenosaunee, the Métis, and the Mississaugas of the Credit First Nation.

This book was published with the generous assistance of a Book Subvention Award from the Medieval Academy of America.

University of Toronto Press acknowledges the financial support of the Government of Canada, the Canada Council for the Arts, and the Ontario Arts Council, an agency of the Government of Ontario, for its publishing activities.

Canada Council for the Arts   Conseil des Arts du Canada

Funded by the Government of Canada   Financé par le gouvernement du Canada   Canada

For Pete

~

IN MEMORIAM

Tina Coggeshall Khachiev, first friend

Contents

Acknowledgments

This book owes its existence first and foremost to the support structures I have found during my time at Florida State University. I am indebted to my extraordinary colleagues in the Italian Program – Reinier Leushuis, Mark Pietralunga, Katy Prantil, Silvia Valisa, and Irene Zanini-Cordi. Their sacrifices helped to give me the time and space to write the book, and their friendship heartened me through the project. I also thank the graduate and undergraduate students in our program, our administrative staff in Modern Languages and Linguistics (especially Jeannine Spears and Jenny Morton), as well as my colleagues and friends across the department and the humanities departments at Florida State as a whole. In particular, I want to recognize my colleagues in the Medieval Studies Workshop, who have been so willing to cross disciplinary boundaries for collaboration and community. I am also honoured to have received institutional support for this project in the form of two grants from FSU's Council on Research & Creativity.

I remain exceedingly grateful to the committee that helped me develop the earliest articulation of this project. I thank Sepp Gumbrecht, Carolyn Springer, Heather Webb, and above all Robert Harrison, for their mentorship throughout my time at Stanford University and beyond. My many unforgettable interactions with Robert – his anecdotes, his talks, his teaching, his toasts, his advice – changed the way I think about what it means to be a humanist, and I will be forever in his debt. My development as an early career researcher at Stanford also owes much to Dan Edelstein, Joshua Landy, and the teaching team and students in the Structured Liberal Education Program, from whose relentless curiosity and intellectual stamina I learned so much.

There are three additional individuals that I would single out for their interventions in the various stages of my early career. I would not be where I am today were it not for meeting Christian Moevs in my first year as an undergraduate at the University of Notre Dame. It is entirely his doing that I ever wanted to be a *dantista*, and I aspire to be a shadow of the teacher and thinker that he is. I thank him for his wisdom. Throughout my PhD and in the years following it, Teodolinda

Barolini intervened in brief but immeasurably impactful ways. On paper there was no reason for her to stand in my corner, and nevertheless she went out of her way to provide me her guidance and her advocacy. I thank her for her encouragement. Lastly, Arielle Saiber has been my most supportive mentor, my fiercest champion, my most stimulating interlocutor, and my most trusted confidante in the field. Despite meeting her when I was still a graduate student, and formalizing our collaboration only shortly after, she has always treated me as her colleague and equal. I thank her – profoundly – for her friendship.

For reading and commenting on my writing, as well as for their conversations, questions, mentorship, and advice over these many years of my early career, I thank Albert Ascoli, David Bowe, Francesco Ciabattoni, Alison Cornish, Christopher Kleinhenz, Akash Kumar, Anne Leone, Dennis Looney, David Lummus, Simone Marchesi, Kristina Olson, Deborah Parker, Guy Raffa, and Mary Watt. I want to warmly thank the organizers and participants in the seminar on "Dante's Theology" held at the Tantur Institute in Jerusalem, sponsored by the University of Notre Dame in the summer of 2013. I give special thanks to Vittorio Montemaggi and Matthew Treherne for their intellectual and interpersonal generosity. I am also grateful to Catherine Adoyo, Thomas Graff, and Laura Ingallinella, for an inspiring conversation at a late stage of the production of this book. Each of these discussions still resonates loudly in my thinking on the *Commedia.*

I was lucky to be introduced early in my time on the tenure track to the resources of the National Center for Faculty Development and Diversity (NCFDD), especially those that run the Faculty Success Program (FSP), which I joined in spring 2018. The resources provided by NCFDD and the mentors in FSP helped me to cultivate stronger, more sustainable, and more productive writing habits, as well as a healthier relationship to work. Beyond this, FSP introduced me to two friends, Hilary Barnes and Alison Greene, whose weekly telephone check-ins continue to sustain me through the more challenging aspects of writing.

This book also benefitted from the professional services of first-rate developmental editors. The brilliant team at TextFormations, Amyrose McCue Gill and Lisa Regan, provided critical assistance framing the book in its early stages. As I began working through chapter drafts, I had the great fortune of meeting the incomparable Julia Boss. Julia pored over every page of the manuscript, rooting out mixed metaphors and faulty logic. Her attention is worth its weight in gold (and of course every remaining error and stylistic infelicity is mine).

I thank Suzanne Rancourt of the University of Toronto Press for sharing her extensive expertise as a shepherd of projects through the publication process. Arianna Contreras and Jonathan DaSo provided priceless help with the bibliography. I am also indebted to two anonymous readers, whose shrewd insights made this a better book.

I am extremely fortunate to boast the following friends, who have provided kindness, support, brilliance, and humor, as well as a resolve I could lean on when mine was lacking: Sheila Bock, Michelle Bumatay, Mac Carley, Melanie Conroy, Matt Goldmark, Lisa Hicks, Michaela Hulstyn, Virginia Lewis, Merry Beth Low, Katie McKeown, Ciara Murphy, Chris Onorato, and Virginia Ramos. My parents, Linda Guetterman and Mark Coggeshall, my sister Christine Khachiev, my grandmother Myra Coggeshall, my stepmother Teresa Corcoran, my uncle Mike Coggeshall, and my in-laws Ted and Barb Maiers, have been a source of infinite love and unconditional support. I thank each of them for the providing me and my family with a stable base from which to navigate everything from cross-country moves to the first two years of COVID-19, not to mention the writing of this book.

Three final names deserve special mention. This project had its roots in my friendship with Christy Wampole. Thank you, Christy, for your nourishing generosity, your vibrant mind, your keen sense of discernment, your unshakeable confidence in me, and your outrageous puns.

For Annabel, who was born at the same time this book was and has grown alongside it, I thank you for your fancy, creativity, curiosity, and laughter. Without you the world would be much smaller.

And my greatest debt is to Pete, whose partnership makes the ground – wherever it may be – more solid beneath my feet. If I am pressed to say why I love him, I feel that I cannot better express it than by answering: "Because it is he; because it is me." This book is dedicated to him.

Parts of chapter 1 were previously published in "Jousting with Verse: The Poetics of Friendship in Duecento *Comuni*" in *Italian Culture* 38.2 (2020): 99–118. Parts of chapter 4 appeared in "'Eternal Hate Created Me As Well': In Search of Hate in Dante's *Commedia*," in *Dante's Volume from Alpha to Omega: Inscriptions on the Poet's Universe*, edited by Carol Chiodo and Christiana Purdy (Tempe, AZ: Arizona Center for Medieval and Renaissance Studies, 2021), 153–70. I thank the editors of these presses for permission to reprint.

ON AMISTÀ

Introduction: The Dilemmas of Friendship in Dante's Italy

At the beginning of Dante's *Inferno*, the pilgrim famously finds himself lost in a dark wood, profoundly and terrifyingly alone. The opening scene of the *Divine Comedy* is a fearful confrontation with solitude, the forced exclusion and estrangement of the individual from the community because of sin. But that paralyzing solitude is quickly remedied when the shade of Virgil suddenly appears, explaining to the fearful and awe-struck pilgrim the reason for his coming: Beatrice, the pilgrim's long deceased love, has enlisted Virgil's assistance in guiding her friend from the deserted shore to the safety of the city. "L'amico mio," she calls him, "my friend, and no friend of fortune."[1]

While even the earliest commentators sought to disentangle the thread of Beatrice's expression that Dante is not a friend "de la ventura," her self-definition as "amico" of the pilgrim has seemed warranted, perhaps even expected, by many scholars. Recently several contributions have sought to demonstrate the consistency of her use of the term "amico" with contemporary sources on friendship: primarily with Aristotelian-Ciceronian claims of mutuality and virtue, reconsidered, transmuted, or transformed in the light of Christian salvation.[2] Furthermore her use of the term "amico" to describe, or even recast, an erotic relationship seems to derive directly from Cicero's own etymology of the term "amicitia," which, he claims, gets its very name from the word "amor" ("Amor enim, ex quo amicitia nominata est").[3] Beatrice's self-definition likewise accords with the term's usage among the Provençal troubadours, for example, who frequently referred to lovers as "amis," charging the terms of friendship with erotic voltage. In Heloise's letters to Abelard, she claims that she would prefer that Abelard call her "amica" rather than wife; the word is frequently translated as "mistress."[4] And it shares echoes with the Song of Songs, where the Bridegroom refers throughout to his beloved as "amica mea." Indeed, it seems that Beatrice could have scarcely called the pilgrim by any other name.

And yet Beatrice's use of the term "amico mio" to describe the pilgrim is one of the most complicated uses of the term we find across Dante's corpus, precisely for its distinction from the ways he had employed the term in previous contexts. This is the only time in his corpus he will assign the name "friendship" to his relationship to Beatrice, and Beatrice is the only figure in the entire *Divine Comedy* to call the pilgrim by the name "friend."[5] Furthermore, in the latter half of the Italian Duecento, the term had taken on great ambivalence in other spheres of literary activity. For the vernacular poets of Dante's generation, the terms of friendship – *amicizia, amistade,* and *amistà* in Dante's Italian – not only pervade literary discourse; they are constitutive of that discourse. In other words, poets relied on their so-called "amici" to promote and circulate their poems, calling on "friends" to solidify their claims to entry into and centrality within literary networks, whether the figurative *piazza* of lyric exchange, the academic Studium, or the signorial court. For these vernacular writers, *amistà* and its related terms were redolent with tensions – network-building inclusivity or dyadic exclusivity, disinterestedness or personal advantage, hierarchical status or implied equality, harmonious uniformity or distinctive multiplicity – that would have practical social consequences in the various literary milieux of northern Italy at the turn of the fourteenth century.[6]

In *On Amistà* I examine the strategic ways that Dante, in conversation with his peers, employs the terminology of *amicizia* over the course of his literary career as indications of an emergent and disruptive contestation over the value of friendship in the competitive literary communities of the northern Italian urban centres. This contestation, in the decades preceding the momentous cultural shift towards secular humanism, ultimately secured the value of preferential, individual, and instrumental attachments (*amistadi*) within the poetic agora of northern Italy.[7] In other words, if we want to understand how Petrarch could become the "first modern friend," as Hannah Chapelle Wojciehowski has notably described him, we have to look carefully at the ways his immediate predecessors thought and wrote about their "amici."[8] Where Petrarch and other early humanists – a movement that was seeing its earliest stirrings in these decades – would come to view even instrumental friendships as critical to healthy human sociability and moral development, the writers and thinkers of Dante's generation discussed friendship as a much more fraught relationship than has previously been considered, complicated by certain sociopolitical tensions specific to this pivotal time and place.

In this book, I consider the labels *amico* and *amicizia*, as well as related terms, as these appear in four of Dante's works: *Vita nova*, *De vulgari eloquentia*, the Epistle to Cangrande, and the *Commedia*. Each of these texts uses the terms of *amistà* or *amicizia* as a practical intervention in a particular field of social engagement. By inscribing each of these works within the sociohistorical conditions of its composition – with all the attenuating disputes around the definition and use of *amicizia* in that particular literary milieu – I show how one of the most prolific authors of the Italian Middle Ages carefully integrated and strategically deployed competing models of friendship to different ends and in diverse social contexts.

I focus on the emergent theory of friendship across Dante's corpus not because his innovations in friendship theory were more impactful than those of his peers, nor because his writing on friendship was especially representative of its period. Rather, in Dante's corpus we have the most complete representation of a single individual's evolving perspective on the strategic values of friendship in specific social milieux.

Traditional Christian models of sociability – derived from a reading of Ciceronian *amicitia* in a moralizing key – generally relied on notions of universality, equality, and disinterestedness in friendships. Cicero's dialogue *Laelius sive de amicitia* (44 BCE) had circulated in the medieval Christian West for centuries. But when Aristotle's *Nicomachean Ethics* and other writings on friendship became newly accessible in Robert Grosseteste's mid-thirteenth-century Latin translation, they produced what historian Bénédicte Sère rightly calls "un choc sensible" [a perceptible shock] on the intellectual landscape of medieval Christendom.[9] Unlike Christian-Ciceronian models of friendship, Aristotelian friendship permitted qualities like individual preference, social inequality, and certain forms of self-interestedness or instrumental advantage. As Aristotelian ethical theory was mapped onto Christian intellectual societies, authors in the nascent vernacular tradition were presented with contradictory tenets which demanded negotiation and resolution. They conducted these negotiations in the exchanges of texts – letters, correspondence poems, dedications, narratives, and even treatises, which pretend to a kind of universal reach – where late medieval authors would contest, both implicitly and explicitly, the ethics of friendship practices like agreement and dispute, praise and reproach, flattery and self-promotion. The picture of friendship that emerges over the course of Dante's works favours exclusivity, competition, self-interest, and hierarchy. These preferences challenge the theoretical notions of *amicitia* espoused by classicizing and Christian authors alike, and the strategic pursuit of such qualities in friendship provides the ethical rationale for the "expanding menu" of types of *amicizia* that could be claimed and exploited by writers in the early Renaissance.[10]

For humanist writers, *amicitia* would become the most capacious and adaptable descriptor of human relationships. Friendship would not be treated as the uniquely moral bedrock of human society we might imagine, but as a sometimes disingenuous, often self-interested, and always dynamic frame for all manner of social relations, both those that strove towards a certain universal kind of virtue and those that did not. But, as these chapters will demonstrate, the possibilities and the pitfalls of such a capacious category of human sociality had been mined by the writers of the generation preceding. The *literati* of Dante's generation inherited certain theoretical disputes around the problems and possibilities inherent to the conception of *amicitia*. They employed the terms "amico," "amistà," "amistade," and "amicizia" as instrumental means to negotiate reputation, fame, and honour – the most coveted currencies of symbolic capital within the competitive society of the northern Italian urban centres. Relationships within the community of *literati* were most commonly framed in the language of *amistà*, and, particularly with the rediscovery and integration of Aristotle's broad notion of *philia* (in Latin, *amicitia*), which could encompass not only morally improving relationships with peers but also instrumental and pleasurable friendships across the social spectrum, the term "amico" became the most flexible category through which to negotiate one's social standing within diverse and overlapping social and intellectual networks.

The language of friendship offered writers like Dante a set of terms adaptable to particular strategic ends in the specific milieux of literary networks. Among this earlier generation of thinkers, Dante's appears to have been a prominent voice, even if not the only one, on the question of friendship's practical and instrumental value. He employed the terms pointedly across his major works. Furthermore, Dante's network connections are numerous, as are his surviving works, and together they touch a number of the crucial spheres of social relations within the interrelated networks of literary production and dissemination. What makes his works compelling as the centre of a study of late-medieval vernacular *amicizia*, then, is that they reveal the variety of strategic moves employed by writers within and against the social conventions of the period, as they sought to negotiate the integration of the Aristotelian spectrum of social relationships with existing Ciceronian and Christian sensibilities.

To study the ways that Italian vernacular writers of the last decades of the medieval period and the first decades of secular humanism negotiated friendship's demands, we must read texts as practical interventions in the specific social milieux in which they are embedded. In taking this historical and sociological approach to the study of these texts, distancing them from idealizing and artificial discourses on *vera amicitia* to see how they represent specific engagements in sociohistorical fields, I follow the recent work of Teodolinda Barolini, whose commentary on Dante's early lyrics unveils his ambiguous use of the term "amico" in the late Duecento poetic agora.[11] Building on the groundwork Barolini has laid in a series of articles and essays, I would further emphasize that, for Dante as for the majority of writers in the late Duecento, *amicizia* or *amistà* was the primary social matrix for a poet's formation and development. What was unique to the literary communities in which he began his career was their relative independence from the oversight of sponsors or patrons, in comparison to other contemporary vernacular literary traditions. Within the independent poetic circles of the northern Italian *comuni*, absent the sponsorship of a lord, poets were obliged to rely on internal means to settle disputes and to negotiate power. It was in these agonistic conditions that Dante and his interlocutors crafted a new language of hierarchies, allegiances, collaborations, and rivalries. Their negotiations in what we might think of as the figurative *piazza* of literary exchange went forward under the guise of *amicizia*.

Beyond their own competitive literary circles, the Italian vernacular poets of Dante's generation also engaged with intellectual networks in other social fields that could prove critical to literary production and dissemination, such as the academic *Studia* and, especially, the signorial courts. As *signori* consolidated power in certain urban centres, poets who sought sponsorship in a court – both for the promotion of their work and also, for exiles, to meet basic needs like bread and shelter – were compelled to align themselves strategically with the locally specific and targeted political interests of their sponsors while also looking to edge out peers with whom they would compete for the patron's affection and the comparatively limited resources that came with it. Each of these fields of social interaction – from the self-governing communal networks, to the well-regulated academic corporations, to the hierarchically ordered courts – inscribed the literature of the period with its own currencies and systems of exchange, as both texts and reputations circulated within and between a number of interrelated, ever-evolving networks. A sociological approach, then, clarifies how the concept of *amicizia* could evolve from the strict, virtue-seeking relationship termed *vera amicitia* by Cicero and his adherents to become "the loosest and most ambiguous frame" that the secular humanists would subsequently have at their disposal.[12]

In *On Amistà* I propose that the negotiations of Dante and his interlocutors created the conditions of possibility for the *literati* of the generation to follow, the founders of secular humanism, to make use of the terms *amistà*, *amicitia*, and the like across many genres, applying the term to an array of social, political, and strategic relationships that would be far afield of what was thought of as *vera amicitia.* These writers would come to utilize the epithet "amico" freely, employing it under the flexible and accommodating Aristotelian framework that permits the application of the term "friend" to a great number and variety of relationships, and not merely those that seek the other's moral good. Renaissance Italy would see a vast expansion of the application of friendship terms such that, as Carolyn James and Bill Kent suggest, "friendship in its several senses was becoming more important to Renaissance Europeans than it had been to their ancestors."[13] The increased importance of friendship's "several senses," as well as the expanded notion of what friendship is and does, are anticipated in the vernacular exchanges of the generation preceding the earliest humanists, whose use of friendship's terminology helped to integrate into the Christian world view classical and secular notions of preferential, hierarchical, and transactional relationships.

Reflecting backward from the humanist perspective on *amicitia* can be valuable to help identify key turning points in the intellectual history of friendship as these came about in the prior century. In debates on friendship sustained in verse and in prose through the political and intellectual flux of the second half of the Duecento, writers advanced and defended the theoretical positions from which would emerge the epistemic shifts in social thought and practice characteristic of civic humanism. This book focuses on northern Italian writers in the late

Duecento and early Trecento not only for what Italy, remarkably, would become – the birthplace of secular humanism and the Renaissance of classical culture ushered in by that intellectual tradition – but also for what Italy was prior to the large-scale social reorganization of the Renaissance – a chaotic handful of independent *comuni* and emerging *signorie cittadine*. Throughout the Duecento, as their experiments in autonomous governance devolved into factionalism, citizens of the northern Italian city-states expressed a commitment to cultivating ethical discourses that would resolve sociopolitical conflict. Towards this end, the theory of virtuous *amicitia*, regulated by the principle of reciprocity *do ut des* [I give so that you may give], held great promise, and its integration into the sociopolitical practice of the period was treated as a matter of urgency.

Friendship's Many Faces

Philia, *amicitia*, *amicizia*, and friendship all differ from one another across times, spaces, and contexts, and their practices depend on the social milieux in which they are expressed and performed. Each of these historical terms carries with it its own attitudes and obligations. Each also has its own reception history. Thus, they must be teased apart carefully in order to identify the specific ethical and practical expectations that accompany the use of that particular term in the milieux in which it is expressed. An analysis centred on *amistà* – the vernacular Italian term for the reciprocal affection and goodwill that theoretically existed between two like-minded equals – necessarily draws on several related concepts: chiefly Ciceronian *amicitia*, especially as it had been theorized by Christian monastic writers in the twelfth century and onward; and Aristotelian *philia*, reintroduced to the Christian West through the Latin translation of Robert Grosseteste, and ushering in new debates about the nature and possibility of friendship within larger communities. Grosseteste and other translators and commentators – including, importantly, Thomas Aquinas – would render Aristotle's term *philia* as *amicitia* in Latin, allowing parallels to be drawn with Cicero's terminology, itself informed by the Greek texts which had preceded it. But Aristotle's notion of friendship is not perfectly commensurate with the Ciceronian term, however much the two have been conflated. Attention to these differences will yield a more nuanced view onto how writers like Dante negotiated around the conflicts and dilemmas raised by the integration of a dyadic, individualized social structure like friendship into greater Christian societies.

In Dante's time it was nearly impossible to write about friendship without referencing Cicero. Any analysis of friendship as experienced and articulated by Dante's generation, then, must logically begin with Cicero's dialogue *Laelius sive de amicitia*. Indeed, Dante would himself cite *De amicitia* in *Convivio* 1.12.3 as one of his chief philosophical authorities, alongside books eight and nine of Aristotle's *Ethica Nicomachea*. In his allusion, he presents the two *auctores* as in fundamental agreement with one another, as least on the generation and intensification of love. But Dante's elision of the two classical authors in this passage obscures the disruptive impact that Aristotle's *Ethica Nicomachea* would produce on medieval notions of friendship, as it was received by thinkers including, most influentially, Thomas Aquinas, and then later – chiefly for Dante and his interlocutors – Brunetto Latini. This section's goal is thus to distinguish Ciceronian *amicitia* from Aristotelian *philia*, examining how each came to be known to the vernacular literary circles of Dante's Italy.

Friendship, of course, has its own distinct tradition in Christian thought, and it has been held as a value in Christian communities since the time of Christ. The Gospel of John cites Christ as celebrating friendship as a sacrificial love that is premised on loyalty, trust, and equality: "No one has greater love than this, to lay down one's life for one's friends. You are my friends if you do what I command you. I do not call you servants any longer, because the servant does not know what the master is doing; but I have called you friends, because I have made known to you everything that I have heard from my Father" (John 15.13–15). Christ figures love for the twelve as an intimacy in which the Apostles are welcomed into his special confidence as loyal followers, but also as equals, who would sacrifice for him as he would for them. As Christian communities grew, however, and especially as they expanded the doctrines of faith and universal love, suspicions around the value of particular friendships followed. The early patristic writers, for example, had disputed the value of the private, intimate, and exclusive social experience entailed by *amicitia* for the good of the community at large. Monastic communities in the early Middle Ages sought to mitigate the impact of individual friendships on the community, discouraging them (but rarely expressly forbidding them).[14]

The suspicions around monastic friendship were challenged in the twelfth century, the so-called "age of friendship," when Cicero's dialogue entered into the mainstream of Christian intellectual thought.[15] *Amicitia* in its several forms came to be celebrated in the letters of twelfth-century luminaries in and proximate to monastic communities: Bernard of Clairvaux, John of Salisbury, Peter of Celle, and Peter the Venerable, among others.[16] Although none of these figures presented a comprehensive theory of friendship, each corresponded with a range of interlocutors – allies, antagonists, acquaintances, intimates, and strangers – employing the ambiguous terminology of *amicitia* to communicate requests, recommendations, rebukes, and other formal matters.[17] Aelred of Rievaulx – relying explicitly on Cicero's *De amicitia*, which he sought to make accord with Christian ethics – would go the furthest in his treatise *De spirituali amicitia*, offering a radical notion of the "true law of friendship," which James McEvoy summarizes thus: "In a word, it is that spiritual friendship is the highest created likeness of God's life: *Deus amicitia est*."[18] Aelred, Bernard, and other prominent intellectuals promoted the ideals celebrated in Cicero's dialogue as commensurate with Christian ethical precepts, although radical views like Aelred's did not meet with universal acceptance across monastic communities. The resistance, even among his own brethren, to his encouragement of special friendships is indicative of a larger cultural suspicion around *amicitia*, especially but not exclusively in monastic life.[19]

The works of Aelred and other prominent monastic writers of the twelfth century elevated Cicero's dialogue, composed in the tumultuous last years of his life (44 BCE), as the predominant classical authority on friendship and its value for the good Christian seeking to live a happy life in accordance with God's commandments.[20] In the dialogue, Cicero defines friendship as "omnium rerum humanarum et divinarum cum benevolentia et caritate consensio" [agreement with goodwill and affection between people about all things divine and human], a definition that later Christian writers, from Augustine onward, would frequently appropriate.[21] Cicero's account stresses the public nature of the virtue-seeking model of *amicitia* for which Laelius, the dialogue's principal speaker, advocates.[22] In Laelius's account, the most virtuous forms of friendship always promote the greater good of the community: each man helps and is helped by his friend towards moral improvement, which makes both men into model citizens. Such a friendship would, in turn, promote internal societal stability and moral integrity within the public realm. Ciceronian friendships take shape in the public sphere and have public concerns.[23] Friends are responsible for one another's good actions in the community, each competing to outdo his friend in goodness and reproving the friend when he falls short of the mark of civic virtue. In fact, in Cicero's account, friends pursue the good so fervently as to compete with one another in virtue – what Laelius, in one of his most rapturous passages, refers to as an "honesta certatio" [honourable competition], in which the friends become so desirous of doing good for each other as to compete in their goodness, expecting nothing in return.[24] The rigorous demands of friendship – agreement in all things under heaven and earth, a complete lack of any self-interest, an unwavering commitment to civic virtue, a thorough dedication of the self to one's companion that would make of him an "alter idem" – assure that few relationships will meet the standards the dialogue sets forth. Indeed, Laelius claims that in all of human history only "tria aut quattuor" [three or four] pairs of perfect friends have been known.[25] He expresses hope that his relationship to Scipio will be counted among these.

Despite the apparent difficulty of establishing and maintaining perfect accord between self and other on all things human and divine (Cicero's "omnium rerum humanarum et divinarum cum benevolentia et caritate consensio"), medieval treatises on friendship relied heavily on the Ciceronian model as setting the goalposts for those seeking *vera amicitia* in earthly life. As I mentioned above, the virtue-oriented model of friendship the treatise sets forth was especially influential in twelfth-century monastic culture – and intellectual culture more broadly – precisely for its emphasis on the relationship between the cultivation of virtue and the good of the community at large.[26] But as the Christianized model of Ciceronian *amicitia* was carried back outside the cloister walls and into the politically and socially diverse urban spaces of late medieval Italy, it confronted a population who were otherwise pursuing ambitious agendas and divergent goals; this divergence of pursuits would undermine the unified sense of *amicitia* as a perfectly disinterested "honesta certatio" seeking only the good of the other.[27]

The *amicitia* that would emerge from such competitive spaces would look more like that presented in the early thirteenth-century *Amicitia* of Boncompagno da Signa, noted Bolognese rhetor and a fierce critic of Ciceronian idealism. Boncompagno's *Amicitia*, composed very early in his literary career during a sojourn in Rome in 1205, is without question the most innovative of the responses to Cicero's dialogue, among the many late medieval Italian sonnets, *poemetti*, dialogues, sermons, dedications, and prosimetra that reference the ancient work.[28] Other authors of the era might eschew practice in favour of theoretical, idealized, or theological discussions of friendship.[29] By contrast, Boncompagno, in his polemic with Cicero, focuses on urban and especially academic life to elucidate the pragmatic uses and widespread patterns of friendship in the early thirteenth century, observed from the perspective of an abiding cynicism about the possibility of cultivating *vera amicitia* in this life.[30] In the fictional setting of the dialogue, Body and Soul are engaged in a dispute about *amicitia*, which they ask Reason to arbitrate. Body proceeds to ask Soul a series of questions, first about the theory of *amicitia* (its name, its origins, its effects, and so on), and then about its practice, in the form of the various types of *amicus* to be found in civic life.

Soul classifies some twenty-six types, few of which come anywhere near the Ciceronian ideal of *vera amicitia*. The problem with defining the word "amicus," explains Soul, is that it can take on different meanings, which, she claims, "yronia vel equivocatio generator" [gives rise to irony or ambiguity].[31] Irony and equivocation open the door to all manner of expressions of inauthentic friendship under the guise of true affection. Thus, we find a cynical picture of social relations in urban life, as Soul derides such insincere friends as the "vocalis amicus" [vocal friend] who offers you a place to stay only after he knows you are already well housed, and the "versipellis amicus" [turncoat friend], who greets you with praise and disparages you as soon as you pass by.[32] Of the twenty-six types of friend Soul enumerates, twenty-three turn out to be false friends.

Arbitrating the contest in the final chapter, Reason extends the ambiguity of the term "amicus" to the very idea of "amicitia" itself ("hoc nomen amicitia est equivocum ut amicus").[33] In her concluding judgment, she divides heavenly friendship from earthly friendship, which, she says, expresses itself in flattery, ambition, greed, and rivalry, among other vices. Earthly friendship foolishly aims to love those outside of one's rank (Reason calls this choice "stultius" [quite foolish], a clear jab at Ciceronian theory, which is premised on the equalizing potential of friendship even across class divides).[34] Reason summarizes the cynical portrait of friendship most succinctly in the sardonic closing line of the dialogue: "fragilitati subiacet omnis amicitia mundanorum" [all friendship of the inhabitants of this world is prone to frailty], a banal observation, perhaps, but one that represents a marked departure from the ubiquitous tradition of Ciceronian idealism.[35]

Despite Boncompagno's criticisms of its idealism, Cicero's *Laelius* continued to dominate theoretical discussions of *amicitia* well beyond the thirteenth and fourteenth centuries.[36] Indeed, Dante himself cites his reliance on the dialogue not only for theoretical but also for practical ends: in Cicero's treatise he seeks comfort for his grief following the death of Beatrice.[37] This profession has led scholars like Domenico De Robertis and Filippa Modesto to read Dante's presentation of *eros* as dependent on the Ciceronian concept of disinterested *vera amicitia*, particularly as filtered through the views of Aelred of Rievaulx and Peter of Blois, two great champions of Ciceronian *amicitia* in monastic life.[38] Aelred and other monastic writers tended to disregard Cicero's concern over the political effects of friendship or friendship's agonistic nature and focused instead on the mutual cultivation of virtue at which the dialogue aims. But as Aelred and his interlocutors idealized friendship within the closed spaces of twelfth-century monastic cloisters, cultural and intellectual shifts outside of the monastery's walls would bring new attention to the limitations of Cicero's virtue-seeking model in the public sphere. The expansion of cities, rising literacy rates, and the emergent mercantile economy would contribute to greater sophistication and scepticism among the reading public.[39] The increased sophistication and diversity among readers, whose social and ethical concerns were not limited to what might be permitted under the strict guidance of monastic law, coincided with the rediscovery of Aristotle's *Ethica Nicomachea* (first translated into Latin by Robert Grosseteste in 1246–7), which – like Boncompagno's treatise had proposed to do some forty years earlier – expanded the definition and range of *amicitia* within larger and more diverse urban social spheres.

Unlike Cicero, who wrote only about the "true" form of friendship, which aims at virtue, Aristotle sees fit to divide the goods of friendship into three categories: the useful, the pleasurable, and the noble, of which he considers only the third a stable object for friends to pursue.[40] In diversifying the ends of friendship, Aristotle's work represents an expansive spectrum of human relationships, all of which may be counted under his wide-ranging category of *philia* (*amicitia* in its Latin translation), and which, as we will see, carry with them a number of attendant convolutions and queries.[41] Friendship, in Aristotle's view, requires mutual, and mutually recognized, goodwill (*benevolentia*). In 9.5, Aristotle specifies that goodwill "principium esse amicicie, diuturnam autem et in consuetudinem advenientem fieri amiciciam" [is only the beginning of friendship, although it may become friendship through long-lasting companionship].[42] It is not enough merely to admire a friend: friendships of all types require sustained contact and activity, and the most exemplary friendships Aristotle describes even require living together. In this way, friendship can be understood as a virtue in the Aristotelian sense of a *habitus electivus*: a stable, practical disposition oriented towards virtuous activity, and falling under the category of justice.[43] While Cicero's account proclaims that *vera amicitia* is limited to the most excellent citizens and restricts friendship's occurrence in history to three or four pairs of friends, Aristotle's definition extends far more broadly, encompassing to varying degrees all persons, regardless of gender, age, or social standing. Cicero saw friendship as the ground of civic virtue in the model behavior of individual pairs of friends, but Aristotle viewed the connections between citizens in the *polis* – like the Mantuan Sordello and his compatriot Virgil in *Purgatorio* 6 – as a form of friendship itself (*politikē philia*), which bound states together.[44] In principle, Aristotelian friendship embraces the greatest number of participants: for all persons in the Aristotelian *polis*, differences of status, intention, and objective are consistent with the varied experiences of friendship encountered in civic life.

Although Aristotle's definition is more expansive than Cicero's – applying the term *philia* equally to transactional and pleasurable friendships, or friendships between unequals in rank, age, or gender, as to the kind of friendship defined by Cicero as "vera amicitia" – it nevertheless insists that friendship is both premised on and productive of equality. For Aristotle, friendship presupposes the equality of its participants; importantly, where that equality doesn't already exist, friendship produces it: "Sic autem utique et inequales maxime erunt amici. Equabuntur enim utique. Equalitas autem et similitudo, amicicia" [Thus it is that even those who are of unequal standing will become friends, for they will undoubtedly be made equal. Moreover friendship is a kind of equality and likeness].[45] In Aristotle's account, equality is both condition and consequence of friendship. And it is on the question of equality in friendship that the medieval commentators leave their most decisive mark on the reception of Aristotelian friendship theory in the Middle Ages.[46] Indeed, the reception of Aristotle's account across the Christian West pivots on a central question that was disputed among and variously resolved by the commentators: how to reconcile the hierarchy of medieval social structures with the equality Aristotle's theory requires. Can one be friend to one's superior, and if so, what are the conditions of that friendship?

In his *Sententia libri Ethicorum* (1271–2), the most widely accepted medieval authority on the *Nicomachean Ethics*, Thomas Aquinas permits a certain asymmetry within relationships, without going so far as to admit true friendship between persons of unequal standing. His argument hinges on the idea of proportionality: friendship, Thomas argues, consists more in loving than in being loved, and each friend must love the other in accordance with what his friend is due.[47] Friends of lower station may rise to meet their superior counterpart through the fervent activity of their loving. But, for his part, Thomas rejects the idea that friendship can exist if social distances are too great; friends must at least approach equality ("oportet quod ad aequalitatem accedant").[48] For this reason, Thomas, closely following Aristotle, denies that men can be friends of God or of kings.[49]

Related to the question of equal status was that of equal virtue, and Aristotle's medieval commentators pushed his theory towards a new definition of the relationship between friendship and virtuous activity.[50] Aristotle's term *philia* is multifaceted, representing an expansive range of types of friendship beyond the Ciceronian ideal of virtue-seeking *vera amicitia*, which Aristotle and his medieval commentators nevertheless recognized as the most durable and stable, indeed the truest, form of friendship. *Philia* was for both Hellenic and later Stoic authors an individual, reciprocal love between equals, to be contrasted with a love like *agape*, which was held to be universal and undifferentiated.[51] Christian Scholastic authors like Albert the Great and Thomas Aquinas retheorized the Aristotelian term, focusing their interest on the premise of friendship as a training ground for virtue, and seeking to justify a universal form of friendship, emanating from God, that would encompass all, even one's enemies.[52] Aristotle's medieval Latin commentators reduced his tripartite model to a single type of *amicitia perfecta*: virtue-seeking friendship.[53] They dismissed Aristotle's other two ends of friendship – utility and pleasure – as, at best, incomplete, and, at worst, false.[54] The interpretation that reduces friendship to its virtue-seeking model maps friendship practices – like mutual support and encouragement, praise and reproach, dialogue and dispute – onto the sphere of moral behavior, moving the practice of friendship away from the tightly regulated monastic community and decidedly into the public, political sphere.[55] Although Aristotle ultimately rejected the notion of a universal form of friendship, highlighting the need for reciprocity as its basis, the Christian commentators' emphasis on the universal reach and moral richness of friendship in the public domain is perhaps consistent with Aristotle's notion of *politikē philia*, or civic friendship.[56] But the reduction of Aristotle's capacious category of *philia* to a Ciceronian *vera amicitia* excludes a critical aspect of his theory: the possibility for friendship to seek other goods, however diminished and unstable these goods may seem.

Even as Christian authorities such as Aquinas sought to integrate Aristotelian theory with Christian ethical sensibilities, the disruptive impact of the *Ethica Nicomachea* on the intellectual life of the mid-thirteenth century and beyond can be read across late medieval Europe.[57] The decisive influence of Aristotle's notion of *philia*, which is to be distinguished from Ciceronian *amicitia*, can be felt in Dante's works, particularly from *Convivio* onward.[58] As such, one must attend with care to the differences between the two theories, where they cohere and where they do not.

In the generation before Dante, early civic humanist Brunetto Latini integrated friendship theory into communal political discourse in his *Li Livres dou Tresor* (ca. 1261–5), among other works, leading the shift towards celebrating Aristotelian virtue-friendship as the foundation of civic life.[59] Within the vulgarization of Aristotle's *Ethics* that Brunetto presents in the second book of the *Tresor*, he reflects broadly on friendship as an ethical precept within communal institutions.

Like Thomas Aquinas, Brunetto excludes friendships for profit or pleasure, first dismissing them as "amistié par accident" [friendship by accident],[60] then developing a vehement critique, even more emphatic than that of Thomas: he compares instrumental friends "au corbel & au voutor, qui tosjors sivent la caroigne" [(to) the crow and the vulture which always follow carrion],[61] and asserts that a friend for pleasure, "maintenant qu'il a fait sa volonté charnelment il s'enfuit au plus tost qu'il puet, & ja plus ne l'aime" [once he has satisfied his carnal desires, flies away as fast as he can and loves her no more].[62] Brunetto's insistence on virtue as the only true object of friendly affection pushes him towards sweeping formulations about the definition of friendship and its operations within civic life. When one is without a friend, he writes, he is all alone in carrying out his affairs. But when he is with his good friend, "il est acompaigné & en perfete aide a achomplir ses euvres, car de deus parfés & buens naissent parfete euvres & parfete entension" [he is accompanied and has perfect help to accomplish his work, for from two perfect and good people come perfect works and perfect intention].[63] In his project of recuperating ancient forms of discourse and thought, Brunetto stresses the morally improving virtue of friendship, the security it provides, the praise it bears, and the harmony it engenders. He does not, however, seem to differentiate between individual modes of friendship and communitarian ones, and indeed many of his claims focus on the necessity of loving all men in the community according to the precepts of friendship. In this way, his account mirrors Aristotle's notion of *politikē philia*, which embraces equally all members of the city and treats them all in accordance with the virtues appropriate to civic life: steadfastness, loyalty, openness, and equality, the last of which is one of the ten "mainieres" [requirements] Brunetto assigns to friendship.[64]

Dante and his interlocutors were convinced by thinkers like Brunetto Latini of the theoretical power of certain forms of *amicizia* to forge allegiances and heal civic wounds. And yet they came of age in an Italy where communal governments were overrun by dispute and discord, and where oligarchs consolidated power in the vacuum left by factionalism. They saw tensions between the theoretical possibility of *amicizia*, on the one hand, and the realities of social mobility, hierarchy, and community, which were inscribed in all social and institutional structures of medieval life: political, personal, professional, and so on. The confrontation between theoretical possibilities and social realities created dilemmas for thinkers striving to articulate the value of friendship in late medieval public life: was friendship an exercise of preference and exclusion – admitting only two or at most a few, into its circle – or was it a love that could bind many, even all, within its expansive reach (akin to Aristotle's *politikē philia*)? Was friendship uniquely tied to the mutual pursuit of virtue, or could it permit of other, less stable, ends? Was friendship possible between friends of unequal rank, or did the introduction of inequalities promote self-interest, flattery, even deception among the ostensible friends, such that the friendship was nullified by rivalry?

Some of these dilemmas may have been resolved in theory. But in the public practice of friendship, Dante and his peers struggled to assimilate theoretical precepts into the sociopolitical realities of civic life. Friendship was the object of reverence – insofar as it was productive of moral excellence and civic virtue – and of suspicion, as regards its ability to inspire rivalries (even seemingly virtuous or noble ones), to integrate larger communities, and to exist within hierarchies. The problems and the possibilities raised by *amicitia* proved a theme to which late Duecento writers would return repeatedly in their correspondence, commentaries, treatises, and dedications. Within these complex literary negotiations, Dante's justifications of friendship as simultaneously unifying and exclusive, transactional and yet morally legitimate, equalizing while retaining social hierarchies help to pave the way for the broad-scale recuperation of *amicitia* we see in humanist social thought.

A Sociological Approach: The Fields and Practices of Friendship

Previous scholarship on both the theory and the practice of friendship in Dante's works and in the medieval Italian context more broadly has tended to treat professions of friendship either thematically or biographically. Thematic approaches apply classical friendship theory – typically the idealized and idealizing view of *vera amicitia* promoted by Cicero's dialogue – as the intermediary between Dante's notion of *eros* and the cultivation of Christian *caritas*, a universal form of love that is mediated through Christ and shared with all, even one's enemies.[65] These studies argue that Dante reconciles erotic desire with spiritual fulfilment through what is often characterized as a "transformation," in which Dante discovers a "new, special" "spiritual friendship" with Beatrice.[66]

The second approach takes friendship in biographical terms, expressed either authentically – as an affective or intellectual bond between two individuals – or inauthentically, an ironic disguise over what is at best dissimilarity and at worst aversion.[67] Many biographical studies implicitly or explicitly use as their point of departure a definition of friendship taken from Cicero's work and appropriated by Augustine: that friendship is "omnium rerum humanarum et divinarum cum benevolentia et caritate consensio" [agreement with goodwill and affection between people about all things divine and human].[68] These studies focus on ideological and epistemological sympathies or antipathies, equating "true" friendship with either intellectual or affective affinity, and sometimes conflating the two. Such idealized relationships may be discoverable in theoretical works, but they are difficult to locate in the historical sources. Following the logic of this approach, some scholars have identified the truest expression of friendship across Dante's works in the fictional persons of Beatrice and Virgil, whose displays of compassionate concern for the pilgrim's wellbeing and spiritual betterment have been interpreted as unique expressions of the highest forms of friendship.[69]

Emphasizing the ambivalence in the broader medieval discourse on *amicitia* and *amicizia* – particularly among monastic writers, who disputed the value of personal attachments for the moral good of the community as a whole – we can both divorce *amicitia*, *amistà*, and related terms from our modern notions of deep, private intimacies and restore to the practices of friendship (exchanges of letters, favours, and services) their public functions as they existed in Duecento and Trecento Italy. These "friendships" may not bear with them any of the sentimentality or intimacy we would now attribute to such relationships; they become, rather, those relations most instrumental to the sharpening of ideas, the promotion of work, and the advancement of careers. Such a reevaluation clears the way for us to investigate the complex role that the *literati* of Dante's generation imputed to instrumental friendships as they were put to use within larger social and institutional structures. Dante's own innovative applications of the terms of friendship – both those that succeed and those that do not – invoke the range of strategies available to writers of the late Duecento and early Trecento. Dante's deep attention to *amicizia* and *amistà* across his works not only affords us an opportunity to examine the negotiations around the pitfalls and promise of *amicizia* in the decades preceding its proliferation in humanist writings, but also reminds us, repeatedly, that writers in the Italian vernacular were then evolving – in both theory and practice – an understanding of *amicizia* that was distinct from the idealized Christian-Ciceronian *vera amicitia*. Their efforts anticipate the humanists' subsequent celebration of friendship in its many senses, be it equal or hierarchical, disinterested or instrumentalized, public and open or private and exclusive.

In contrast to previous studies, Teodolinda Barolini's recent work on the semantics of friendship in Dante's lyrics usefully moves towards sociology, historicizing "amicizia" by divorcing the term from its sentimental heritage and instead evaluating the usefulness of the term "amico" in the social contexts in which lyrics were produced and circulated. My own approach follows Barolini's in its historicizing and sociological turn, though I will expand the generic range of works considered here beyond Dante's lyrics, to encompass his whole body of work and the evolution of that work over time. I will put those works in conversation with the interventions of Dante's contemporaries, also writing in the northern Italian cities at the turn of the fourteenth century. My approach, engaged with the work of historians of medieval friendship and informed by Pierre Bourdieu's sociological theory, takes into consideration the specific fields in which each of these texts intervened, thus making clear how the authors of this period positioned friends and friendships within their texts, and how they utilized the duties and benefits these friendships proffered. By highlighting the contemporary ambiguity around the term "amico" and the dependence of that term on the field of its expression, I focus not on what friendship is, so much as what it does, how it is used, and what ends it serves.

As with all forms of exchange, the practices of literary friendship – imitation, dedication, praise, critique, reproach, dispute – are enmeshed in systems of strategic intervention. As Bourdieu has suggested, practices are structured by both the field (*champ*) in which they take shape and by embodied dispositions towards patterns of perception and behavior (what Bourdieu calls *habitus*).[70] Within a particular field, individuals are positioned relative to one another, in objective relationship to other participants. Position is determined by the distribution of multiple forms of capital (for example, wealth, reputation, fame, virtue, education, the esteem of one's peers or of one's patron), all of which are valued and exchanged differently in their respective social systems. One's practices may be improvised and innovative, but they are governed by the rules of the particular field, and by one's position in that field relative to the other players, determined by the accumulation and exchange of one's stock of economic and symbolic capital. Within specific fields of practice participants must negotiate their positions relative to one another through a series of strategic moves in what Bourdieu calls "the game of honour."[71] Positions on the field are negotiated with more or less strategic mastery, according to one's sense of the game. Each intervention within the field issues a challenge to another player, which contains within it "the possibility of a continuation, a reply, a riposte, a return gift, inasmuch as it contains recognition of the partner (to whom, in the particular case, it accords equality in honour)."[72] A reply recognizes the honour of the giver and restores the honour of the recipient.

That practices are embedded in fields where agents are differently positioned according to the various types of capital they have acquired, and where particular sets of rules regulate participants' behavior, does not imply that practices are mechanized. Neither, however, are those practices fully conscious and freely chosen. Rather, like well-trained players of a game or sport, participants develop a "practical mastery" within social fields, an embodied set of regularized behaviors and perceptions that governs but does not fully determine their interventions in the field. Practices, then, are strategic, but also structured by and within the specific field in which they are undertaken.

Treating professions of friendship in these medieval Italian texts as strategic practices within particular arenas of symbolic exchange allows us to chart these vernacular poets' negotiations of contradictory socio-ethical claims in this period of great cultural, intellectual, demographic, and social change. In approaching specific sites like the literary "piazza," the academic network, and the patron's court as "fields" in Bourdieu's sense, and examining literary practices like praise and reproach as motivated by the desire to accumulate symbolic capital, this project complements what has been dubbed the "new agenda" in the history of medieval friendship.[73] Historians of friendship – Julian Haseldine most prominently, along with C. Stephen Jaeger, Antonella Liuzzo Scorpo, James McEvoy, John McLoughlin, Margaret Mullett, Bénédicte Sère, and others – have examined the ambivalence around friendship discourse in different fields of medieval life, especially the monasteries, courts, and universities of the preceding centuries.[74] Friendship's role in the composition and exchange of letters in both the medieval and early modern periods has provoked much scholarly interest, particularly regarding diplomatic efforts, power relations, and social networks.[75] In their emphasis on strategy over biographical intimacy or ideological affinity, these histories uncover the complications involved with the integration of broad Aristotelian models of friendship, which would include even instrumental relationships, with Christian theological ones.

We have not seen this "new agenda" in the history of medieval friendship thoroughly applied to the investigation of *amistà* in the Italian urban centres at the turn of the Trecento, in those crucial interstitial decades between the Middle Ages and early modernity. And yet, Florian Hartmann's studies of the semantics of *amicitia* among the twelfth-century *dictatores*, along with Barolini's scholarship on Dante's early lyric engagements and Bénédicte Sère's work on the reception of books eight and nine of Aristotle's *Ethica Nicomachea* within thirteenth- and fourteenth-century philosophical circles, make clear the need for a large-scale investigation of the complex negotiations of friendship among the Italian *literati* in these decades, when what Sère calls a "decisive epistemic shift" began in Italy and then echoed across the rest of Europe.[76] This shift would allow the civic humanists of the later Trecento and Quattrocento to revere private friendship as the pinnacle of human sociability, and to accept instrumental friendship as morally justifiable and even valuable for particular social and ethical ends.[77] Humanist writers would use the language of *amicitia* to delineate idealized portraits of kinship, marriage, patronage, political accord, even commerce.[78] This is not to suggest that these later humanist friendships were not themselves contested and rife with ambiguities. But the value of *amicitia* as a framework for writing about all manner of social relationships would no longer, even by the time of Petrarch, be controversial. What had happened to make this possible? *On Amistà* proposes an answer to that question.

Where secular humanism – which was seeing its earliest stirrings in these decades – would come to view even instrumental friendships as critical to healthy human sociability and the wellbeing of the state, late medieval writers and thinkers experienced friendship as a much more fraught relationship, complicated by rigid social hierarchies, entrenched political factionalism, fierce struggles for communal autonomy, and the localized consolidation of power into the hands of oligarchs. The conditions of late medieval Italy's sociopolitical environment allowed for the proliferation of concerns about who was to be counted among one's *amici*. Voluntary bonds and allegiances (often construed as *amistadi*) held critical strategic value in Italy's unstable political configurations, which were shifting between *comuni* – where citizens had for centuries experimented with the possibilities of self-government – and the emergent *signorie cittadine*, which would soon replace communal governments in many of Italy's northern cities. Self-governance conflicted with strict social hierarchies; the interests of the nobility collided with those of the rising merchant class; communities were fractured by civil dispute. Meanwhile, writers and intellectuals competed with their peers for both recognition and resources, all the while also disputing questions related to stylistic expression, ideological position, and political affiliation. The civil disputes and sociopolitical instability of these decades fractured communities, creating an urgent demand for a set of terms through which writers could articulate the boundaries around and the bonds within their networks. Articulating voluntary bonds through the terms of *amistà* could present a more stable alternative that might supersede sociopolitical divides, or, in the best case, function broadly as a healing mechanism for a body politic that has been racked with factionalism.

To examine these new rhetorical formulations of social bonds, *On Amistà* engages in close readings of four of Dante's key texts: *Vita nova*, *De vulgari eloquentia*, the opening paragraphs of the Epistle to Cangrande, and the *Commedia*.[79] I contextualize those readings with additional investigation of contemporary sources, some well-studied and some less known: *tenzoni*, epistles, encomia, dedications, and treatises, both secular and religious. Brunetto Latini, Guittone d'Arezzo, and Guittone's imitators feature prominently in the corpus of texts gathered here, as do Dante's principal *amici*: Guido Cavalcanti, Cino da Pistoia, Cangrande della Scala, Forese Donati, his sister Piccarda, and, with important caveats, Beatrice Portinari. In each of these cases, what is more important than the biographical reality of Dante's private, affective attachments to one friend or another is the fact that he conceived of those relationships as friendships, with all of friendships' attendant benefits and duties, as they were formulated following Aristotelian precepts: reciprocal good will, trust, and loyalty, and the equal exchange of goods and services. Attending to the practices of friendship in which Dante and his interlocutors engaged – practices like dispute, critique, self-promotion, and dedication – means sorting through the sources to uncover the inconsistencies, equivocations, and contradictions that underlie theoretical aspirations to disinterested, reciprocal, and morally improving *vera amicitia*. When we read Dante's articulations of friendship in key passages of his major works against and alongside the works of contemporaries like Brunetto and Guittone, we see late medieval vernacular *amistadi* as embedded in political, economic, and social realities that bear with them contractual obligations and instrumental advantages, as these transactional friendships had been articulated in theoretical form in dictatorial manuals in the twelfth century and as they had since developed into actual exchanges of symbolic capital parading as friendship. While arguably these tensions are universal to friendships in complex communities, writerly attention to *amicizia* in Duecento and Trecento Italy demonstrates the function and nature of the language of friendship during an important phase of social and political redefinition and reorganization. A study of the strategic employ of the language of *amicizia*, *amistà*, and related terms in specific fields of social interaction reveals how Dante and his interlocutors dramatically widened *amicizia*'s semantic range, introducing to friendship a new breadth of instrumental advantages while still striving to preserve its Christian-Ciceronian heritage. Attention to the language of friendship thus reveals the ways that individuals like Dante paved the way for the recuperation of individualized, hierarchical, and instrumental friendship, which would become commonplace among Renaissance intellectuals.

Each chapter that follows examines a particular social field in which the ethical demands around friendship are put to the test. In designating these environments as "fields," I refer specifically to the concept of *champs* I alluded to above: Bourdieu's theory of social structures in which knowledge, services, and status – in the form of the different types of economic and symbolic capital – are produced and negotiated.[80] Each field (networks of lyric exchange, academic or scholarly circles, courts of patrons, and so on) functions relatively autonomously from the others, but they often overlap, as actors are simultaneously enmeshed in multiple spheres of negotiation. For example, Dante was at various times a poet in dialogue and in competition with his fellow Tuscans, an aspirant to recognition by the intellectual society of Bologna, an exile dependent on the generosity of patrons in northern courts, and a pilgrim journeying up the mountain of Purgatory towards his own redemption. These systems and the exchanges that take place within them not only structure the relationships between the actors in the system, but also condition their particular practices.[81]

Bourdieu's theory considers the relative positions between individuals within a field, not specific individuals themselves. This study will proceed in the same way: I am not interested here in teasing out the affective, personal relationships shared between Dante and individual figures. Nor will I dwell on the many candidates to be counted among Dante's biographical friends, alluded to by the poet himself or by his biographers: fellow poets and artists like Lapo Gianni, Lippo Pasci de' Bardi, Giovanni del Virgilio, or Giotto di Bondone; allies and associates from his later days in Ravenna, like Dino Perini, Pietro Giardini, Menghino Mezzani, or Fiduccio de' Milotti; patrons in his exile, like Moroello Malaspina or Guido Novello da Polenta. I will also not explore the allegorical or fictional constructions of friendship in texts like the *Fiore* or the *Convivio*. What I am interested in, rather, is how Dante and his fellows use the terms of friendship (*amico*, *amistà*, and the like) to position themselves alongside and against other nodes in their networks. When we identify and differentiate between the various social systems in which poets participated, a clearer picture of the structure of social relations within each system emerges. We are thus able to track the different ways that friendship was employed in this crucial period of rapid intellectual transformation and multilayered political change.

The book's chapters proceed by examining the institutional milieux in which the discourse of friendship, with all its attendant ambiguities and complexities, dominated ways of thinking and speaking about social bonds and obligations. Each of the first three chapters considers one of the interrelated networks in which poets on the emergent Italian literary scene were enmeshed: the poetic marketplace of the republican *comuni*; the community of literary scholars surrounding the university; and the Northern Italian court system, with its gifts and favours offered under the auspices of patronage. The final chapter turns to an imagined (and yet, for its author and its reading public, no less real) field in which poets engaged with the ambiguities of friendship according to eschatological concerns: the three distinct realms of the afterlife. These are the crucial environments in which the poets who were the standard-bearers of intellectual culture in the period would circulate and contest their ideas. It is in these four fields that theories of friendship most visibly undergirded contemporary social interactions, and it is from these fields that the civic humanists of the succeeding generations would draw their re-articulations of the benefits and obligations inherent to social life.

Readers influenced by the widespread Ciceronian doctrine of friendship as a salve to heal the larger civic community would have found themselves puzzled by Dante's portrait, in his earliest works, of his friendship with Guido Cavalcanti, his so-called "first friend." As I argue in the first chapter, "Exclusivity: The Piazza," the concept of *amistà* articulated in Dante's *Vita nova* (1292–4) and his pre-exilic lyrics is rooted, counterintuitively and inventively, in anti-sociality, exclusivity, and hierarchy. Unlike previous discussions, which dispute the biographical details of the friendship between Dante and his "primo amico," this chapter undertakes the essential reading of Dante's dubious claims to Guido's *amistà* within and against their contemporary social and historical context. Such a contextualization requires, I argue, an attention to the sociopolitical structure in which networks of literary exchange took shape. By contrast with the earlier generations of vernacular lyricists, whose exchanges were conducted under the aegis of imperial or seigneurial authority, the poets of the late thirteenth-century Italian *comuni* autonomously oversaw the operations of their own networks, conferring on participants and aspirants recognition, honour, and fame – their primary forms of symbolic capital in the "piazza," the figurative site of literary exchange. Within this self-regulating network, poets relied on the language of friendship as a means to extend their networks and cement their reputations, referring to strangers, intimates, and rivals univocally as "amico." In their correspondence with other established or aspiring versifiers, poets would employ the terminology of friendship to increase their centrality within the literary network, seeing strength in diversifying their connections and striving for productive modes of intellectual dispute. This web of weak-tie connections, inclusive in its reach, contrasts with the linear, bilateral bonds Dante describes in his pre-exilic works, especially the poem *Guido, i' vorrei che tu e Lapo ed io*. Where other exchanges of the period employ the terms of friendship to reconcile diverse opinions, heal rifts, and neutralize rivalries, ultimately reaching towards greater social cohesion, Dante's claims to Guido's friendship in the sonnet and the prose narrative of the *Vita nova* strategically exclude, divide, and elevate two above the crowd. Dante's works, in other words, treat friendship as an isolating and rigidly hierarchical modality that performs an exclusionary role within larger societal structures. Ultimately, though, Dante cannot reconcile this isolationist model with the dialogic and disputatious sphere of the "piazza," and the unsuccessful attempt at asserting the value of an exclusive model of friendship within the rivalrous sphere of literary exchange leaves the narrator of the *Vita nova* estranged from all, even his "primo amico."

Chapter 2, "Self-Interest: The University," looks at how claims to *amicitia* worked to mitigate competition and rivalry among peers, participants in the extended network in and around the Studium of Bologna. This chapter examines friendship practices – specifically, here, collaboration, recommendation, and mutual promotion – in the academic field, taking as its point of departure the infrequent but pointed assertions of friendship in Dante's *De vulgari eloquentia.* In this ambitious but unfinished work, Dante positions himself as "amicus" of a well-connected node of the social network of individuals within and around the Bolognese university, the jurist and poet Cino da Pistoia, precisely at a time when such an allegiance would have been most advantageous, not only to the poet's career but to his very survival. If in the pre-exilic *Vita nova* Dante used the language of *amistà* to portray allegiance to Guido as exclusionary, hierarchical, private, and privatizing, in *De vulgari eloquentia*, written in the years immediately following his exile from Florence in 1302, he presents his *amicitia* with Cino in the form of a public, horizontal, extensive bond, premised on non-competitive collaboration. But is the disinterested collaboration *De vulgari eloquentia* envisions possible in the academic sphere? In the treatise, Dante employs the term "amicus" as a tool for personal advancement and self-promotion, staking a strategic claim about his own poetic-philosophical alignment with a well-established literary figure. The language of *amicitia* in *De vulgari eloquentia* suggests that an individual who aligns himself with a prominent friend – and asserts consensus with that friend on matters of intellectual weight – will advance his position within the field of "doctores illustres" that the treatise attempts to define. The author can prove himself worthy of accreditation by attempting to draw his own direct line to the authority of one who is already validated by the system. At the same time, *De vulgari* uses the epithet "amicus eius" to differentiate the universal authority of the treatise's author from the specific expertise of the supposedly anonymous poet the treatise wishes to promote: for nearly two-thirds of the treatise Dante maintains a distinction between Cino's "amicus" (Dante himself, the newcomer worthy of inclusion in the elite group) and the "nos" who authors the treatise. That Dante decides first to disguise and then to reveal his own identity as one of the two vernacular poets celebrated in the treatise, employing the epithet "amicus eius" to strategically align his poetic reputation with Cino's star, permits him to straddle two opposing constructions of *amicitia*: as both a category of disinterested collaboration and a tool for strategic self-promotion and self-interest.

Chapter 3, "Hierarchy: The Court," examines the hierarchical friendship between lord and client, locating Dante's most innovative use of the term "amicus" across his corpus in the first four paragraphs of his epistle to his patron Cangrande della Scala. Here I argue that while friendships in the communal and academic social fields were characterized by ambiguity, friendship between patron and client at the turn of the Trecento was marked by categorical contradictions. Even within the space of the *signoria cittadina*, where all relationships between peers were mediated by their strictly hierarchical relationships to the lord, friendship would come to dominate the discourse of social organization, and in the generation following Dante's, lords and clients alike would speak of their *amicitia* with one another. But such friendships are philosophically vulnerable, as the underlying principles of Aristotelian friendship – equality and reciprocity – are necessarily weakened, even contradicted, by the hierarchical nature of patronage. Attending to conflicts surrounding the ethical demands of equality and reciprocity in friendship, this chapter analyses documents including *dictamen*, encomia, and petitions, as these illustrate the strategies clients employed in negotiating the hierarchy inherent in courtly patronage. Taking the court of the Veronese lord Cangrande della Scala as an especially well-documented case in which to examine modes of speaking about and to one's patron, this chapter examines the structure of request, the language of praise, and the frames for dedication that clients used to position themselves vis-à-vis their sovereign. In particular, I highlight the Epistle to Cangrande, which presents a daring argument for equal and reciprocal friendship between patron and client. I demonstrate that a theoretical framework for the exchange of symbolic capital underpins this letter and its claims to friendship with the sovereign. In defending reciprocity even in relation to the (seemingly unreciprocable) gifts of patronage, the Epistle stakes a claim for the possibilities inherent in dedication itself. In re-theorizing the relationships of equality and reciprocity in a friendship between a patron and his client, rendering them coherent within the hierarchical order, the Epistle lays the groundwork for the rigidly hierarchical and yet non-preferential attachments Dante will describe in *Paradiso*, and prepares a pathway for humanist writers and artists to assert friendship with the *signore*.

Where the first three chapters look at real fields of social interaction between historical individuals, chapter 4 focuses on the afterlife, an imagined field that, for all its artifice, stakes real claims about the interactions between individuals in the here and now. Within the imagined communities of the three realms of the afterlife, friendship practices – now expanded to embrace the reciprocal support of penitence and the mutual delight in salvation – take on new forms and serve new functions. Friendship practices are especially prominent in the field of Purgatory. As is seen through the numerous and varied examples of friendly encounters across the purgatorial journey, from Dante-pilgrim's brief exchanges with Casella and Belacqua at the base of the mountain to his crucial later encounter with Forese on the penultimate terrace, particular attachments become crucial to each pilgrim's progress up the mountain. But the language of *amistà* goes nearly silent in *Purgatorio*, applied in a limited number of cases to characterize a small subset of the preferential, affective, and often intense private relationships celebrated across the canticle. Personal attachment, framed in the familial language of *fratellanza* and thus distinguished from the expansive range encompassed by the terms *amistà* or *amicizia*, becomes a mechanism for the moral improvement of the individual, a rehearsal for the submission of individual desires to the divine will. Once the will has successfully been aligned, private attachments, while productive of delight when concordant with the divine will, become accidental: no longer serving the tactical purposes of those social fields that unfold in and across time, they are therefore eclipsed, even if not dissolved. Viewed in this way, the *Commedia* becomes a compendium of the social formulations that the other chapters have examined: social relations in the *Commedia* are simultaneously inclusive and exclusive, collaborative while still strategic, hierarchical and yet equalizing. The poem also introduces a new distinction: the tension between likeness and difference in the recognition of a friend as an *alter idem*. The modes of personal attachment presented in the *Commedia* sit with but do not resolve the dilemmas and ambiguities of friendship practice in Dante's era. They do so by constructing new formulations for private attachments, which can be distinguished from the instrumentalizing friendship practices of the period.

In its eschatological presentation of friendship's irresolvable dilemmas, however, the *Commedia*'s presentation of personal attachments would not ultimately make a long-lasting impact on the theories and practices of sociability, particularly as they are expressed through *amistà* or *amicizia*, that would come to dominate early humanist social and ethical discourses. It is the practices of friendship that Dante and his interlocutors model elsewhere – in Dante's *opere minori* and the texts and ideas with which they are in dialogue – that would instead most closely anticipate the strategic practices of their humanist successors. As I discuss in the book's epilogue, the friendships later celebrated by early humanist writers like Petrarch and Boccaccio would demonstrate the wholesale recuperation and use of the expansive range of possibilities for secular friendship – not the idealized divine friendship articulated by Beatrice in the opening scene of the *Commedia* – that had been opened by their late Duecento predecessors. By attending to the ambivalence surrounding friendship in Dante's works and works by his contemporaries with which his are in direct dialogue, we see how Dante and his interlocutors navigated the integration of secular values with previously dominant Christian ethical attitudes, paving the way for the following generation to revere private friendship as the pinnacle of human sociability, and to accept instrumental friendship as morally justifiable and even valuable for particular social and ethical ends.

1
Exclusivity: The Piazza

"Every real friendship is a sort of a secession, even a rebellion."

C.S. Lewis, *The Four Loves*[1]

The *Vita nova* asserts Beatrice as its apparent and undeniable focal point. Yet it is nearly impossible to imagine, much less to grasp, what this work would be without the looming presence of Guido Cavalcanti. If Beatrice is the centre of the *Vita nova*, then Cavalcanti is its circumference, delimiting the *libello*'s scope. Although Dante mentions Cavalcanti explicitly in the text on just a few notable occasions – and never by name – he specifies throughout that the work is addressed to Guido, his "primo amico" [first friend] according to what he calls the "gradi dell'amistade" [degrees of friendship].[2]

Dante's claims of devotion to Guido in the *Vita nova*'s prose represent the most conspicuous declarations of *amistà* across his *oeuvre*. He will rarely, as emphatically as he does here, rely on the terminology of *amistà* to describe figures we consider his friends. The *Vita nova* insists on Guido's *amistà* from the prose narrative's early pronouncement of the "principio dell'amistà" [the beginning of our friendship] between Guido and the speaker: the sonnet Guido penned in response to Dante's open request for dream interpretation.[3] Dante vocally asserts Guido's role as his most respected peer and must trusted confidant, calling on Guido as "primo amico" in six different passages across the work and alluding to Guido and his works, both directly and obliquely, from the first chapter.[4] And yet these assertions of *amistà* with Guido are anything but clear: within the pages of the *Vita nova* itself, the author neglects to name Cavalcanti outright, despite his frequent reference to his "amico" and the distinctly Cavalcantian influence on certain sections of the text. More importantly, Dante appears at times to undercut his friend's position, avowing his loyalty to his "primo amico" out of one side of his mouth while subverting that same loyalty out of the other by undermining – even perhaps mocking – the intellectual positions that his friend most passionately affirms.

What, then, to make of the *amistà* that the *Vita nova* so insistently proclaims? For all the declarations of friendship Dante puts forward in the text, their friendship appears a far cry from that of Laelius and Scipio, idealized by Cicero in *De amicitia*, where Dante claims to have sought consolation while composing the *Vita nova*.[5] After reading the *Vita nova*, one would struggle to call the bond between Dante and Guido *vera amicitia*; it appears at best insufficient, and at worst inauthentic. In accounting for Guido's ambiguous presence in the *Vita nova*, some scholars take a biographical approach, claiming that the references to Guido represent a longstanding intimacy, with evidence of a personal dispute, culminating in a falling out.[6] Others emphasize the ideological over the biographical, insisting both on the abiding influence of Cavalcanti's (Averroist) philosophy across the full trajectory of Dante's career, and on the ways that Dante sets his work apart from such ideological commitments.[7] Some readings of the elder Guido's influence over the young Dante emphasize rivalry over friendship, placing Guido in the role of poetic "Father" in an "Oedipal drama," waiting to be chased out of the "nido" [nest].[8]

The divide among scholars on the question of Guido's friendship with Dante can be traced to the equivocal language of "amistà" in the literary culture of the *comuni* of Northern Italy at the end of the thirteenth century. Declarations of friendship abound in the literature of the period, both among newcomers on the scene and among more established, acknowledged poetic authorities. These declarations are especially common in the correspondence poems of writers such as Guittone d'Arezzo, Monte Andrea, Guido Orlandi, and Dante da Maiano, as well as some lesser-known versifiers, all of whom frequently referred to their peers as "amici" even, as Teodolinda Barolini has discussed, when confessing ignorance about their interlocutors' names or identities.[9] Poets incorporated calls to "amistade" or "amicizia" into epistolary poems intended to reproach or antagonize their interlocutors. They employed the terminology of friendship strategically, as a means to negotiate their prominence of place within the network of poets active in communal circles. Such practices were especially critical within the communal sociopolitical structure, which – unlike its courtly counterpart – relied on internal mechanisms for establishing renown and exchanging honour.

While the biographical and intellectual affinities between Dante and Guido have rightly been of interest to scholars, this chapter centres instead on the theory of *amistà* that undergirds Dante's claims to Guido's friendship in the *Vita nova* and elsewhere in his early career. I argue that, through its portrait of friendship with the "primo amico," the *Vita nova* articulates a vision of exclusionary, hierarchical, and antisocial friendship, which stands in sharp relief to the prevailing usage of the terminology of *amicizia, amistà*, and *amistade* in the lyric exchanges of the period. In placing Dante's notion of friendship in its larger socio-historical context, I follow the work of Teodolinda Barolini, who, in a series of recent essays, uses a sociological approach to analyse Dante's use of the term "amico" in his lyrics.[10] In this chapter, I build on Barolini's insights on the declarations of *amistade* between a young Dante Alighieri and his peer Dante da Maiano, applying her concept of the "poetic agora" to the field of communal poets composing and exchanging lyrics in the late Duecento.[11] Within the "piazza" of lyric exchange, which would come to supplant the imperial court as the primary space of vernacular lyric engagement in Italy, communal poets negotiated honour in contentious public disputes.[12] In the absence of a sovereign arbiter, literary communities sought other methods for determining "sovereignty" in the field, establishing their own centres of gravity within decentralized networks that lacked clear hubs. These methods are most evident in the exchange of *tenzoni*, correspondence poems through which well-established poets and newcomers alike would stage disputes over poetic ideologies and techniques as a means of negotiating their primacy. *Tenzone* exchanges – however antagonistic they may have become – were frequently construed by even the earliest practitioners as an exercise of friendship.[13]

Rooting expressions of *amistà* in dispute has often resulted in the mischaracterization of these expressions as inauthentic or ironic. By contrast with these characterizations, I argue here that dispute, antagonism, and reproach should instead be viewed as central practices of friendship emerging in the literary communities of urban Italian centres in the latter half of the Duecento and coming into fruition at the turn of the Trecento. And yet, the exclusionary impulses of a sonnet like Dante's *Guido, i' vorrei che tu e Lapo ed io* – which, while it grounds friendship in the ideological disputation common to *tenzoni*, also insists on an antisocial distancing from civic life – were at odds with prevailing accounts of *amistà* in communal lyric, where friendly poetic exchange was treated as a salve that would heal the strife of the community. Where Guittone d'Arezzo and his imitators would use calls to friendship as an instrumental means to extend one's network, always reaching outward to catch others in its grasp, in *Guido, i' vorrei* Dante asserts a friendship that has an exclusionary appeal, as the small coterie of friends seeks to distinguish themselves from the group at large. In contrast to prevailing modes of discourse, Dante's appeals to *amistà* in some of his earliest works serve to isolate two friends from, rather than integrate them into, the larger social whole. In this way, friendship becomes, to borrow a phrase from C.S. Lewis, a "sort of secession, even a rebellion."[14]

When such a secessionist model is then reintroduced to the rivalrous communal sphere, however, it ultimately fails, collapsing into solipsism, and leaving the poet estranged from all his previous interlocutors in the piazza, including his "primo amico." Ultimately, Dante's early attempt to shift *amistà* away from a civic model and towards a private, exclusive, and exclusionary model founders in the rivalrous agora of late Duecento lyric exchange.

In what follows, I will first lay out the dominant theories, emerging out of Ciceronian idealism, of the restorative possibilities of friendship in communal public squares, which had been marred by factional violence and civic strife. Then I will demonstrate how such theoretical positions were put into practice by lyric poets in their contentious exchanges of correspondence poems. In these exchanges we will see how *tenzone* participants preferred dispute and antagonism – under the auspices of an expansive and inclusionary notion of *amistà* – to isolation, avoidance, and disengagement. Such a contextualization makes clear just how innovative and unusual Dante's depiction of his *amistà* with Guido was. By contrast with his peers, Dante will employ the terms of *amistà* not for greater, more expansive reach, but for creating and maintaining social barriers. Although in his earliest exchange with Dante da Maiano, Dante likewise uses the language of *amistà* to invite engagement in the game of honour, he soon shifts strategy, developing a vision of friendship that was designed to disengage, to segregate, and to exalt two or three friends above the community. Seen in this light, the *Vita nova* represents an attempt to reinscribe this exclusive *amistà* – articulated in the magical and artificial space of the sonnet *Guido, i' vorrei* and other lyrics – into the social field of the public square. But attempts to translate the fictive cohesion of the small coterie of friends into real social spaces would fail, causing the narrator to retreat further into isolation and into imagined intimacies with unknowable strangers. The *Vita nova*, a text which ostensibly celebrates exclusive and intimate private friendship, in fact points towards the impossibility of such cohesion when it is carried back into the agonistic piazza.

Friendship as Civic Medicine

In the context of Duecento *comuni*, where political factionalism created antagonism and strife that reached into all areas of sociopolitical life, the intellectual class found attractive the theory of civic friendship celebrated by classical authorities like Cicero, Aristotle, Seneca, and others. In sermons, treatises, and poems, authors relied on classical commonplaces to testify to the healing work friendship could foster not only between individuals but also among groups. Friendship, both for the ancients and their medieval disciples, was first and foremost a morally improving enterprise, and a growing contingent of late-medieval vernacular authors testify to the goods of friendship across genres, especially in verse treatises.[15] One such treatise is Fra Guittone's late thirteenth-century sonnet *Amistade d'envidia è medicina.* Part of a cycle on the subject of the vices and their opposing virtues, Guittone's sonnet places friendship as the inverse of envy, and sings its praises in what is mostly a series of truisms deriving from ancient and contemporary authorities: friendship is the highest good of human nature, Guittone writes.[16] It is the fountain of all moral worth and refinement.[17] Its lack spells poverty for the rich, wretchedness for the strong, and worthlessness to whatever is held most dear.[18]

In this case, what is interesting about Guittone's poem is not these truisms, but the incipit: "Amistade d'envidia è medicina / e de leggero piaga onni sua sana" [Friendship is the medicine for envy and easily cures all her wounds]. Conventionally, *invidia* was associated with women's natural inferiority and the resulting corruption of female friendships.[19] But in his sonnet cycle, Guittone evokes *invidia* also in predominantly male spaces, as the vice that most disrupts attempts at establishing a civic peace. Like its embodied form on the second terrace of *Purgatorio* and drawing from its etymology, *invidia* for Guittone is a blinding emotion that arises from pain at another's good fortune.[20] It derives from the kind of voracious, bottomless lack that characterizes the she-wolf in *Inferno* 1, where *invidia* is posited as the force that calls the she-wolf forth from hell, which the *Veltro* will chase back: "Questi la caccerà per ogne villa, / fin che l'avrà rimessa ne lo 'nferno, / là onde 'nvidia prima dipartilla" [He will drive her from every town until he has put her back in Hell, whence envy first sent her forth].[21] Contrasting it against envy's infernal lack, Guittone's sonnet premises friendship on fullness: it is the very "pane de vita" [bread of life]. Where envy makes all virtue appear as vice, friendship produces the opposite effect, as the friend selflessly rejoices in the good of another ("so' gaud' è l'autrui come 'l su' bono").

Guittone positions friendship not merely as envy's opposite but more precisely as its cure or antidote, the *medicina* of *envidia.* Guittone asserts that the wounds created by envy can be healed by the cultivation of friendship, which inspires a disinterested sense of joy at another's good fortune. The sonnet does not distinguish friendships between individuals from those between groups; instead, it seems to want to harness the broadest formulations of the term, to suggest that a general civic investment in the cultivation of this virtue will encourage the eventual defeat of envy, the plague of the *comune.*[22] More than merely creating a secondary community alongside these other institutional structures, friendship has, in Guittone's view, the ability to heal those structures, fractured as they are by rivalry and conflict.[23]

Brunetto Latini likewise posits a polarity between envy and friendship, but he clarifies what mediates between them: rhetoric. Brunetto's *Rettorica* (1260), an incomplete vulgarization of and commentary on Cicero's *De inventione*, champions Ciceronian pronouncements on the social value of rhetoric, conceived of in the broadest terms, as the art of persuasion not only in speech but also in writing.[24] Brunetto aims to carve out a space within social and political formation for rhetoric, recuperating it as an "adversarial art" in the service of ethics, combatting envious rivalries and laying the groundwork for friendship.[25] Following Victorinus's twelfth-century Latin gloss of *De inventione*, Brunetto offers two definitions of social relations that are of interest to the present study. The first, "compagno," describes what might best be called a "civic friend," one whose friendship, formalized in a pact, arises as a result of a common stake in a shared project: "Compagno è quelli che per alcuno patto si congiugne con un altro ad alcuna cosa fare; e di questi dice Vittorino che se sono fermi, per eloquenzia poi divengono fermissimi" [A companion is one who unites himself with another through some pact aimed at accomplishing something; of these, Victorinus says that if they are determined, through eloquence they then become even more resolute].[26] Much as they were for the twelfth-century *dictatores*, for Brunetto instrumental friendships like these are not to be taken cynically (although they are, of course, easily feigned, abused, or dissolved, as seen in Boncompagno da Signa's *Amicitia* and Brunetto's own *Favolello*).[27] In his Ciceronian civic optimism, Brunetto takes the instrumentality of such relationships one step further, presuming that such pacts encourage citizens to perform services for the community at large and may be directed towards public ends, as a form of political or civic friendship.

Brunetto then differentiates the "compagno" [companion] from the "amico" [friend] by means of the private stake the friend has in the well-being of the other:

> Amico è quelli che per uso di simile vita si congiugne con un altro per amore iusto e fedele. Verbigrazia: Acciò che alcuni siano amici conviene che siano d'una vita e d'una costumanza.... [Q]uella amistade ch'è per utilitade e per dilettamento nonn è verace, ma partesi da che 'l diletto e l'uttilitade menoma.[28]

> [A friend is one who, because of a shared way of life, unites himself to another person through a just and devoted love. That is, to be considered friends it is fitting that they share their lives and their habits.... (F)riendship based on usefulness or pleasure cannot be true friendship, but takes flight from that which pleasure and use diminish.]

The definition of "amico," likewise borrowed from Victorinus, derives from a distinct Ciceronian heritage: a similarity of customs, habits, and values serves as the groundwork; on this ground are built honesty, loyalty, and affection. Above all, Brunetto's "amistade" is consistently characterized by disinterestedness: friendship is indifferent to personal gain and hostile to dissolute pleasures, an emphasis that signals its debt to Cicero's *De amicitia*.

In Brunetto's view, rhetoric is the tool that both companions and friends can use to uncover and cultivate their common projects, similar habits, and faithful bonds.[29] He stakes this claim on rhetoric's ability to mitigate envy and overcome dispute: "Rettorica," he claims, "è scienzia d'usare piena e perfetta eloquenzia nelle publiche cause e nelle private: ciò viene a dire scienzia per la quale noi sapemo parlare pienamente e perfettamente nelle publiche e nelle private questioni" [Rhetoric is the discipline of using full and perfect eloquence both in public cases and in private ones; that is, the science by which we know how to speak completely and perfectly on public and private matters].[30] Brunetto's emphasis on rhetoric as a route to resolving controversy and mediating between envy and friendship reminds us that he was writing in the immediate aftermath of the Guelph rout at Montaperti in 1260, when civic factionalism would bring armies to the battlefield, resulting in the exile of principal civic leaders like Brunetto himself. The author calls attention to his own autobiographical circumstances in an aside in the first book, where he notes that the "cagione" [cause] of the book's very existence is Brunetto's discovery, in his exile, of "uno suo amico della sua cittade e della sua parte, molto ricco d'avere, ben costumato e pieno de grande senno, che lli fece molto onore e grande utilitade, e perciò l'appellava suo porto" [a friend of his, from the same city and political party, a man of great wealth and resources, very well-mannered and full of great wisdom, who bestowed on him great honour and great assistance, and for that he would call this friend "his port"].[31] Friendship, particularly the very useful friendship between Brunetto and "suo porto," presents a private resolution to the author's civic banishment, and he uses that private resolution to great public consequence, by writing a manual instructing in the "adversarial art" of rhetoric.[32]

Brunetto's conceptualization of rhetoric as an "adversarial art" is entirely appropriate to the deliberations of the communal context, as its councils and assemblies work to negotiate the governance of cities overrun by factionalism, which tended to resolve dispute by exile or, in the extreme, battle.[33] The civic reality of communal life necessitated such an art, marked as it was by public disputes over property and law, as well as by the perpetual threat of compulsory exclusion from the *comune*, an exclusion that effectively, although often only temporarily, rendered the exile stateless. Brunetto sees such disputation as the means to the restoration of civic peace: as Stephen Milner notes, "For Latini, the symbolic construction of community, therefore, involved the marshaling of rhetoric, which was necessarily contentious, as a central part of the imagination of communal government as the preferred form of social ordering."[34] When the "adversarial art" of rhetoric is guided by wisdom, dispute may become the foundation of like-mindedness, which is in turn the cornerstone of an idealized civic identity. Eloquent argumentation is, then, much like *amistade* for Guittone, the salve that will heal the *comune*.

Indeed, following Cicero's treatise, Brunetto identifies rhetoric as a constructive social force in the communal context. What enables rhetoric's functionality as a social salve is Brunetto's extension of its reach from public controversies to include controversies between individuals on private matters. In Brunetto's historical scheme, resolving private dispute through the exchange of opinions and perspectives on truth defeats *invidia* and creates *amistadi*. Through eloquence and wisdom, Brunetto glosses, men first came to organize themselves into cities, which prospered through the cooperative work afforded by living in society. Such prosperity inevitably led to envy, from which arose conflict. Rhetoric was put to good use, to extinguish the battles wrought by envy among the populace. Cooperation and commerce flourished, and "di queste compagnie cuminciaro a ffare ferme amicizie per eloquenzia e per sapienza" [from these associations they began to form strong friendships through eloquence and wisdom].[35] Overcoming disputes, which is the aim and end of the art of rhetoric, is the essential precondition for friendship, at both the interpersonal and the greater civic levels. For Brunetto, friendship finds its home where eloquence and wisdom are employed to resolve controversy: rhetoric generates like-mindedness between individuals, instructs in conflict resolution, teaches strategies for negotiating opposing political wills both at the level of the *comune* and in private controversies, and so on.

This general optimism notwithstanding, the strife of political factionalism infected the *comuni* at all levels, and literary communities were not exempt from this. Poetic disputes mirrored political ones, in which struggles for enfranchisement led to open conflict in the public square. Likewise, poets competing for prominence engaged one another in open dispute. It is under these combative conditions that we see the promise of a broad-based civic friendship most clearly: as the poets of the *comuni* struggled to negotiate their own ties with one another, they also strove to found a literary community that could supersede those bonds that were infected with the great poison of civic structures, envy.

Creating Networks

In the agonistic conditions of the *comune*, where poets did not vie for the patronage of a sovereign, literary communities were left to establish other tacitly agreed-upon methods for integrating newcomers, forging connections, and determining the centrality and influence of certain figures within their poetic networks. The *tenzone* emerged as the principal tool through which these negotiations took place.[36] In a typical *tenzone* exchange, two or more poets traded lyrics (most frequently sonnets, but also occasionally longer-form poems like *canzoni*), modeling their response poems on the meter and rhyme scheme of the original proposal.[37] This collaborative and dialogic literary practice, imported from the troubadours of Provence by way of Sicily, was particularly well suited to the political and ideological formation of the *comuni* of the late Duecento, with the back-and-forth exchange of ideas in literary form echoing the practice of strategic negotiation among civic counselors across communal institutions and offices.[38] Writing in *tenzone* with one's peers and betters was readily adopted as standard practice by communal literary circles; a community of poets competing for recognition coalesced around the practice and the exchange of *tenzoni* became common among educated laymen of all stripes as they sought attention in the poetic agora.[39] Even the greatest poets on the scene – including Guittone d'Arezzo, Guido Cavalcanti, and Dante – cut their literary teeth in *tenzoni*, asking questions, requesting revisions, experimenting with form, and disputing ideology and terminology in dialogue with their colleagues, in both supportive and antagonistic terms.

The poetic jousting of *tenzoni* served multiple, overlapping functions. Receiving a response to one's *proposta* implied that a poet was a respected contributor to the marketplace of lyric circulation. Participation in these exchanges increased the poet's centrality in the greater literary network, as he showed himself to be a combatant worthy of engagement. Crafting replies improved each poet's skill, as he honed his language to meet the language of his friend. The *tenzone* allowed younger, greener poets to test their mettle – both philosophical and poetic – against the more established poets of their generation, and it opened a space for novices to establish themselves as voices to be reckoned with. Exchanges could be bilateral conversations between two participants or multivocal discussions, involving a wide number and variety of stakeholders. Scholars have reconstructed *tenzoni* made up of only two poems: a proposal and a response. Others appear to have comprised extensive engagements including dozens of sonnets. In the most optimistic view, the *tenzone* modeled productive intellectual dispute. On the whole, these exchanges promoted a broadly inclusive model of sociability that was beneficial for all parties involved: participating in these public exchanges drove up the value and visibility of one's own poems as well as those of one's interlocutors, and permitted poets to create and maintain ties with a wide range of peers, friends, and rivals, despite partisan rancor, ideological dispute, and class (or even gender) difference.[40]

Much as contemporary political communities were sites of consensus and conflict between fellow citizens, *tenzone* exchanges were explicitly construed as a practice of friendship and interpersonal obligation. From the earliest attempts at defining the practice in the mid-Trecento, rhetoricians emphasized the social obligations implicit in the address of a *proposta*. Antonio da Tempo's *Summa artis rithmici vulgaris dictaminis* (1332), for one, insists that upon receipt of a proposing sonnet a poet "debet respondere" [ought to respond], as if bound by a mutual obligation.[41] In his vernacular translation of da Tempo's *Summa*, the Veronese poet Gidino da Sommacampagna adds a contextual note here, which emphasizes the specific social bond between the interlocutors: "quando l'omo receve alguno soneto lo quale gli fia mandado *da alguno suo amico*, l'omo dée respondere alo dicto soneto" [when the man receives some sonnet which will have been sent to him *by some one of his friends*, the man ought to respond to said sonnet].[42] Gidino's translation, with its redoubled emphasis on obligation and its addition of the terminology of *amicizia*, does not imply that all cases of *tenzoni* in the late fourteenth century were initiated between poets who were already friends. But we might suggest that the recipient's obligation to reply is both constitutive of and contingent on the friendship that the proposing sonnet puts on offer. In other words, the act of initiating a *tenzone* can activate the bond of friendship and its concomitant expectations of response.

To analyse the social stakes of the exchange of correspondence poems in the literary communities of late Duecento *comuni*, it is important to consider what exchange means to the context of *tenzone* culture. *Tenzone* exchange, like any practice of non-commercial exchange, is premised on an economy of symbolic capital, as theorized by Pierre Bourdieu. For Bourdieu, practices of exchange operate according to "a fundamental principle, that of equality in honour, which, although it is never explicitly posited as an axiom of all ethical operations, seems to orient practices, because the sense of honour gives practical mastery of it."[43] Exchanges occur within specific fields of practice, where participants constantly negotiate their positions relative to one another through a series of strategic moves in what Bourdieu calls "the game of honour."[44] Positions on the field are negotiated with more or less strategic mastery, according to one's "sense of the game."[45]

In Bourdieu's view, one must obtain the right to enter any field of practice, like the competitive arena of Duecento communal literary exchange. Such a right is won through the accumulation of symbolic capital: honour, virtue, reputation, recognition, and so on. To enter and move within the field of literary production, poets would issue challenges to one another in the *tenzone* form: by initiating an exchange – either directed at a specific individual or group, or a generic call to the field at large – a poet aimed for recognition by established members of the group whom he wanted to consider his peers. He put up his symbolic capital (his name, reputation, and skill level) to be weighed against that of his interlocutor. The success of such an endeavor was characterized by its response (or lack of response). Bourdieu clarifies:

> The exchange of honour, like every exchange (of gifts, words, etc.) is defined as such – in opposition to the unilateral violence of aggression – that is, as implying the possibility of a continuation, a reply, a riposte, a return gift, inasmuch as it contains recognition of the partner (to whom, in the particular case, it accords equality in honour). The challenge, as such, calls for a riposte, and is therefore addressed to a man deemed capable of playing the game of honour, and of playing it well: the challenge confers honour. The converse of this principle of reciprocity is that only a challenge issued by a man equal in honour deserves to be taken up. The act of honour is completely constituted as such only by the riposte, which implies recognition of the challenge as an act of honour and of its author as a man of honour.[46]

What begins as an act of aggression, then, calling into question the honour of both the poet and his interlocutor, contains within it the possibility that the challenge might be converted into an honourable exchange. The initiating sonnet, in Bourdieu's terms, confers honour on the recipient, but only if the recipient replies in kind. Reciprocating the original challenge stands as a recognition of the partner's honour, the reply turning the challenge into a dialogue and converting the aggression of civic dispute into the honourable and mutually beneficial exchange of symbolic capital within the literary field.

For all the tense negotiations of poetic honour and competitive ascendancy underlying *tenzoni* – marked as they are by debate and strife – poets from the Duecento onward regarded these combative verse exchanges as a practice of friendship, frequently hailing their interlocutors as "amici." The Sicilian poets of the previous generation had similarly employed the epithet "amico" in a mode that has been treated as an ironic disguise masking aggression.[47] The Abate di Tivoli, tossing out the term in a heated moment in his exchange with Giacomo da Lentini, blends his call to friendship with reproach, as he admonishes the man he calls "amico" for having taken his censure too far (*Qual om riprende altrui ispessamente*, 3). The tension of the middle sonnets of the *tenzone*, with the Abate's oblique "amico" and the Notary's sharp criticism of boastful but superficial lovers, is frequently remarked.[48] But the about-face of the Abate's final sonnet *Con vostro onore facciovi uno 'nvito*, in which he calls the exchange to abrupt conclusion by heaping apparently sincere praise on his adversary, belies any cynicism in the reading of the Abate's use of the term *amico* in his previous sonnet, however heated the exchange may have earlier appeared. In this forerunner of communal *tenzoni*, friendship and combat seem largely congruent, if not precisely blended, the one proceeding from the other.

Following from Sicilian exchanges such as these, the communal poets employ the term "amico" according to several strategic uses: as a vehicle for calling friendship into being by hailing a potential interlocutor as a friend, as a means of demonstrating one's preeminence by adopting an advisory role with an inferior, and as a mode of reclaiming one's own honour when it has been impugned by the reproaches of one who affects an air of superiority. The terms of friendship appear with surprising frequency in *tenzoni* where the subject is reproach. Cicero insists that reproaches – "cum benevole fiunt" [when given in the spirit of goodwill], he cautions – are integral to friendship, where virtuous friends are obliged to hold their dedication to truth and rectitude over their interpersonal devotion to one another, or, better, as a consequence of that very devotion.[49] The usage of the term "amico" in sonnets of reproach thus enacts an essential operation of Ciceronian friendship, however much some cases may disrupt the balance of rebuke and goodwill.

The most prolific use of the term "amico" in late-Duecento communal poetry appears in the corpus of Guittone d'Arezzo, whose short treatise on the healing nature of friendship was discussed above.[50] Guittone employs the term in both his prose letters and his exchange poems, frequently pairing the epithet with the name of his interlocutor – opening the door to an intensely personal, individualized usage of the term.[51] He also wrote a number of poems to unnamed friends, referred to in the poems only as "compagno" or "amico." Three such examples are *Compagno e amico, non t'oso vetare*; *Amico meo, vetar non oso*; and *Tutt'el maggiore bono amistà sia*. These three sonnets discuss the pitfalls of friendship with one who is unworthy of a good man's affections, or unworthy of the affections of his beloved lady. In each, Guittone heaps scorn on the man he identifies as his friend, reprimanding him for a lack of virtue in his amorous affairs. Across all Guittone's friendship sonnets – and especially in *Tutt'el maggiore bono amistà sia*, the first nine lines of which read like a mini-treatise on the dissolution of friendship – the lyrics express the same sort of truisms about friendship we saw in *Amistade d'envidia è medicina*, conventional enough to be easily exportable. These three sonnets, lacking individual identifications and incorporating commonplaces as they do, permit a great imitability: the Guittonian poets could well pick up on these modes of speaking to issue their own reproaches to friends who act inappropriately.[52] The exportability of such sentiments contributes broadly to the coherence of the Guittonian poets, those who participate in the great network of influence Guittone seeks to establish for himself through his calls to friendship.[53]

In fact, reproach became a defining modality of Guittonian friendship, as evidenced by a long exchange between two poets who found themselves on opposite sides of the partisan divide: the twenty-four-sonnet *tenzone* between two Florentine contemporaries, the Guelf poet Monte Andrea da Firenze (an avowed Guittonian) and the Ghibelline Schiatta Pallavillani, Monte's political opponent but individual ally.[54] While relatively little is known about Monte – beyond his work in the banking sector, his sojourn in Bologna in the late 1260s and early 1270s, and his frequent poetic correspondence with a variety of contemporaries – Schiatta's biography is even less known, and no trace of his literary activity survives save his *tenzoni* with Monte: one on amorous and meta-literary matters, and the other on politics, which I address here.[55] What the poetic record makes clear, however, is that the two participated in what Peter Hainsworth describes as "a poetic society which enjoyed aggressive as well as decorous exchanges of poems, which set store by technical expertise, but which was open to anyone who felt confident enough to join it."[56] Their exchanges, in which the two poets relentlessly try to demonstrate their own prowess while also offering "friendly" advice, teeter on the delicate Ciceronian edge of rebuke guided by goodwill.

As with Guittone's anonymous sonnets, the subject of this *tenzone* is friendly reproach. In the original *proposta*, Schiatta turns to Monte with a concern and a complaint: Monte is too inclined to "smemorare / ispessamente" [to lose your wits frequently], and Schiatta worries for him since people say he has a "cor di con[i]lglio" [a rabbit's heart].[57] Schiatta reproaches Monte for certain excesses that are ruining his reputation; these seem to extend not only to his amorous behavior but also to his poetry, which Schiatta euphemistically accuses of being plagiarized. Monte, in turn, blames all his actions on Love, who has consumed him and now operates him at Love's will.

In his replies to Schiatta, Monte invariably refers to his accuser as "amico," beginning from the first line of his first reply, *Di ciò che prendi, amico, a dimandare*.[58] The *tenzone* illustrates some of the most complex uses of the term "amico" in late-Duecento *tenzoni*, with its attendant obligations and expectations. The appellation appears both in prudent moments of self-denigration and in heated moments of self-defense. For example, in the concluding tercet of Monte's poem *A me nom piace di, tal triega, fare*, the twelfth in the exchange, Monte pleads with Schiatta to believe him, as a friend:

> A voi, amico, mi do tutto im balia
> (ma volglio che crediate al mi' scritto mandato!)
> ch'io spero pur di voi gran cortesia.[59]

[To your mercy, my friend, I give myself (but I want you to believe what I've written!) for I continue to hope that you will show me great kindness.]

The tercet equivocates on Schiatta's sense of courtesy: either believe what I've told you, Monte seems to say, or you are not the friend I thought you were. Monte thus stakes his appeal to friendship on Schiatta's good name, Schiatta consequently risking an impeachment of his chivalry. Later, in the sixteenth sonnet, Schiatta counters, claiming that his reproaches mean to correct and heal Monte's reprehensible behavior, but that his addressee lacks enough courtesy to recognize his errors (*S'io non v'ò servuto, sì come vi pare*, 1–4). Monte, importantly, retorts that just reproach of a friend's bad behavior can heighten the sense of "amistate" between them, but such is not the case here, where Schiatta unjustly blames Monte (*Lo servisgio, chi 'l sape bene fare*). Were Schiatta's reproach worthy, resolution would be sought, and the *tenzone* would "assai monta[re] amistate" [greatly increase their friendship]. It would, in other words, effect a deeper union of the two friends and, thus, of their community. This piece of the exchange is the most Ciceronian moment of the entire *tenzone*: while the truth of Schiatta's accusations is up for debate, the two do not dispute the place of just reproach in the canons of friendship, and even a critique as seemingly aggressive as this one serves to reinforce the ties between the two friends and thus to strengthen the network even across political divides.

The *tenzone* concludes with a hostile reply on Monte's part, in which he refuses to "muddy himself" anymore in this dispute ("Assai mi pesa, ch'io cosí m'infango, / con voi stare a tenzon"), and lambastes himself for having tried to speak truthfully, as a friend, to Schiatta ("A ben pensare, di dolor sofrango, / a voi porgendo il ver, sí com' a amico"). Schiatta's reproach has only succeeded in moving them further from the truth, and in the final analysis Monte shifts his terminology away from that of friendship, giving Schiatta the title of "vincitor" [winner] of the "giostra" [joust], but removing the title "amico," holding his former friend at arm's length ("sí com' a amico"). Friendship fails to secure a resolution of the matter, and Monte withdraws from both the joust and, seemingly, the bond of friendship.

As the *tenzone* with Schiatta exemplifies, Monte frequently uses the term "amico" in social circumstances that may otherwise appear adverse, even hostile: making appeals for aid in times of distress, receiving reproaches (even those ostensibly given in friendly confidence), refusing requests for solidarity, and so on. In quite the opposite mode as Guittone, Monte frequently appeals to his friends' sense of duty from a position not of superiority but of inferiority. By hailing Schiatta as a friend, Monte seeks to restore his own honour within the dispute, charging that despite the conflict he and Schiatta remain equals in their pursuit of truth and virtue. His strategic use of the term invites his interlocutor to heed his obligations to Monte, arising from the sense of duty shared among friends. Monte's call to friendship does not bring about the desired resolution, and he ends the exchange with his erstwhile friend by drawing himself out of the mud Schiatta has created. The failure of friendship to bring about honourable resolution to the dispute results in Monte's abrupt refusal to engage any further. But the *tenzone*, remarkable in its length, demonstrates the extent of engagement sought between *amici* within these networks, even when the engagement appears to have little to do with what we would expect of *vera amicitia* as Cicero theorized it.

In the two surviving exchanges between Monte and Schiatta, each author refers to the other by the epithet "amico" at least once. Such balance is not the case in the correspondence poems exchanged between Guido Cavalcanti and Guido Orlandi, *tenzoni* which display even more emphatically friendship's failure to assuage the bitterness of reproach, when not perceived to be guided by goodwill. Like their forebears Monte and Schiatta, these two Florentine contemporaries were on opposing sides of the political divide, here the Black-White rift that riled the Florentine Guelfs following the decisive rout of the Ghibellines from the city. The handful of sonnets exchanged between them shows evidence of the aggressive political and ideological enmity that divides them.[60] Despite this enmity, Orlandi twice appeals to Cavalcanti as "amico," once in *S'avessi detto, amico, di Maria*, a reply to Cavalcanti's sonnet *Una figura della donna mia*, and again in *Amico, i' saccio bene che sa' limare*, an intervention in his debate with Cavalcanti on the qualities of lyric poetry. Such uses of the term can appear ironic, hiding a "clearly outraged and defensive response" to Cavalcanti's poetry under the guise of friendship.[61] Nevertheless, the *tenzoni* give evidence – as do the rest of their correspondence poems – of an extensive engagement, even though they find themselves on opposite sides in political, literary, and ideological disputes. To this point, it bears noting that not all of Orlandi's exchanges with Cavalcanti were malicious: *A suon di trombe, anzi che di corno* shows no evidence of antagonism, nor does *Onde si move e donde nasce amore*, which, it is commonly suggested, may have elicited Cavalcanti's masterpiece *Donna me prega* as a response. This last gives no apparent indication of any animosity or irony behind the request.

S'avessi detto and, in a more complicated fashion, *Amico, i' saccio ben* wield the term "amico" as a challenge issued from one rival to another. As in the case of the Monte-Schiatta exchanges, dispute under the aegis of friendship ultimately strives to draw the two into the kind of conflictual dialogue that was sought by the citizens of the *comune*. By contending with one another in these disputes, as "amici" (to take Orlandi's word), communal poets confirm their preference for confrontation over disregard, and they confer honour on one another, converting aggression into exchange by engaging their antagonists in dialogue. In both instances, Orlandi's use of the term projects the image of a friendship that could mitigate the political-intellectual antagonism between them, calling on a bond that might underlie their dispute. In particular, in *S'avessi detto* the call to Cavalcanti's *amicizia* at the outset of Orlandi's response appears as a chastising corrective to the "invidia" with which Cavalcanti's *proposta* concludes. But Orlandi's reproaches, which do not appear to abide the Ciceronian dictum "cum benevole fiunt," have tipped the scale from friendly reproach into direct aggression, and his call to Cavalcanti's *amicizia* rings hollow. Cavalcanti pointedly does not replicate the term; indeed, no evidence of any reply to either of Orlandi's challenging sonnets survives. By refusing to engage, Cavalcanti permits Orlandi's challenge to his honour to remain a marker of aggression, without reconciling such aggression through the kind of extensive dialogue and dispute we see in the Monte-Schiatta exchange. The acrimony of Orlandi's tone seems not to have convinced Cavalcanti that his reproaches are made in the spirit of Ciceronian goodwill, but the call to friendship, as a force aimed at channeling animosity towards engagement, stands.[62]

Even if the ostensible friendships performed in *tenzoni* are not resolution-seeking disputes like those anticipated by Brunetto's theory of rhetoric, nor explicit attempts at healing the envy rife among the citizenry, as Guittone's sonnet had hoped, they are, however, evidence of greater connectivity across partisan divides. Networks are agnostic on the affective value or sincerity of ties between their nodes, and these pairs of "friendly" rivals grow more integrated into the broader network through their interactions, as do Dante Alighieri and Dante da Maiano, for example, in spite of Alighieri's refusal to recognize his interlocutor by name.[63] Even when the epithet is seemingly wielded as a taunt, an insult, or an outright attack, it nevertheless serves the function of increasing one's centrality in the literary network. Setting aside sincerity or sentiment, what we see between these poets is engagement, a joust that draws two combatants into a tighter network relation, using the terminology of friendship to do so.[64] The affective aspects of these friendships – their basis in goodwill, loyalty, and trust – sometimes fail, as poets overstep the mark of courtesy in their reproaches of their fellows. But these exchanges promote engagement over aversion, and in doing so move towards rebuilding social bonds among the citizens of the *comune*.

These strategies for negotiating one's position in the field of literary production and circulation were employed as often by the most successful poets in the field as by the least. Acknowledgment in a *tenzone* provides the right to enter the network of active poets, and obsequious praises become important currency in the economy of recognition within which these poets maneuvered. These praises were mutually beneficial: the recipient of a proposing sonnet would benefit from the publicity offered him by the *tenzone*, which would further incline him to reply to the proposal in the first place. Proposing poets would overstate the reputations of even relatively unknown addressees, as appears to have been the case in the exchange initiated by the Pisan poet Geri Giannini to a certain Si. Gui. of Pistoia:[65]

Magna ferendo me tuba 'n oregli
d'orrato ch'ognor in te pregio regna,
lo cor mi stringe, pur volendo vegli,
com'eo pensando tuo conto devegna,
e con onni argomento m'aparegli
pugnando c'ad amico t'aggia e tegna,
in guisa c'amistà mai non envegli,
ma fra noi sempre fresca si contegna.
Und'ho pensato de l'acontar mostra
il dir sia pria, ché 'n ciò vegliat'ho e veglio,
parendo me grand' amistansa n'èsca.
E, perc'ho ditto de l'amistà nostra,
responsion chero qual ti sembra meglio:
vèglia tuttor la mantegnamo u fresca.

[A great trumpeting, sounding in my ears the honoured praise that continues to reign in you, presses on my heart – which even wills such attention – thinking how I may become your confidant,

And I furnish myself with every argument, fighting to have and to keep you as a friend, in such a way that our friendship may never grow old, but between us may always be renewed.

Whence I thought that, as a sign of our trust, speech may come first, so I kept and keep vigil, as it seems to me that a great friendship may arise.

And since I have spoken of our friendship, I ask you to reply as it seems best to you: so may we let it grow old or stay new.][66]

The recipient of the sonnet, Si. Gui., has been variously and uncertainly identified by scholars,[67] not least because he left behind few traces of his poetic output.[68] And yet the sonnet *Magna ferendo* insists on Si. Gui.'s great fame and "orrato … pregio" [honoured praise], which resounds so loudly in Giannini's ears that he can no longer ignore his desire to become the "conto" – the trusted companion or confidant – of this supposedly great poet. Giannini's loud praise of this otherwise unknown poet prompted Zaccagnini to remark that the practice of over-praising one's correspondent was so common as to be seen even among "poeti mediocrissimi" [very mediocre poets].[69]

Perhaps the presumed mediocrity of the poem and its author has led to its being largely overlooked.[70] And yet no exchange, I would contend, better demonstrates the agonistic dynamic at the base of friendship in the urban centres of medieval Italy than this *tenzone*. The *tenzone* has as its very subject friendship itself, and in its theorizing about friendship manages also to be a declaration of friendship-in-act. It is not, as has been suggested, a private conversation, but instead a public performance of friendship in which the correspondents engage in a discussion of what constitutes literary friendship.[71] Unlike Guittone's mini-treatise on friendship's opposition to envy, Giannini's sonnet does not put forth the traditional platitudes about friendship's value as a morally improving enterprise. Rather, it pivots on a vocabulary that makes explicit the relationship of conflict and antagonism to late-Duecento *amicizia.*

Giannini's sonnet is replete with lexical repetitions, and his diction reflects an attention not to the theory of friendship but to its practice. The sonnet conceives of relationships between men (and, to be precise, between poets) as a struggle, in need of constant attention and renewal. In fact, Giannini repeats twice the adjective *fresca* to describe his friendship with Si. Gui., both times contrasting it with *enveglia* or *vèglia* (here semantically related to the idea of growing old and dull). Likewise, Giannini repeats three times the verb *vegliare* [to be awake, to attend to, to keep vigil], claiming that the friendship demands his constant attention and care, particularly at this crucial moment of its inception. The repetitions bring to light an anxiety behind the desire for friendship's maintenance: that without devoted attentions friendship is always under threat of losing its luster, growing dull or dim. This is already surprising for a sonnet on the subject of friendship, about which it is commonplace to use expressions of ease, sweetness, and intimacy, as Guittone's sonnet *Amistade d'envidia è medicina* does. The sonnet, in other words, emphasizes not the pleasures but the difficulties of friendship.

The struggle, however, is not described merely in terms of some abstract arduousness or strain; rather, the sonnet pushes friendship squarely into the sphere of conflict. Much as Brunetto's *Rettorica* had done in its account of the healing power of rhetoric, the sonnet systematically employs a military lexicon in its account of the friends' camaraderie: the trumpet that rings out in Giannini's ears recalls that of the herald sounding the victory of Si. Gui.'s "orrato … pregio" [honoured praise], and in contemplating how he will become the "conto" [confidant] of a poet of such high esteem, Giannini claims that he must equip himself with arguments ("con onni argomento m'aparegli"), suggesting that he anticipates entering a battle of words and philosophies with this newfound friend.[72] But the word that most clearly indicates the combative drive at the heart of this sonnet of friendship appears in verse 6: "*pugnando* c'ad amico t'aggia e tegna" [fighting to have and keep you as a friend]. Such a confrontational verb is surprising in a sonnet about friendship. Though the verb could simply mean "to endeavor" or "to strive," in the context of the rest of the poem's pugnacious imagery the verb carries the specific resonance of the language of combat.[73]

In his reply, Si. Gui. replicates the confrontational language of the initiating sonnet, emphasizing in particular the notion of the "giostra," a word he repeats twice in the poem in *rima equivoca.* Si Gui. claims that his impulse to reply springs not from the worth of Giannini's poem, which he pretends he could not match, but "per lo tu' valor" [because of your valor], which has so captivated Si. Gui. that it awakes in him a loving call to arms, without any contest ("me 'l desti 'n insegna / piena d'amor e sens'alcuna giostra"). He closes by asserting how much friendship pleases him, precisely for the way it encourages a healthy competition ("giostra") for similarity of affections: "Unde mi piace l'amistà, poi g[i]ostra / tanto con le du' l'una per pareglio" [And so I like friendship, because one competes so much with the other to be his equal]. In his last verse, he heartily wishes that their friendship "fresch' e vèglia fra noi sia" [remain between us fresh and new], replicating the adjectives of Giannini's proposal.

Taken together, these references to friendship as combat, contest, and joust confirm the evolution of this strand of thought on literary friendship, as a corollary of the diffusion of the *tenzone* from its Sicilian origins to its fruition in communal circles. Giannini's sonnet anticipates, even desires, a battle of words and wits with Si. Gui. as the very constituent act of friendship itself, and Si. Gui. replies in kind, claiming that friendship itself is a form of joust. Their friendship consists in combative dialogue, in which one must arm oneself with arguments before entering into the public arena to joust with his friend and adversary. It is in the very pugnaciousness of this engagement that we can think of friendship as combatting the disputes and envy rife within the literary network, by acknowledging the spaces of lyric exchange as a battleground in which combatants arm themselves with language and ideas, transforming battle into a practice of friendship. Like rhetoric, this literary practice of friendship is itself disputatious, but ultimately strives to bring about the kind of civic healing called for across the political, social, and ideological spectrum. It is inclusive and expansive in its reach.

In her discussion of the rivalrous subtexts of *tenzone* culture, Barolini claims that the usage of the terminology of friendship in certain of these exchanges "has nothing to do with *amicitia* in the Ciceronian sense of the word."[74] This practice of friendship is, indeed, a far cry from the Ciceronian ideal of the friend as partaking in "omnium divinarum humanarumque rerum cum benevolentia et caritate consensio" [agreement with goodwill and affection between people about all things divine and human]. The Ciceronian view of *amicitia*, however, is not strictly limited to this idealized relationship between two individuals; it also incorporates a greater ambition, aimed at cultivating civic friendship through dialogue and dispute. Each of the pairs of interlocutors considered above – Giacomo da Lentini and the Abate di Tivoli, Guittone and his various anonymous friends, Monte Andrea and Schiatta Pallavillani, Guido Cavalcanti and Guido Orlandi, Geri Giannini and Si. Gui. – uses the term "amico" as a gesture of outreach, with the aim of extending one's network beyond partisan divides and despite ideological differences. Although many of the exchanges that survive from the period characterize friendship as a form of antagonism or rivalry, like Giannini's sonnet does, this characterization in fact participates in a larger Ciceronian project: that of cultivating civic friendship through increased dialogue among the citizenry, much like the "tencione" of Brunetto's *Rettorica*, itself an interpretation of Ciceronian social theory. Even with the dispute that accompanies these dialogues, the practice of *tenzone* exchange functions as a means of retraining the intellectual class in ethico-political modes of speech that allow for the broad contestation of the values of urban life.[75] The kind of dialogue practiced in the exchange of *tenzoni*, as Brunetto's *Rettorica* argued several decades before the mass proliferation of these exchanges, is a fundamentally Ciceronian enterprise, not only desirable but even necessary for the health of communal politics. It could become, in other words, the *medicina* for *envidia*.

The Ship of Friendship

Given the ethical ambivalence with which late-Duecento authors approached *amistà* and *amicizia* in their literary practices, it is perhaps not surprising that a group of poets would wish to revitalize friendship's moral substance. As Guittone and his imitators instrumentalized the language of *amistadi* in the service of increasing their network connections – with little apparent regard for the depth or durability of those connections – their sprawling networks diffused and diminished the moral force of a term like *amistà*. As is especially evident in Guittone's corpus, in *tenzone* exchanges the word "amico" was deployed as a tool for extending one's network: to call one's interlocutor "friend," as Guittone frequently did with both named and unnamed interlocutors, did not imply an already-established, intimate connection. On the contrary, the term served a generic function, an appellation a poet would use to hail another as a peer, united with the initiator of the exchange in literary fellowship, however performative or even insincere that fellowship may appear. These friendships met the expectations for the kind of disputatious dialogue hoped for in optimistic discussions of expansive and healing civic friendship.[76]

The *dolce stil novo* poets would replace the inclusionary, expansive approach of Guittone and his imitators with an exclusionary and restrictive one. Dante and his fellow *stilnovisti* use the vocative "amico" seldom in their lyrics, relative to the frequency with which the term appears in the poetry of their contemporaries, especially Guittone, Monte, and the other adherents of their school. Though terms of friendship appear infrequently in their lyrics (not least of all because, as Barolini has argued, the term "amico" was charged with the rivalries and oppositions of the broader community of Tuscan writers), these poets nevertheless sought to reinstate a practice of individual, private friendship that moved its participants towards moral and intellectual perfection.[77] In principle, friendship in the stilnovist mode no longer aspired to unite large communities of writers in dialogue, but instead sought to purify and intensify a limited number of connections, favouring depth of rapport over quantity of ties. Emilio Pasquini sees in this tightknit group a "rapporto corale, fatto di sorridente complicità e di sapidi ammicchi" [harmonious rapport, made up of smiling complicity and knowing winks].[78] Such a definition, though, glosses over the highly contentious, even antagonistic, nature of these seemingly harmonious bonds. The stilnovists' increased focus on individualism, critique, and competition complements rather than diminishes the sense of unanimity between the adherents of the group. The *stilnovisti*, and particularly Dante, promoted an exclusionary and isolationist mode of friendship, which competed for moral worthiness with the expansive civic friendship advocated by Guittone and his imitators.

No text from the period celebrates this exclusionary mode of friendship quite like *Guido, i' vorrei che tu e Lapo ed io*, Dante's sonnet penned to Guido Cavalcanti presumably in the mid-1290s around the time of the *Vita nova*'s composition. That this sonnet on friendship evades direct use of the terms *amico*, *amistà*, *amicizia*, and the like, may, Barolini has suggested, indicate that the term remained too tightly connected to its contemporary usage as a thin disguise for poetic rivalries.[79] We might also read this ostensible omission as a subtle critique of the theoretical idealizations of friendship that arise from readings in the Aristotelian-Ciceronian tradition. Regardless, *Guido, i' vorrei* paints a singular portrait of friendship that distinguishes it not only from the theoretical literature on friendship (following writers like Brunetto and Guittone), but also from its praxis in contemporary *tenzone* culture, which I have described above.[80]

Modeled in part after the Provençal *plazer*, *Guido, i' vorrei* performs in its dream landscape the desires at the base of the kind of morally and intellectually improving friendships sought by ancient authorities and their medieval counterparts alike.[81] Yet the crucial exchange between the speaker, Guido, and their friend Lapo also anticipates the pitfalls on the way to realizing such a desire:

Guido, i' vorrei che tu e Lapo ed io
fossimo presi per incantamento,
e messi in un vasel ch'ad ogni vento
per mare andasse al voler vostro e mio;
sì che fortuna od altro tempo rio
non ci potesse dare impedimento,
anzi, vivendo sempre in un talento,
di star insieme crescesse il disio.
E monna Vanna e monna Lagia poi
con quella ch'è sul numer de le trenta
con noi ponesse il buono incantatore:
e quivi ragionar sempre d'amore,
e ciascuna di lor fosse contenta
sì come credo che saremmo noi.

[Guido, I wish that Lapo, you, and I
were carried off by some enchanter's spell
and set upon a ship to sail the sea
where every wind would favour our command,
so neither thunderstorms nor cloudy skies
might ever have the power to hold us back,
but rather, cleaving to this single wish,
that our desire to live as one would grow.
And Lady Vanna were with Lady Lagia
borne to us with her who's number thirty
by our good enchanter's wizardry:
to talk of love would be our sole pursuit,
and each of them would find herself content,
just as I think that we should likewise be.][82]

As the final tercet makes plain, the sonnet places dialogue at the centre of friendly activity.[83] The *ragionar d'amore* that these friends share in their endless and aimless sea voyage is akin to the practice of dialogue that Brunetto's rhetor seeks: the goal of such dialogue is not to unite the participants' opinions, arriving at some truth that we might call objective, but rather to achieve concord within one's own opinions, discovering in the process what these opinions have in common with those of the friend. In an essay on Socratic dialogue and its role in generating social cohesion, Hannah Arendt explains that the object of a dialectic like this one is not to replace *doxa* – which she defines as the ways one "comprehend[s] the world as it opens itself to me" – with truth, but to better understand and better articulate one's idiosyncratic perspective on the world, finding the truth within that perspective.[84] This activity, she contends, is generative of friendship. "It is obvious," she explains, "that this kind of dialogue, which doesn't need a conclusion in order to be meaningful, is most appropriate for and most frequently shared by friends."[85] This shared occupation is generative of the concord that the classical authorities celebrated as the foundation of friendship, and it is this sense of cohesion that is the object of the *ragionar d'amore* that Dante and his companions share. Dialogue, even dispute, is the fuel that sustains the desire to remain in their little company.

In his *Rettorica*, Brunetto Latini connects such dialogic activity back to the polis, presenting eloquence as the arm that would fight for ("pugnare") the good of the State, and the eloquent speaker as one who is "uomo e cittadino utilissimo et amicissimo alle sue et alle publiche ragioni" [a very useful man and citizen, deeply committed to his own interests and to those of the general public].[86] In *Guido, i' vorrei*, however, Dante notably departs from Brunetto's concern for the "publiche ragioni." In fact, *Guido, i' vorrei* lays bare the paradoxically anti-civic, antisocial nature of such friendships, a mode of friendship that C.S. Lewis, centuries later, would characterize as "a pocket of potential resistance."[87] For all of the incantatory power of the poem's impulse towards the unification of the three friends and their beloved ladies, the fellowship formed among them is premised on their exclusion from society at large.[88] The poet desires that he and the two friends he individuates in the *capoverso* are magically removed from their society, to the exclusion of all societal cares – figured as "fortuna od altro tempo rio" [thunderstorms or cloudy skies] – that would threaten their unanimity. In the magic space of their exclusive society the friends find the governance of their affairs entirely within their own power ("ch'ad ogni vento/ per mare andasse al voler vostro e mio"). The kind of friendship celebrated in *Guido, i' vorrei* seeks to individuate and elevate certain individuals from among the larger social group, drawing them away from their peers in an exclusionary, preferential mode.

At stake in the sonnet is the tension between the two social impulses of friendship: on the one hand the individualizing, preferential desire of two (or at most three) friends to remain in each other's close company, and, on the other, the cohesion of society at large. The sonnet negotiates between the tight exclusivity of the most virtuous forms of Ciceronian friendship and the risk that such friendships might be too inward-looking, and hence antisocial. Such cliquish friendships represent a threat to the cohesion of the group as a whole. In its yearning for the isolation of the three friends and their ladies from any "impedimento" brought by public concerns or social responsibilities (Brunetto's "publiche ragioni"), the sonnet removes the potential for the most virtuous friendships to open out to a greater sociability.

The exclusionary impetus at the heart of *Guido, i' vorrei* shares its impulses with certain claims made by the classical authorities on friendship, chief among them Cicero. In *De amicitia*, for example, Laelius claims that friendship derives its strength from its exclusivity: "ita contracta res est et adducta in angustum, ut omnis caritas aut inter duos aut inter paucos iungeretur" [friendship is selective so that its affection joins together only two or at most a few people].[89] *Guido, i' vorrei* follows this pattern, accentuating the small number of its company by restricting the three to a single verse, at least in the octave: "tu e Lapo ed io," the three mentioned in rapid succession, highlighting their particularity before gathering them into the implied "noi" of the following verse.[90]

The exclusionary impulse at the heart of this friendship forms part of what Barolini calls the sonnet's "desire for a magic space of impossible and perfect non-difference," a radical unification of the three friends' wills that elides the differences in their desire while simultaneously insisting on their individuality.[91] According to her Trinitarian reading of the sonnet, Dante has envisioned a perfect union of three persons through the harmony at the base of friendship.[92] For Barolini, the focus here is on the imaginary aspect of the voyage and the impossibility of realizing the fantasy of unity. Where Barolini rightly insists on the contrary-to-fact condition of this desire, which ultimately points to the sonnet's tragic impossibility, I would highlight the clarity of the sonnet's position on friendship, which contrasts sharply with Ciceronian precepts: the fellowship the speaker desires is an exclusionary, distant, non-civic friendship. Isolation from their social group, which is unambiguously desired by the speaker, begets their unity; the magic spell separates them from their peers and contemporaries and places them in a boat on an imagined sea, where they pass their days as they please. The sonnet removes any trace of the ambivalence that we may have been able to detect in others of Dante's "social" sonnets, like that Barolini identifies in *Sonar bracchetti*.[93] The separation of the three from the collective only increases the bond they feel with one another: it is in one another's company that their desire becomes one, and "di star insieme crescesse il disio" [our desire to live as one would grow].

While the unity of the group increases with time and distance – as Barolini's Trinitarian reading recognizes – so does their voluntary exile from the rest of communal life. It is that exclusionary impulse that requires our further attention as we work to disentangle this dilemma of friendship theory as Dante understood it. Within the dream-landscape of the sonnet, such self-imposed exclusion from public (and especially political) cares is the driving force behind the friends' longing for such radical unity. The desire for one another's company is continuously multiplied in the absence of worldly concerns, concerns of both the domestic and the public spheres. Such tempests represent the "impedimento" [the power to hold us back] to the friends' dialogue, obscuring the clarity of their disputations and driving them back towards the rocky shores of communal vicissitudes. In the sonnet's dreamscape, the friends' unified will – not the uncertainties of communal conflict – is the only wind that will fill their sails. Their energies are directed to a single end, steering the ship away from shore in an endless "ragionar d'amore" [talk of love]. The sonnet simply removes any obstacles to exerting these energies by magically transporting the friends to a sphere outside greater social concerns.

Indeed, the same forces that facilitate the formation of an exclusionary, isolated, virtuous friendship like the one envisioned here would prevent any of its participants from using that friendship in transactional engagements with others in the larger society, like those described in the *tenzoni* we saw above. In *tenzoni*, poets sought to dispute, praise, and reproach in a deliberately public forum, engaging in these contentious dialogues as a form of asserting one's centrality to the network and negotiating poetic ascendancy. Jousting with one's peers and betters in the piazza of lyric exchange integrated a poet more fully into the literary community and granted him a stage on which to compete for recognition.

By contrast, *Guido, i' vorrei* draws its competitive edge from the three friends' withdrawal from the piazza – their refusal of its petty, public jousting in favour of what they style as authentic dialogue. Guido's reply, *S'io fosse quelli che d'Amor fu degno*, then doubles down on withdrawal, even further distancing the speaker from the community envisioned in Dante's dream by refusing to count himself one of Love's favoured courtiers.[94] Guido's reply seems to vie with Dante's for separation and isolation, as a marker of the speaker's uniquely intense, shattering experience of love.

The desire to remove oneself from the vicissitudes of urban life and from the kind of transactional, disputatious friendships celebrated in *tenzoni* is comprehensible in light of the reality of the Florentine *comune* at the end of the Duecento. The life that *Guido, i' vorrei* envisions is one that is removed from the piazza, with all its political turmoil and commercial bustling, especially in a hub like thirteenth-century Florence. The statesman Laelius, however, would scarcely tolerate such a self-imposed exile from civic society; in this sense, Dante's sonnet violates one of the principal precepts of Ciceronian republicanism: the political drive towards participatory politics and the inclusion of all voices within civic society.[95] Such an exclusionary model shifts away from the optimism of civic friendship, which hopes to unite citizens in dialogue (however pugnacious), to employ their *ragionar* to reach a broad consensus, ultimately aiming to heal the tensions that threaten the unity of the whole. Instead, Dante's sonnet desires to exclude the friends, elevating them above the fray. Only in separation, the sonnet suggests, will they discover the moral force of *vera amicitia.*

Friendship's Secret Chambers

The *Vita nova* represents the young Dante's attempt to transport such an exclusionary, isolationist friendship from the magical seas of dreamscapes back into the interpersonal engagement of the piazza. Much as readers might expect of a young poet attempting to break onto the literary scene of the late Duecento Florentine *comune*, the speaker of the *Vita nova* begins his autobiographical account with a gesture of outreach. Signaling towards the social structures of the *comune*'s literary world, the speaker sends his first sonnet to "tutti li fedeli d'Amore" [all of Love's faithful], those who were the "famosi trovatori in quel tempo" [well-known poets of that time].[96] But unlike the sonnet that it introduces, which is as expansive in its outreach as are the Guittonian exchanges considered above, the prose commentary that contextualizes and reframes this poem presents the community at large as having strict social boundaries that must be maintained. The speaker claims to have already publicly demonstrated his ability ("che io avesse già veduto per me medesimo l'arte del dire parole per rima");[97] he has thus surmounted the barrier to entry that would prevent just any amateur rhymester from participating in the marketplace of exchanges that Love's faithful servants might enjoy. The prose narrator boasts that his sonnet generated intrigue and attracted many replies offering diverse explanations ("A questo sonetto fue risposto da molti e di diverse sentenzie"), presumably thanks to the subtlety and complexity of the original proposal.[98] Among these replies, of course, we find that of Guido Cavalcanti, "quelli cu' io chiamo primo delli miei amici" [somebody whom I consider my best friend].[99]

What appears at first glance to be an act of outreach to the community at large in fact reveals an even more restrictive picture of social relations in the *comune*, one that focuses almost exclusively on the relationship between the prose narrator and his pointedly unnamed "primo amico." The prose narrative of the *Vita nova* represents, I argue, an attempt by the narrator to reinscribe the exclusionary vision of friendship with Guido celebrated in the sonnet *Guido, i' vorrei* into communal literary society. The contours of that restrictive picture will emerge more clearly as the narrative progresses. The narrator strategically abandons the outreach model of friendship that dominated *tenzone* culture in the late Duecento and embraces an increasingly hierarchical, exclusive, and antisocial model – one which will, in the final analysis, alienate all others from its grasp. Ultimately, the attempt to integrate the imagined model of exclusive friendship with Guido into the rivalrous sphere of literary exchange will fail, resulting in the self-imposed alienation of the speaker from all his previous interlocutors in the piazza, including his *primo amico*.

Following from seminal studies by Domenico De Robertis and Charles Singleton, critics have seen in the modes of friendship predominant in the *Vita nova* a preparatory model for the *caritas* that will be sung in the *Commedia*.[100] And yet, as I will show, the *Vita nova*'s presentation of *amistà* does not share in the optimism of the *Commedia*'s disinterested, universalizing *caritas*. Neither does it share in the optimism of *Guido, i' vorrei*'s antisocial longings, even as it retains the earlier lyric's emphasis on exclusion from public life for the sake of friendship's moral force. Reinscribing the antisocial imaginings of *Guido, i' vorrei* into the tensions of communal life ushers in ambiguity, isolation, and alienation, qualities which hang over the idealizing gestures towards Guido's friendship in the early parts of the *Vita nova*'s prose narrative.

The *Vita nova* enacts a series of exclusionary literary practices that conflict with the expansive and morally ambiguous *amistà* central to *tenzone* culture. The conception of friendship developed in the prose narrative is consonant with the restrictive, even cliquish, portrait celebrated in the visionary sonnet. In other words, the self-marginalization envisioned and desired by the speaker of the sonnet is put into practice in the *Vita nova*'s prose commentary, developed as a response to the *maldicenti*, "pieni d'invidia" [full of envy], who constantly threaten the narrator's relationships.[101] The marginalization the earlier sonnet imagined, however, extends in the *Vita nova* even to the gradual exclusion of the poet's closest *amici*, who throughout the narrative repeatedly misread both texts and situations, emphasizing their lack of *concordia* [harmony] and *consensio* [agreement] with the speaker. The *Vita nova*'s performance of such a restrictive theory of *amistà* is enacted in four principal movements: the hierarchization of the speaker's *amistadi*; the voluntary marginalization of the speaker and his closest allies; the systematic erasure of other interlocutors from the text, including, eventually, his closest friends; and the recurrent episodes of self-dialogue. Taken together, these four movements work actively to separate certain individuals from society at large, allowing their private dialogue to draw them away from the public aggressions of the piazza and into the secret chambers of noble homes and hearts.[102]

Rather than revel in the public, open performances of disputatious dialogue that were characteristic of *amici* in *tenzone* culture, the prose of the *Vita nova* strategically restricts its audiences and gradually silences its interlocutors. The prose narrative destabilizes the celebratory notion of *amistà* as public engagement established by *tenzone* exchanges, shunning the expansive framework of existing network structures in favour of a discriminatory and fundamentally antisocial model of exclusive poetic circles. And yet, this antisocial model is equally doomed to failure, as the narrator will find himself unable to reconcile his opinions with those of his friend, in their restrictive circle. The exclusionary premises celebrated in Guido's friendship fail to provide the *Vita nova*'s narrator with the withdrawal from social jousting – and its concomitant moral force that evading the petty joust promises – that he appears to have sought in both his poetry and its accompanying prose. In its failure he finds a unique condition of estrangement.

The earliest marker of Guido's friendship, in *Vita nova* 2.1 [3.14], is tied to the idea of a hierarchical vision of friendship that the speaker will maintain for the duration of the prose commentary, referring to Guido always as "primo amico." Such a hierarchized vision of friendship is made explicit in the discussion of what the speaker calls the "gradi dell'amistade," introduced in reference to another friend: "secondo li gradi dell'amistade," the poet announces, "è amico a me immediatamente dopo lo primo; e questi fu tanto distretto di sanguinitade a questa gloriosa che nullo più presso l'era" [in degree of friendship, is the friend of mine right after the first. And he was such a close blood relation of the glorious one that nobody was closer to her].[103] Here, as elsewhere in the *Vita nova*, the speaker underlines questions of proximity, in both voluntary (friendship) and involuntary (familial) ties. Proximity is calibrated according to precise degrees ("gradi"), with some individuals ascending to the top of the preferential scale and others falling below.

The notion of the "gradi dell'amistade" is easily dismissed as simply congruous with the medieval world view, with its obsessive drive to categorize and order nature. But the *Vita nova*'s unusual presentation of the degrees of preference in friendship marks a pointed departure from discussions of the *gradus amicitiae* or *gradus charitatis* of its Latin predecessors. Guglielmo Gorni identifies possible sources of Dante's term *gradus* in relation to a hierarchical concept of love, typically correlated with *caritas*, in several works included in the *Patrologia Latina* and the *Thesaurus Linguae Latinae*.[104] Of those he lists, only one uses the term in a mode similar to Dante's: where Bernard of Clairvaux, Aelred of Rievaulx, Richard of Saint Victor, Livy, and Valerius Maximus all use the term *gradus* to mean "step" or "stage" of *caritas*, *amor*, or *amicitia*, only John Cassian's *Collationes patrum* [*Conferences*] employs *gradus* to refer to the degree to which one individual is loved more than another.[105] The term appears in the title of one of the sections of the *Conferences*, dedicated to the question of friendship. The text develops the term's figurative meaning, as part of a gradation or ranking, a way of indicating preference among one's loves. If all are due our love (*agape/dilectio*) – even, Cassian insists, our enemies – among those we love it is fitting that we show affection (*diathesis/affectio*) to only a few:

> Διάθεσις autem, id est, affectio, paucis admodum, et his qui vel parilitate morum vel virtutum societate connexi sunt, exhibetur, licet etiam ipsa affectio multam in se differentiam habere videatur. Aliter enim parentes, aliter conjuges, aliter fratres, aliter filii diliguntur, et in ipsa quoque horum affectuum necessitudine magna distantia est, nec uniformis parentum dilectio erga filios invenitur.
>
> [But Διάθεσις, or affection, is shown to very few, to those who are linked by a similarity of behavior and by the fellowship of virtue. Yet even Διάθεσις itself seems to have many divisions. For parents are loved in one way, spouses in another, brothers in another, and children in still another, and within the very web of these feelings, there is a considerable distinction, and not even the love of parents for their children is uniform.][106]

Cassian concludes the section on the degrees of affection by articulating clearly his notion of a hierarchy among friends: "quaeque cum generaliter diligat cunctos, excipit tamen sibi ex his quos debeat peculiari affectione complecti, et rursum inter ipsos qui in dilectione summi atque praecipui sunt, aliquos sibi qui caeterorum affectui superextollantur excerpit" [Although it loves everyone in a general way, nonetheless it makes an exception for itself of those whom it should embrace with a particular affection. And, again, among those who are highest and chiefest in this love it chooses for itself some who are set apart from the others by an extraordinary affection].[107] A preferential hierarchy of friends, for Cassian as for Dante, implies the exclusion of many, even most, for the sake of the elevation of a chosen few.

I am not concerned here with establishing the exact provenance of Dante's use of the term "gradi dell'amistade," nor do I wish to suggest that the young poet derived his concept of the degrees of friendship directly from a reading of John Cassian's *Conferences*.[108] Rather, I would emphasize how greatly his conception differs from that of the other authors on Gorni's list: while most of these theologians use the term to designate the stages of friendship, as pairs of friends ascend in a hierarchy towards the most intimate forms of friendship, for Dante, as for Cassian, the degrees of friendship establish a hierarchy of preference and proximity among friends, separating first from second, second from third, and so on. The emphasis for the young poet was on creating a hierarchical order among his confidants, ordering them not according to the stages of their intimacies but to their degree of proximity within the speaker's network.

The same exclusionary impulse seen in *Guido, i' vorrei* animates the ways the speaker arranges his hierarchy of friends according to degrees. The speaker's classification system does not take an expansive view of friendship like that anticipated within the communal literary sphere, one that would unite a larger network of individuals who engage in contentious debate around a shared set of concerns. Rather, the thrust of the "gradi" is one of distinction and differentiation, establishing clear boundaries between in-group and out-group, and then further subdividing the in-group according to rank. Dante's principal concern in speaking of *amistadi* in the *Vita nova* is in limiting his innermost circle, in precisely the opposite way we see the term used in exchanges in the period. Here, as elsewhere in the *libello*, Dante employs the notion of "gradi," not in relation to fellowship and commonality, but to create hierarchies of intellection.[109]

That the speaker hierarchizes his inner circle leads him to a second restriction placed on social structures in the prose of the *Vita nova*: the exclusion of outsiders.[110] Where the poets of *tenzoni* often desired to increase their centrality in the literary network by acts of outreach, entering into public disputes with the renowned poets of their age, the speaker of the *Vita nova* strives to impede the public's access to the meaning of his lyrics. Indeed, after recording the pivotal *canzone* of the *Vita nova*, *Donne ch'avete intelletto d'amore*, the speaker confesses explicitly his desire to limit the size of his audience: "tuttavia chi non è di tanto ingegno che per queste [divisioni] che sono fatte la [canzone] possa intendere a me non dispiace se la mi lascia stare, ché certo io temo d'avere a troppi comunicato lo suo intendimento pur per queste divisioni che fatte sono, s'elli avenisse che molti le potessero udire" [However, it does not bother me if anyone who is not insightful enough to understand the poem by using the divisions already provided leaves off trying, since in fact I fear I have already communicated its meaning to too many people – assuming, that is, it should ever have a large audience].[111] The poet's admission of modesty (genuine or feigned) at the conclusion of this passage is obvious and has garnered the attention of commentators.[112] But the poet's supposed modesty obscures his primary motive: the narrator articulates here his explicit intent to set barriers between his lyrics and their audiences, as a filter for the intellectual discernment that he requires of his interlocutors (which he will elsewhere call *discretio*, as I discuss in the following two chapters). Beyond expressing a modest concern over his possible future readership, the speaker here strives actively to limit the number of readers who have full access to the text and its meaning.

Dante elaborates on the question of access to meaning in his brief digression on the origins of vernacular poetry in *Vita nova* 16. Following a discussion of the rhetorical cloaks with which poets beautify their rhymes, the speaker concludes, "grande vergogna sarebbe a colui che rimasse cose sotto vesta di figura o di colore rettorico e poscia, domandato, non sapesse denudare le sue parole da cotale vesta in guisa che avessero verace intendimento. E questo mio primo amico e io ne sapemo bene di quelli che così rimano stoltamente" [it would be shameful for one who wrote poetry dressed up with figures or rhetorical color not to know how to strip his words of such dress, upon being asked to do so, showing their true sense.

My best friend and I are only too well acquainted with poets who write in such a stupid manner].[113] As in *Guido, i' vorrei*, here the speaker distinguishes his friend and himself, setting their "noi" – an elite brotherhood of two – explicitly apart from "quelli che così rimano stoltamente."[114] Even among the "fedeli d'amore," the "primo amico" is set apart as a particular connoisseur of rhyme, rhetoric, and meaning. More than a statement about their mutual lyric acumen, or about the intensity of their like-mindedness, the statement works to set Guido apart as the primary, even singular, audience of the text, one who can "denudare" its words to draw out its "verace intendimento." The systematic elevation of Guido to the position of *primo amico* – and hence *primo lettore* – works simultaneously to marginalize and debase the rest of the literary community.

That Dante elevates Guido to *primo lettore* hinges on Guido's implicit agreement with the narrator on the matter of literature – its questions and its forms – even if the two do not precisely agree on its content. Previous conversations, pointedly not recorded in the prose of the *libello*, elevate Guido in the speaker's hierarchy thanks to his judicious agreement with the speaker. Claudio Giunta has argued that the *Vita nova*'s innovation is its insistence on monologism: that the *libello* writes out the dialogic elements of the lyrics included in the collection, with the exception of the first.[115] Even in the *tenzoni* included in the *libello*, Giunta points out, Dante only includes *missivi*, ignoring his own *responsivi* and those of his interlocutors as if they have no place in the monologic space of this new *canzoniere*. To Giunta's suggestion I would add, however, that whatever its claims to monologism, the narrative retains markers of dialogism throughout, both in the speaker's performed self-dialogue – the episodes of which are the motor of the narrative's movement – and in markers of excised dialogues that have been strategically erased from its structure.[116] I will first turn attention to the latter.

Within the prose of the *Vita nova* are scattered references to critiques that would have arisen in the piazza of public exchanges, where poets were frequently censured for choices of both form and content. The most famous case of these behind-the-scenes critiques is Dante's prose clarification of the sonnet *Oltra la spera che più larga gira*, which had been criticized, immediately upon its circulation, in a polemical sonnet by Cecco Angiolieri.[117] The speaker uses the later prose narrative to reframe the original composition, giving clarity to the apparent contradiction in the poet's ability to "intendere" [understand] the words spoken in his ecstatic vision, a contradiction for which Cecco had maligned the sonnet. Dante uses the prose narrative to respond to Cecco's accusation of inconsistency, thus silencing Cecco's critique without naming him, nor alluding directly to the dispute.

Where *tenzone* exchanges would have placed such antagonistic and friendly dispute front and centre, airing grievances and staging debates in the most public fashion, the prose narrative of the *Vita nova* erases dialogue and dispute, leaving the reader to imagine the lyric critiques behind some of the defensive moves in the prose commentary. With the early exception of the narrator's explicit request for interpretation of the *Vita nova*'s first poem, the remainder of the prose narrative actively excises dialogue with interlocutors like Cecco, who might discredit the poet or his claims. Like the prose explanation of the apparent contradiction in chapter 30, the explanatory gymnastics the speaker must do in chapter 27 seem to suggest another silenced debate. Here, the narrator is at pains to justify the substitution of the pair *cuore-anima* [heart-soul] in *Gentil pensero che parla di voi* for the *occhi-cuore* [eyes-heart] of the sonnet recorded in chapter 26 (*L'amaro lagrimar che voi faceste*). The speaker concludes his explanation of the substitutions by forestalling a possible accusation of contradiction: "onde appare che l'un detto non è contrario a l'altro" [therefore it is apparent that one statement does not contradict the other].[118] Where *tenzone* exchanges permitted such dispute to happen openly, here the narrator elects to pre-empt and thus silence critique. Such silencing further restricts the social engagement of the speaker, limiting his friendship to an elite inner circle of worthy interlocutors.

At best, antagonists who may have voiced previous criticism of the *Vita nova*'s poems are rewritten into the prose narrative as imaginary interlocutors. Such an imagined dialogue follows on the heels of the poem *Ballata, i' vo' che tu ritrovi Amore* (chapter 5), where the narrator pre-empts a dispute with an imagined interlocutor:

> Potrebbe già l'uomo opporre contra me e dire ch'e' non sapesse a cui fosse lo mio parlare in seconda persona, però che la ballata non è altro che queste parole ched io parlo; e però dico che questo dubbio io lo 'ntendo solvere e dichiarare in questo libello ancora in parte più dubbiosa, e allora intenda qui chi qui dubita o chi qui volesse opporre in questo modo.
>
> [It is true that someone might object, saying he does not know whom my words are addressed to in the second person, since the ballad is none other than the words I speak. And so I say that I still intend to resolve and clarify this ambiguity in an even obscurer section of this little book. And at that point may whoever has such doubts here, or wishes to object in this manner, understand what is said here.][119]

The passage, the first of its kind in the *Vita nova*, bears all the markers of a prior exchange with another poet, an anonymous and generic "uomo" who could object and yet is erased from the "libro de la mia memoria" [book of my memory] from which the narrator is ostensibly copying.[120] Because of its correlation to chapter 16 – the "parte più dubbiosa" [even obscurer section] to which the poet refers in the passage cited above, in which he claims he will resolve the doubts that his imagined interlocutor has raised – this passage appears to have been added on as an emendation to chapter 5, where the poet meditated on the question of Love's figuration in the *libello*. In both cases, the poet speaks directly to a reader whom he sees as worthy of serious engagement in dialogue; in fact, in chapter 16 he specifies that this reader is a "persona degna da dichiararle ogni dubitazione" [a person worthy of having every doubt clarified]. The speaker affords his interlocutor here great dignity: this reader is deemed capable of subtle understanding, and his criticisms merit the poet's response. Such affordances have led Gorni to suggest that the *persona degna* could be no other than Guido Cavalcanti.[121] And yet, while the speaker accords his critic great worthiness, he simultaneously effaces this worthy critic from the narrative by refusing to identify him beyond generic terms: the "persona degna" of chapter 16, and the even less specific "uomo" of chapter 5. By leaving the identity of the opponent so obscured, the speaker manages to erase him from the dialogue.

While the *libello* seeks to elevate the status of Guido Cavalcanti as *primo amico*, it simultaneously erases even his voice, allowing him to appear explicitly only in the arguments in which he and the narrator find agreement – and even so, never by name. With the notable exception of *A ciascun'alma presa*, anywhere that Guido – or some other *persona degna* – appears in opposition to the speaker's ideas, the evocation is indirect, nonspecific, and certainly not correlated to the narrator's friendship, as "amico." Although Guido haunts every page of the *libello*, his presence is only evoked for it to be shadowed: he is never named, as he is prominently in lyrics like *Guido, i' vorrei*, where his name announces the particular importance he holds in his very special friendship with the speaker.[122] In the *libello*, by contrast, there is no mention of Guido's name and only scant reference to his poetry. His identity in the text only exists in its specific relation to the speaker, as the speaker's "primo amico," but not as a full-fledged participant in exchange as he is figured in *Guido, i' vorrei*. The silencing of Guido's voice and the erasure of his name removes the real Guido Cavalcanti even further from the speaker's inner circle, replacing him with a fictional interlocutor that the prose commentary positions as united with the speaker on all questions, both literary and philosophical. As the speaker attempts to reinscribe the exclusionary friendship imagined in *Guido, i' vorrei* within the contentious urban space of the *Vita nova*, the disputatious dialogue of that *amistà* impedes his authorial voice. The *primo amico* and all others must be silenced so that the speaker might achieve his goal of composing a fiction that would cement his place in the literary hierarchy.

The *Vita nova* replaces the productive public disputes of *tenzoni* with private, behind-the-scenes dialogues, held not in the public square but in quiet chambers found in homes and hearts. In fact, the most prominent interlocutor of the prose commentary is not the *primo amico*, as Mazzotta has suggested, but the speaker himself, who eschews the care and affections of his friends for the sake of cultivating solitude, where he can more carefully attend to the inner dialogues he enjoys with himself.[123] After having heard the voices of the various spirits crying out from the most secret chambers of his body, the speaker finds himself withdrawing from the crowded spaces of the city "al solingo luogo d'una mia camera" [away to the solitude of my room], where he reflects on the lady's courtesy.[124] He returns frequently to the solitary space of his *camera* (in itself likely a self-aggrandizing fiction of the narrative, as Dante's own family would scarcely have had the resources to provide the young man with a quiet space all to himself).[125] The prose commentator obsessively seeks his own seclusion, away from the inquisitive eyes and gossiping lips of his contemporaries, who are the drivers of the few turns in an already very slight plotline. By so doing he brings about his own estrangement, highlighting the uniqueness of his position, singular both in his suffering and in his selection.

The solitude the speaker seeks is also, however, generative of a particular kind of exclusive dispute within his own thoughts. Such internal dispute, which he twice refers to as a "battaglia delli diversi pensieri" [battle of various contending thoughts], recurs at crucial moments in the narrative.[126] Occasionally the dialogue is formulated as a dialogue proper, a *tenzone fittizia* between faculties of the speaker's person who take on their own voices: *occhi, cuore, appetito, ragione, anima*, and other faculties dispute with one another about the psychic state of the speaker.[127] On other occasions the speaker participates in a *tenzone* with a higher power, like Lord Love, figured as a separate entity; or with an imagined person, a vision produced by his imagination, as in the case of the man who appears to the speaker in the delirium of his fever dreams to proclaim Beatrice's death. In the lyric, the herald is an unspecified "omo" [man], rendering the vision all the more terrifying for the anonymity of the apparition: "ed omo apparve, scolorito e fioco, / dicendomi: 'Che fai? Non sai novella? / Morta è la donna tua, ch'era sì bella'" [a man appeared, spectral and colorless / who said: "Come on. Do you know what befell? / Your lady's dead, who was so beautiful"].[128] In the prose, by contrast, the corresponding figure appears in the guise of an unnamed friend: "E maravigliandomi in cotale fantasia e paventando assai, imaginai *alcuno amico* che mi venisse a dire: 'Or non sai? La tua mirabile donna è partita di questo secolo'" [And marveling over that fantasy, and full of fear, I imagined that *a friend* came to say: "Don't you know now? Your miraculous lady has left the world"].[129] The speaker projects his own thoughts, concerns, and anxieties onto imagined figures who come to stand in as his ideal interlocutors, *amici* who challenge the poet in the kind of productive dispute we saw in *tenzone* exchanges of the period. While celebrating dispute and exchanges – practices of *amistà*, as we have seen – he nevertheless narrows its practitioners, eventually settling only upon himself. The dialogism and antagonism of the public square does not disappear; such antagonism is instead internalized in the private chamber of the poet's mind.

The poet's self-dialogue is often the product of a generative discussion held with himself, a living-together with his own thoughts that, through meditation, gain clarity. In the essay on Socratic dialogue that I alluded to above, Hannah Arendt describes such moments of self-dialogue as the product of a kind of friendship with oneself, an ongoing inner dialogue between two sides of the self that negotiate together to form opinions: "Insofar as I am one, I will not contradict myself, but I can contradict myself because in thought I am two-in-one; therefore I do not live only with others, as one, but also with myself."[130] In the *Vita nova*, these episodes of self-contradiction and self-dialogue are fixed with a formulaic expression, "dicea fra me medesimo" [I told myself]. The phrase repeats, with slight variation, eight times throughout the text, with more prominence in the latter half, particularly after the disappearance of other interlocutors: the Lord Love, the *primo amico* and other friends, even the competing voices of the speaker's own faculties.[131] They are most frequent in his discussion of the penultimate sonnet of the *Vita nova*, *Deh peregrini che pensosi andate*, which positions its fictionalized reader as unknown and unknowable, "not a friend, an acquaintance, or even an adversary but an alien, a stranger, the other," enhancing the marginalization of the speaker from his audiences.[132] By giving prominence to the *tenzoni fittizie* he enjoys with himself, and silencing those he may have enjoyed with others, the poet severely restricts his inner circle, first excluding all but the two highest rungs on the scale of *amistadi*, then marginalizing even these, focusing his efforts on himself alone. Seemingly, he arrives in the *Vita nova* at the conclusion that he will later state outright in *Convivio* 1.2.5: "nullo è più amico che l'uomo a sé: onde nella camera de' suoi pensieri se medesimo riprendere dee e piangere li suoi difetti, e non palese" [No one is a better friend than one is to himself; therefore it is in the chamber of one's thoughts that a person must reprimand himself and bemoan his faults, and not openly].

For all its talk of friendship, the *Vita nova* celebrates exclusion, solitude, and self-marginalization. The theory of *amistà* articulated in the prose commentary oscillates between the pull of two spaces of friendship: the open piazza, where friendship is a public battle engaged with civic concerns, and the private enclosures and secret chambers of the heart and the home, where two friends engage in a quiet, elite *ragionare* that avoids the commotion of urban life to focus its discussion on matters of philosophical discretion. Gradually, the poet retreats even further from the urban, disputatious piazza and towards isolation by alienating even his first friend: the narrative concludes with a series of episodes of self-dialogue, as the speaker retreats further and further into his own meditations. He excludes all his former interlocutors, including the *primo amico* and the Lord Love himself. His *ragionare* concludes with a silence imposed by his inability to speak in a way befitting the dignity of "questa benedetta" [this blessed lady].[133] The *Vita nova* narrates the gradual retreat of the speaker, first into the company of a few elect friends, then into a discreet and undisclosed dialogue with one, finally repudiating even this one, ultimately driving the narrator further into his own company and his own mind.[134]

If Domenico De Robertis is right to read in Dante's love of Beatrice an elevation of disinterested *amicizia* to the universalizing *caritas* of the *Commedia*, with the rest of Dante's social circle we see quite the opposite: a highly interested notion of *amicizia*, governed by an elitism that drives towards the exclusion of all others from the innermost circle. As *Guido, i' vorrei* suggests, friendship is enacted in a certain *ragionar* among the closest of friends, and yet the *Vita nova* works to conceal even that private dialogue, allowing the author to emerge as the unique authority in the text.[135] The *Vita nova* moves towards a radical inwardness, an exclusive and hierarchized vision of friendship that would eventually go so far as to exclude all others, even the *primo amico*, from its vision of fellowship. The text presents the speaker's negotiation between companionship and solitude, as well as the values of each for poetic composition. The *Vita nova* performs the importance of dialogue, especially dialogue with oneself, to literary pursuits: by alluding to exclusive conversations with his select friends and staging dialogues with himself, the speaker highlights the possibilities and limits of that *ragionar* that had been celebrated in *Guido, i' vorrei*. In the final analysis, the poet in fact finds himself falling silent in the face of the *mirabile visione*, unable to continue his *ragionar*, even with himself. The narrator's failure to reinscribe the exclusive and private friendship of the dream-vision into the public square of literary engagement leaves the narrator at risk of collapsing into solipsism. In the final pages of the *Vita nova*, the silence of the secret chambers wins out.

Epilogue

The exclusionary impulses of Dante's early thinking on friendship find their way back into his reflections on poetry in the famed encounter he stages with Bonagiunta da Lucca in *Purgatorio* 24. In contemplating his own poetics, Dante sets himself apart as having a particular, individualized, direct engagement with Love – a friendship, if we wish to characterize it as such. Whatever conclusions may be reached about the poet's intention to include others in this exclusive company, he insists on the individual relationship he enjoys with the *dittator* [he who dictates]: "I' mi son un" [I in myself am one], he begins, underlining the uniqueness of their connection with the quadruple stress on his singularity.[136] Bonagiunta picks up on the exclusivity of Dante's claim, firmly placing himself in the out-group, held back from proximity with the *dittator* by the *nodo* [knot] that holds him and many others away.

Dante's active – and effective – erasure of others from his company in *Purgatorio* 24 is part and parcel of the same impulses he showed in the *Vita nova* and in the sonnet *Guido, i' vorrei*: the desire to separate and elevate two from the company of the many. In many ways, this was a privilege of the man living in civic society, where one could dream of excluding the *gente noiosa*, as Guittone famously called them, precisely because one was surrounded by them. The dream of a willing withdrawal from civic life would change when withdrawal was forced, and when the possibility of civic participation was removed. In the immediate aftermath of exile, Dante's views on the integration of friends into larger communities would shift, as his reliance on these communities, and the networks to which they gave access, grew. This shift will be the subject of the next chapter.

2

Self-Interest: The University

The exigencies of Dante's exile from Florence in January 1302 would dramatically shift how he perceived strategic social interactions in the literary community. If in the pre-exilic *Vita nova* the narrator seeks to cultivate exclusive, hierarchical, and closed friendships within a tight-knit circle, in his post-exilic works, especially those immediately following his departure from Florence, Dante would reassess the strategic value of openness and public engagement in his relationships to literary interlocutors. In this recalculation he relaxes his attachments to his innermost circle: instead of a small coterie of exclusive and exclusionary relationships within a tightly restricted group, we now see Dante advocating the value of an inclusive alliance with a strategic collaborator – Cino da Pistoia – and envisioning that alliance as embedded within an evolving network of symbolic interactions and affinities.[1]

This chapter examines Dante's repeated self-identification as "amicus" of the well-connected poet Cino da Pistoia in his *De vulgari eloquentia* (ca. 1304–6), a treatise on the eloquence of the vernacular.[2] Stylizing himself as Cino's "amicus" in *De vulgari* permits Dante to straddle two competing conceptualizations of friendship: on the one hand, the Ciceronian claim of a disinterested communion of understanding and collaboration between individuals, which seeks to embrace others in its outreach; and, on the other, the strategic self-promotion of an individual agent, reaching out from a position of precariousness in an attempt to establish his standing in a conservative and competitive cultural field. Although Cino was long framed by scholars as a mere imitator of Dante and the other stilnovist poets, or as a "stopgap" friend embraced only after the death of "primo amico" Guido Cavalcanti, in *De vulgari eloquentia* Cino serves a particularly valuable role, as gatekeeper to the Bolognese intellectual network.[3] When contrasted with his approach to the term as we saw it in the previous chapter, where friendship was an exclusive, closed, and disengaged dialogue between two, here Dante's term "amicus" signals the distinct Ciceronian turn in his thinking on the practical applications of friendship theory in society. But the ambiguous term also signals a strategic self-interest on the part of the author, who employs the epithet as a means to disguise his identity as both the "nos" who authors the treatise and the "amicus" whose lyric poetry is promoted by it. By identifying how the work attempts to intervene in the social field of the university city, this chapter will argue that Dante's claim to Cino's friendship negotiates between a theoretical Ciceronian disinterestedness and a strategic instrumental advantage.

Recent research has reconstructed Dante's strategic self-presentation in *De vulgari eloquentia* as "amicus eius." Albert Ascoli has discussed the difference in the authorities embodied by the two voices of the "nos" and the "amicus," and Teodolinda Barolini has examined the semantic and affective value of the "eius" in the repeated formula, which recuperates friendship from the antagonism of Dante's youthful relationships.[4] I am interested further in the theories and practices of *amicitia* that inform the choice of this particular moniker, what Barolini calls the "semantic and ultimately philosophical content of this remarkable phrase," which had been taken as self-evident until she examined it in her 2015 article.[5] Continuing on from Barolini's suggestion that Dante recuperates Ciceronian friendship in *De vulgari*, we can articulate two competing definitions at play – one disinterested and the other self-interested – in the positioning of the individual vernacular poet as "amicus eius," that is, friend of a poet who was establishing his reputation as practitioner and defender of the "new poetics" that *De vulgari* wishes to inaugurate.

Dante employs his allegiance with Cino da Pistoia as the foundational support out of which he will promote his new poetics to a network of intellectuals that *De vulgari* identifies as "doctores illustres" [distinguished men of learning], a dynamic intellectual network of men bound by a shared commitment to creating a vernacular Italian literary culture. *De vulgari* imagines that this culture will emerge out of the learned community of vernacular writers centred around the Studium in Bologna.[6] The historical group of "doctores illustres qui lingua vulgari poetati sunt in Ytalia" [illustrious authors who have written vernacular poetry in Italy] is not confined to any specific academic site; these authors are instead dispersed, even exiled, throughout Italy.[7] However, the emphasis on the *doctores'* distinguished learning (their *ingenium et scientia* in the arts of poetry, their *magistratus* in vernacular eloquence) remains a focus throughout *De vulgari*, suggesting that, however dispersed their forebears, the author and his would-be collaborators now aim to assemble a new group of poets trained in the *doctrina* of vernacular eloquence.

In *De vulgari*'s conceptualization, the elite assembly of "doctores illustres" would convene, physically or virtually, around a centre of learning like late medieval Bologna, a city which was renowned across Europe for its university – and especially for the institution's excellence in canon and civil law – and whose renown is central to the treatise's claims about the preeminence of the *vulgare illustre*.[8] It is apt that the dissemination of the *vulgare illustre* would emanate from a city like

Bologna, a "crossroads" city in the terminology of historian Nicholas Terpstra. In a "crossroads" city – as opposed to "terminal" cities like Rome, Florence, or Venice, which are conceived of as destinations – urban geography, politics, and other organizational considerations created porous boundaries. People, with their goods and ideas ready for exchange, would flow through the city, where they would "merge, meet, and disperse again."[9] As Terpstra explains, "we might argue that Bologna's particular cultural characteristic was to be more a point of departure than a point of arrival. If we consider its students, its intellectuals, its artists, its ambitious tyrants and elites, we can see that it was also for each of them a test-tube for experimentation and an incubator of innovation."[10] The university city features prominently in *De vulgari* as precisely this sort of "point of departure" and "incubator" of socio-cultural and linguistic movements: Bologna and her poets are replete with the virtue of *discretio*, the capacity to judiciously craft poetic language, style, and meter.[11] Dante presents the "poetantes Bononie" as precursors to the avant-garde poetics that *De vulgari* aims to establish. The treatise decries Bologna's linguistic confusion and diversity while also praising the city's idiom as a model of equilibrium between extremes, in its citizens' discovery of a unifying language that draws the best from surrounding elements (even though that language remains merely municipal and not "aulicum et illustre" [aulic and illustrious], as would be appropriate to the elevated context of the court).[12] In other words, *De vulgari* celebrates Bologna as a linguistic crossroads, where vernaculars – much like the people who speak them – have the potential to, as Terpstra puts it, merge, meet, and disperse again.

That *De vulgari* aims to make a strategic intervention in the Bolognese intellectual field has been discussed before. Reconstructing the timeline of Dante's early years in exile – a timeline for which we lack concrete records and which is disputed among the poet's biographers – Mirko Tavoni has placed the poet in the city of Bologna from mid-1304 to 1306.[13] He conjectures that Dante composed *De vulgari* during a sojourn in the university city, between the decisive defeat of the exiled Florentine Guelphs at the Battle of the Lastra (July 1304) and Dante's conscription into the service of Moroello Malaspina (sometime between February and October 1306).[14] Tavoni argues that certain markers in *De vulgari* demonstrate that the treatise was written not only "*in* Bologna" but also "*for* Bologna,"[15] and suggests Dante's interventions on political, social, linguistic, and literary matters would have especially resonated with the academic Bolognese audience. He notes the treatise's elevation of the Bolognese dialect; the prominent role accorded to Bolognese poets like Guinizzelli, Ghislieri, Fabruzzo, and Onesto; the put-downs of Bologna's political enemies; and so on.[16] But the most compelling evidence he presents concerns the university: what he calls the text's "evidente interesse per il pubblico universitario" [obvious interest in the university audience], the treatise's display of philosophical and dictatorial concerns, and, above all, the primacy accorded to Cino da Pistoia, who had trained as a jurist in Bologna and had frequently corresponded with Bologna's chief poets, especially Onesto. Tavoni points to Cino da Pistoia as "l'ideale *trait d'union*" [the ideal intermediary] between the poets of the Tuscan and Bolognese literary communities, and he explains that Dante relies on Cino's *amicitia* "perché il suo nome gli apra le porte dell'ambiente bolognese, universitario e poetico" [so that (Cino's) name may open (for Dante) the doors to the academic and poetic spheres of Bologna].[17] Tavoni's speculative suggestions about the practical role Cino served for Dante as liaison with the Bolognese intellectual and literary communities are critical to understanding the agency Dante ascribes to Cino's *amicitia* in *De vulgari*.

Whatever we may think of Tavoni's reconstruction of Dante's location and the dating of *De vulgari*, the relationship of *De vulgari* to the site of the university – or, as I have phrased it, to the field of the university – is indisputable.[18] There are clear indications that the treatise frames its audience quite differently than does the earlier *Vita nova*, which had been directed at fellow poets. Here, repeated calls to the *doctores illustres* [illustrious masters] and *illustria capita poetantia* [illustrious poetic minds] – whose *ingenium et scientia* [talent and knowledge] will serve to *instruere* [instruct] and *edocere* [to teach] the *doctrina de vulgari eloquentia* [doctrine of vernacular eloquence] – suggest that the text is directed at a distinctly learned audience who, even if they are not part of the class of accredited doctors of the Studium in Bologna, would consider themselves part of the *literati* affiliated with academic or intellectual life.[19]

In designating the field of *De vulgari*'s intervention the "university," I do not limit my definition to the officially sanctioned *doctores* of a particular Studium. In cities like Bologna, the university network reached far beyond the strict limits of its formal body, encompassing a large and fluid swath of civic society in each of the cities which housed a Studium.[20] While the Studium itself had fairly strict barriers to entry, informal networks of university affiliates grew around the Studium, and university cities boasted lively intellectual exchange in the public square. The professoriate itself was hierarchical, with scholars striving to join the ranks of the *doctores* but often obtaining only the ability to give *lectiones extraordinarie* or to teach as *repetitores*, a practice that was most frequent in the schools of medicine, arts, and grammar.[21] *Doctores* enjoyed great prestige and power not only among the scholars and students of the Studium; they were also recognized as figures of significant social, cultural, and political authority around the commune and beyond.[22] Professors would compete for disciples, to the point that, Guido Zaccagnini observes, some teachers resorted to bribing students with financial loans to cover their fees in exchange for the students' attendance at lectures.[23] Pride and envy would inspire rivalries and oppositions at all ranks, and disciples of one master or another would occasionally tussle in defense of their teachers, with whom they often developed strong affectionate bonds.[24] The strained social relations of university life are well captured in Boncompagno da Signa's dialogue *Amicitia* (1205).[25] Although composed in Rome, Boncompagno's dialogue is infused with cynical reflections on the sociability of the spheres of academics with whom he was most closely associated throughout his adult life. The dialogue depicts human sociability as a minefield, where infighting and backbiting – underscored by communal political dispute – make trust not only the most valuable asset of friendship, but also the hardest to obtain.

As it had been for Boncompagno a century prior, friendship is central to Dante's appeal to this new, learned audience in *De vulgari eloquentia.* He addresses the new social field by employing different theories, terms, and strategies than he had in *Vita nova.* In the treatise he divides his authorial voice into two distinct subjects: on the one hand, the first-person plural "nos" who authors the treatise, an objective and analytical voice of authority on the vernacular literary tradition; and on the other, the particular practitioner of that tradition, an unnamed third-person vernacular poet, who is designated in the treatise as "amicus" of the other worthy practitioner cited throughout, Cino da Pistoia.[26] The latter Dante is mentioned in the text by the formula "amicus eius" [his friend] six times (1.10.2, 1.17.3, twice in 2.2.8, 2.5.4, and 2.6.6), before the two identities of the dispassionate prose authority and the individual vernacular poet (Cino's "amicus") are united under the single designation "nos" late in the treatise (2.8.8 and following).[27] Shortly thereafter, the author abandoned the project of the treatise, likely moving on to focus his attentions on *Convivio*, which he had already begun while composing *De vulgari*, and which he would likewise abandon in a short matter of years in favour of the *Commedia.*[28] *Convivio* and *De vulgari eloquentia* overlap not only in the timeline of their compositions, but also in their thematic concerns, including and especially their engagement with theories of friendship.

Following his study of Cicero's *De amicitia*, which in *Convivio* 2.12.3 he claims to have pored over in his grief over the death of Beatrice, Dante reorients his thinking on friendship around the Ciceronian principle of disinterestedness. Scholars have identified *De amicitia* as the source for his new *stile della loda*, inaugurated in the pivotal *canzone* of *Vita nova*, *Donne ch'avete intelletto d'amore.* According to this newfound style of praise poetry, Dante commits to shifting his focus exclusively to the praise of his lady, without expectation for receiving anything in return. De Robertis, Modesto, and others suggest that the disinterestedness of the new *stile* derives from the poet's reading of Cicero, Aristotle, and other philosophical authorities, much as Dante himself claims in the pages of *Convivio* where he describes his *amistade* with Lady Philosophy.[29]

But the extent of this turn towards disinterestedness as the guiding principle of friendship is not limited to theoretical reconsiderations of his relationship to the now deceased Beatrice in the *Vita nova* or to the imagined projection of Lady Philosophy in *Convivio.* The ramifications of Dante's long engagement with Cicero's text can also be seen in the ways he reconceptualizes *amistà* or *amicitia* in his post-exilic works, centring his notion of friendship on the principles of disinterestedness, reciprocity, and public engagement, which he gleaned from deep study of Cicero's treatise.[30] Undergirding the sociological claims to *amicitia* in the treatise on language is an implicit understanding of friendship that contrasts sharply with what we saw in *Vita nova*, as I described in chapter 1. As this chapter will demonstrate, the Ciceronian turn in Dante's thinking on friendship is most clearly encapsulated in the scant but pointed assertions of *amicitia* in *De vulgari eloquentia* – a text that, as Teodolinda Barolini observes, does not attempt to theorize friendship, as does the contemporaneous *Convivio*, but instead to perform it.[31] In analyzing how *De vulgari* performs friendship with Cino, I build on Barolini's observation by noting the powerful tension between the disinterested friendship the *De vulgari* theorizes and the self-interested friendship that it performs. It is this contrasting understanding of friendship and its strategic performance in *De vulgari eloquentia* that I intend to examine here.

In what follows, I will begin by laying out the social strategies embedded in *De vulgari eloquentia*. The first book of *De vulgari* structures its claims about language around the goal of restoring an elite ruling class, united through the *amicabilitas* (friendliness) that is promoted through common use of the *vulgare illustre*. As I will show, later passages put this theoretical *amicabilitas* into practice, as Dante's use of the epithet "amicus eius" claims a communion of mutual understanding and moral betterment between the unnamed lyric poet and his well-established friend Cino. The poet's strategy – first to disguise and then to reveal his identity as the *amicus* celebrated in the treatise – permit him to negotiate between two opposing constructions of *amicitia* in the same short text. On the one hand, friendship serves in the treatise as a category of disinterested collaboration between two likeminded, equally ambitious poets, aligned by their mutual project of establishing and promoting the emergent Italian vernacular literary tradition. On the other hand, the poet's *amicitia* with Cino serves a tool for his own strategic self-promotion and self-interest. In this way, we see Dante's use of the term *amicus* as a precursor to the manifold uses and meanings of the term that would come to define Renaissance social theory. From Petrarch onwards, the terms of friendship could simultaneously signal disinterestedness and self-interest, collaboration and competition, moral betterment and instrumental advantage. *De vulgari eloquentia* anticipates the negotiations around *amicitia* as the two Dantes attempt to straddle contradictory positions with regards to Cino's friendship.

Language and *Amicabilitas*

In discussing the theory of *amicitia* that undergirds Dante's strategic claim to his own friendship with Cino, it is helpful to turn to a rarely cited passage early in the treatise, where the poet examines the particular necessity of language for humans in so far as the human being is, in Thomas Aquinas's formulation, an "animal sociale et politicum."[32] Language, the argument of *De vulgari* 1.2 goes, is peculiar to humans, who lack both the immediacy of understanding that characterizes the angels and the identity of behaviors and feelings characteristic of the lower animals. Humans are a species uniquely reliant on *locutio* as "the indispensable bridge between isolated rational subjectivities," a bridge that enables them to articulate to one another information other animals understand by virtue of shared instinct.[33] Across different animal species, language is unnecessary and would in fact be hazardous; Dante explains, "inter ea [animalia] vero que diversarum sunt specierum non solum non necessaria fuit locutio, sed prorsus dampnosa fuisset, cum nullum amicabile commertium fuisset in illis" [among those (animals) of different species, however, not only was speech not necessary, but it would indeed have been utterly harmful, for there could be no friendly exchange between them].[34] The brief mention of *amicabile commertium* [friendly exchange] here deserves pause, for it suggests a critical connection between language and *amicabilitas*: not friendship per se, but a disposition towards friendship or a "friendliness," which is made possible by the mutual understanding of individual behaviors and feelings (*actus et passiones*).[35] *Locutio*, the medium through which human beings bring about the sharing of our *actus et passiones*, permits us to engage in *amicabile commertium*. Such exchange constitutes the discussion (or, perhaps, justification) of our behaviors and feelings, an exchange which creates the conditions of possibility for the kind of *consensio* that serves as the most basic foundation of social, cultural, and political cohesion.[36]

The idea of "friendliness" implicit in this brief reference to *amicabile commertium* was common to many discussions of friendship's place in the social order.[37] Much as Guittone d'Arezzo had figured friendship as the medicine that would treat the envy riling the communal political structure, so Dante here positions language as the antidote to the human tendency to solipsistic thinking and the arbitrary exercise of the individual will.[38] At stake is the kind of "civic friendship" celebrated by proto-humanists like Brunetto Latini, for whom the human disposition towards friendship represents the sense of social solidarity that develops between the individual citizens of the same city.[39] In his *Rettorica* (1260), Brunetto is more explicit in drawing the connection between rhetorical eloquence and friendship than Dante is in *De vulgari* 1.2. Brunetto frames rhetoric as a necessary tool for creating the conditions in which eloquent dispute could lead to like-mindedness, which would turn mere co-inhabitants into companions (*compagni*, who share a mutual commitment to a particular project) and eventually friends (*amici*, whose mutual commitment leads also to trust and intimacy).[40] Much as Brunetto had done, in *De vulgari* Dante shapes claims about social cohesion that hinge on demonstrating the relationship of language to the quality of *amicabilitas*, "friendliness."

As has often been observed, language in Book 1 of *De vulgari eloquentia* is a gift fundamental to our nature as social creatures. Without it we would risk the radical division of community figured in the calamitous scattering of the tower-builders in Babel. But the emphasis here, as Albert Ascoli and Maria Corti have highlighted, is not at the level of collectivities; rather, the wound inflicted by the Babelic *dispersio* of languages is struck at the level of the individual.[41] Language is not merely a social phenomenon; it is what mitigates between the individual and the social. In our post-Babelic condition, the propensity of individuals towards isolation is great. The bisection of language into a wide variety of vernaculars and dialects – a crisis emerging from the calamitous wound Babel inflicted on the human collective – is such that it threatens the individual with a collapse into radical individualism or solipsism, "adeo ut fere quilibet sua propria specie videatur gaudere" [to the point that it seems almost everyone enjoys the existence of a unique species].[42] Language, in *De vulgari*'s formulation, is the medium through which the chasm of individual subjectivities can be crossed. In other words, language enables the possibility of arriving at a communion of mutual understanding between two individuals, who first see and comprehend one another's *actus et passiones*. When two individuals discover in that communion a compatibility, a bond of friendship begins to germinate. Thus language enables human *amicabilitas*, the intraspecies capacity to develop voluntary individual bonds or attachments, either for the instrumental purposes of cooperative endeavor (what Brunetto would call *compagni*), or for the moral purposes of the mutual development of virtue (Brunetto's *amici*).

Another way of understanding the link between language and *amicabilitas* in *De vulgari* is to imagine the converse. Were language so divided as to disallow the sharing of *actus et passiones* between individuals, to compel each to be a species unto oneself, civic structures would descend into division and disorder, a chaos befitting post-Babelic communities.[43] By making possible the sharing of individual subjectivities, language disposes humankind towards a natural *amicabilitas*.[44] Unlike the private and exclusive *amistadi* cultivated in the *Vita nova*, the *amicabilitas* alluded to in *De vulgari* 1.2.5 is an extensive bond, sweeping in its horizon, as a quality shared by all members of the same species. The natural tendency of humankind towards friendship is put forth even more forcefully in *Convivio* 1.1: "ciascuno uomo a ciascuno uomo naturalmente è amico" [each is by nature a friend to each].[45] The two contemporaneous texts suggest that the natural propensity to love is both universally engendered in the human species as a collective and individually directed, each to each.

The connection of language to *amicabilitas* in *De vulgari* 1.2 does not, as it does in *Convivio* 1.1, imply a radically inclusive vision of *amicitia*, at the base level of human nature or at the level of civic societies. Much as Brunetto's *Rettorica* envisions a social structure in which smaller circles of intimacy would coexist within larger social groups, the *amicitia* imagined in *De vulgari* – as Dante's elaboration of the *vulgare illustre* will make plain – exists among members of an "in-group" of highly trained masters of rhetorical eloquence, the "doctores illustres" referred to throughout the treatise, as well as a range of outsiders who approach the training of the *doctores* to greater and lesser degrees.[46] The *doctores* alluded to throughout the treatise have privileged access to the social field which structures their interactions. The structure of the field remains rigidly hierarchical, an individual's position correlated with his expertise in and commitment to the project of establishing the vernacular literary tradition. This social order, which as we will see in the following section is distinctly Ciceronian in origin, centres on the *amicitia* between the two most prominent practitioners of the new vernacular poetics, "Cynus Pistoriensis et amicus eius."

The Ciceronian Turn

The more extensive notion of a natural human *amicabilitas* – as well as a Ciceronian-Brunettian vision of public-facing civic friendship – underlies Dante's assertions of his personal *amicitia* with Cino da Pistoia. Where the closed and exclusive *amistà* cultivated by Dante and Guido Cavalcanti in the *Vita nova* had emerged out of the rivalrous sphere of vernacular literary exchange, the friendship between *De vulgari*'s two exemplars of vernacular eloquence follows the Ciceronian model of disinterested friendship, set forth in the dialogue *Laelius sive de amicitia* (44 BCE). Cicero's dialogue, which Dante claimed to have read in the wake of Beatrice's death, reflects on the moral value of friendship in a world dominated by political ambition and class hierarchies.[47] It defines friendship as "nihil aliud nisi omnium divinarum humanarumque rerum cum benevolentia et caritate consensio, qua quidem haud scio an excepta sapientia nil quicquam melius homini sit a dis immortalibus datum" [nothing other than agreement with goodwill and affection between people about all things divine and human. With the exception of wisdom, I'm inclined to believe that the immortal gods have given nothing better to humanity than friendship].[48] For Laelius, friendship is among the highest goods of human experience, higher even than virtue, which "et gignit et continet" [gives birth … and nourishes] the form of friendship celebrated in the dialogue.[49] This last aspect reveals how Cicero redefined *amicitia*, and especially how medieval thinkers understood Cicero's contributions: the explicit, necessary link between friendship and moral virtue. According to Cicero and his later Christian advocates, only friendships that bring about improvements in one's personal moral character are worthy of the name.[50]

Before looking at how *De vulgari* proclaims a Ciceronian *amicitia* with Cino, we should recall how Cicero defines true, virtue-seeking *amicitia* in his dialogue. According to Laelius's logic, if friendship is to be construed a morally improving exercise it must be a product of one's voluntary choice. Friendship is distinct from – and elevated over – other forms of *propinquitas* or relationship (kinship, citizenship, proximity, and so forth) precisely because it is not a necessary tie: Laelius explains, "namque hoc praestat amicitia propinquitati, quod ex propinquitate benevolentia tolli potest, ex amicitia non potest; sublata enim benevolentia amicitiae nomen tollitur, propinquitatis manet" [Friendship, however, is stronger than kinship since goodwill can be removed from such a relationship but not from friendship. If goodwill is removed from friendship, friendship disappears.

However if you remove goodwill from kinship, it nonetheless remains].[51] In other words, because friendship is a habitual rational exercise – originating in freely given goodwill and not in any pre-existing social ties – it reflects and reinforces one's moral character, and it is to be desired, praised, and preserved for the good it bestows on human experience, both individual and collective.[52] Thus, it becomes all the more imperative to be selective in choosing our friends.[53]

Laelius insists that ideal friendship derives from a natural and spontaneous feeling of goodwill rather than from any sort of weakness or lack in the individual.[54] This allows him to make what would eventually be taken up by Dante scholars as the claim most influential on Dante's thinking on friendship: that *vera amicitia* is entirely free from selfish motive, and instead rests on the genuinely magnanimous nature of both friends. Cicero is adamant about friendship's disinterestedness: "Ut enim benefici liberalesque sumus non ut exigamus gratiam (neque enim beneficium feneramur, sed natura propensi ad liberalitatem sumus), sic amicitiam non spe mercedis adducti, sed quod omnis eius fructus in ipso amore inest, expetendam putamus" [We are not so kind and generous to our friends because we seek favours in return. We are not so petty as to charge interest on our kindness. We are kindhearted because it is the right and natural thing to do, not because we are hoping for something in return. The reward of friendship is friendship itself].[55] Unlike Aristotle's instrumental friends, Cicero's ideal friends are not drawn to one another because of some personal need or insufficiency, nor do they require the repayment of goods given and services rendered. Nevertheless, the two friends are bound to one another through a spontaneous, continuous, and reciprocal exchange of services, offices, profits, and advantages (what Cicero variously calls *utilitates*, *opportunitates*, and *commoditates*). The truest form of friendship will likely have reciprocal benefits for the individuals involved, but if either of the friends enters into the relationship with hope of culling some advantage from his friend, the friendship will be destabilized and will likely fall apart.[56]

Laelius's emphasis on reciprocity is tempered by his insistence that true friendship should not tip into a cold calculus of favours given and received. Such a view, he claims, "definit amicitiam paribus officiis ac voluntatibus. Hoc quidem est nimis exigue et exiliter ad calculos vocare amicitiam, ut par sit ratio acceptorum et datorum" [limits friendship to an equal exchange of actions and feelings. This reduces friendship to a careful and petty calculation of credits and debits].[57] The passage seems to suggest that reciprocity is of limited importance to the friendship. But, he continues, "Divitor mihi et affluentior videtur esse vera amicitia, nec observare restricte ne plus reddat quam acceperit; neque enim verendum est ne quid excidat, aut ne quid in terram defluat, aut ne plus aequo quid in amicitiam congeratur" [I think that true friendship is something richer and more abundant than that. It doesn't check the books to see if it's giving more than it has received; it doesn't fear that some favour will get lost or overflow and spill onto the ground, or that it's pouring more into the other's bowl than it's getting back].[58] Maintaining his idealism, Laelius suggests that true friendship has no need to keep accounts, for each friend gives so generously as to "overflow" what is expected of him, removing any concern that acts of kindness between true friends would not be perfectly reciprocated. In perfect friendship, in other words, it is more likely that the balance of exchange would be exceeded in mutual and reciprocal generosity than undermined by insufficiency.[59]

The boundless generosity that true friends show one another fuels what C. Stephen Jaeger has called "friendships of mutual perfecting."[60] Indeed, such friends pursue the good so fervently as to compete with one another in virtue. Laelius explains the impulse towards this mutual perfecting of character as a longing for virtue:

> Quam qui adpetiverunt, applicant se et propius admovent, ut et usu eius quem diligere coeperunt fruantur et moribus, sintque pares in amore et aequales, propensioresque ad bene merendum quam ad reposcendum, atque haec inter eos sit honesta certatio. Sic et utilitates ex amicitia maximae capientur, et erit eius ortus a natura quam ab imbecillitate gravior et verior. Nam si utilitas amicitias conglutinaret, eadem commutata dissolveret; sed quia natura mutari non potest, idcirco verae amicitiae sempiternae sunt.
>
> [When two people long for such goodness, they seek it out in each other and so draw closer together, so that they can enjoy the company and character of the one they love. They become rivals in doing good for each other, more desirous of doing good for the other than getting something in return – an honourable competition! In this way friendship becomes something quite advantageous, not in the sense of gaining something we need in our weakness but as a relationship deriving from nature itself. If we assume friendship is based merely on gaining advantages from someone, then that friendship will end when that person has nothing left to give us. But since nature cannot be changed, real friendship lasts forever.][61]

Laelius's stipulations about the advantage-driven nature of friendship indicate a delicate balance in the "honesta certatio" [honourable competition] that he describes. Both friends compete equally in this rivalry, driven by delight, affection, and a desire to be worthy of his friend's favour. The balance centres on the notion that "natura mutari non potest" [nature cannot be changed], which assures the stability of virtuous characters and protects the contest from driving towards vicious ends. That central pivot, however, is unstable, and the passage is immediately followed by a discussion of the changes wrought by nature on a man's character, which cause disequilibrium in the balance of friendship's advantages, and may eventually lead to its dissolution.[62]

In Cicero's account, friendship is unstable because it is embedded in the public sphere. Beyond his emphasis on ideological agreement, mutual goodwill, and voluntary election, Laelius insists that the two men not retreat into private cares and concerns but remain deeply engaged in affairs of the state. However much delight and goodness the friends might find in one another's private company, they must also seek to carry their mutual commitment to virtue out to the public sphere, to serve the best interests of the republic. Precisely because they are both good men who share tastes, values, and views, their commitment to virtue extends beyond their private rivalry of goodness and into matters of the State.[63] But Laelius remains clear-eyed about the exacting measures of idealized friendship, and the near impossibility of its realization in the political arena.

Whatever the improbability of perfect friendship existing in the real world of political life, the idealizing discourse Laelius presents would dominate theories of friendship, especially Christian friendship, for centuries.[64] Like many of his contemporaries, Dante will insist on the influence Cicero's treatise had on his thinking, and, as I alluded to above, scholars have focused on disinterestedness as the primary lesson Dante would glean from his reading of *De amicitia*. Domenico De Robertis notably looked to Cicero's theory of disinterested friendship to interpret the gradual shifts in Dante's love for Beatrice over the course of his career, specifically in the crisis of representation that concludes the *Vita nova*. Commenting on disinterestedness in the praise poetry of *Vita nova*, De Robertis notes, "La contrapposizione, intanto, tra amore che nulla chiede all'amato e amore mosso da speranza di mercede, tra amore dell'amato e amore delle cose di costui, era già nel *Laelius*, rispondeva al principio, fondamentale nel libro, e ben fermo in tutto il pensiero ciceroniano, dell'amore disinteressato, cercato per se stesso, che ha in sé il proprio fine" [The contrast, for one, between love that asks for nothing from the beloved and love moved by the hope of reward, between love of the beloved and love of his things, was already in the *Laelius*, corresponding to the principle – fundamental in the book and well-grounded in all Ciceronian thought – of disinterested love, sought in and for itself, that has its own end in itself].[65] This kind of disinterested love for the beloved is also set forth and praised in *Convivio*, where Dante celebrates his *amistade* with Philosophy, loving and hating for the sake of love for her.[66]

But it is here in *De vulgari eloquentia* that the lessons of such a reading seem to have been put to the test of real human sociability. By focusing on the claim to Cino's friendship in *De vulgari* we begin to see how such a theoretical reading of Ciceronian disinterestedness becomes more complicated when considering friendship practices in the real world. Three correlated principles, all of which are expressed in Cicero's fusion of friendship and virtue, are invoked in *De vulgari*: first, because friendship does not depend on any essential kinship tie but is instead elective, it should be considered a rational exercise dependent on the will. Second, although true friendship can also produce instrumental advantages, it must arise from a fundamentally disinterested union between two likeminded people. Third, as a mutually bettering moral exercise among civic leaders, true friendship also has repercussions on the public sphere. Each of these definitional aspects of friendship comes to light in *De vulgari*, marking the sharp Ciceronian turn in the poet's usage of the term in his repeated epithet "Cynus Pistoriensis et amicus eius." At the same time, each of these principles is equally central to the poet's self-interest, who strategically stylizes himself Cino's "amicus" as he strives to gain access to a new intellectual network of which Cino is already an established part. In the doubled signals of the word "amicus" – theoretical Ciceronian disinterestedness on the one hand, and the self-interest of the aspirant on the other – we see the poet straddle two competing social positions in the academic field, generating a tension which may have appeared irreconcilable. Although he does not attempt to resolve the contradictions in his strategic use of the term, he does seek to occupy both positions simultaneously, in a move that would anticipate similar attempts among the early humanists of the succeeding generation.[67]

Amicitia as Disinterested Collaboration

In his repeated use of the epithet "amicus" to disguise his identity in the first three quarters of the treatise, Dante projects Ciceronian disinterestedness, reciprocity, and public engagement onto his collaboration with Cino da Pistoia. By presenting himself as uniquely aligned with Cino in the establishment of a new linguistic standard, he inaugurates a public relationship with Cino as co-conspirators in a shared project. Their mutual positioning as the avant-garde of the new vernacular poetic tradition narrows the general *amicabilitas* that the treatise gestured towards in its opening: the natural human inclination towards mutual goodwill is actualized into friendship by the discovery of concord when two friends lay bare their *actus et passiones*.

Even more to the point, *De vulgari*'s claim to Cino's *amicitia* depends on the two friends' sharing of language itself: in the treatise *amicitia* implies not only shared ideologies and commitments but also shared modes of speaking and writing. As he makes clear across several passages of the work (*De vulgari* 1.9.6, 1.9.10, 1.16.3, 2.1.5, among others), Dante counts *locutio* [language] among human *mores et habitus* [customs and habits]. Because of its association with *mores et habitus*, language is an outward sign of one's moral character.[68] Thus, the sharing of excellent language between the two friends marks a similarity of moral standing, reaffirming the possibility of *vera amicitia* between them. Dante lays this out explicitly when he explains the four attributes of the *vulgare illustre*: that it is *illustre* [illustrious], *cardinale* [cardinal], *aulicum* [aulic], and *curiale* [curial]. He explains its illustriousness in terms of learning and sophistication:

> Magistratu quidem sublimatum videtur, cum de tot rudibus Latinorum vocabulis, de tot perplexis constructionibus, de tot defectivis prolationibus, de tot rusticanis accentibus, tam egregium, tam extricatum, tam perfectum et tam urbanum videamus electum ut Cynus Pistoriensis et amicus eius ostendunt in cantionibus suis.

[That it is sublime in learning is clear when we see it emerge, so outstanding, so lucid, so perfect and so civilised, from among so many ugly words used by Italians, so many convoluted constructions, so many defective formations, and so many barbarous pronunciations – as Cino da Pistoia and his friend show us in their canzoni.][69]

The partnership between "Cynus Pistoriensis et amicus eius" envisioned here entails both a shared sense of discernment (*discretio*, as he will call it throughout the second book) and a mutual striving towards mastery over linguistic craft (here, *magistratus*), which depends on a common language (*locutio*) that would allow the two friends to be fundamentally understood by one another, despite the mutability of language and the arbitrariness of individual will.[70] Their friendship acts as the bulwark against the risk run by all humankind in the post-Babelic condition: that in one's presumption one may become like Nimrod, who through his linguistic isolation became "sua propria specie," a species all his own.[71] The shared language that constitutes their *amicitia* safeguards both "Cynus Pistoriensis et amicus eius" from such a risk, which threatens to undermine their very humanity. That sublime language has been carefully and rationally selected (*electum*) by both Cino and his friend, who find common ground in their rational assemblage of the choicest words, constructions, formations, and pronunciations of the *vulgare*. *Electio*, an essential rational exercise, thus becomes a practice of friendship.

The sharing of language implicit in *De vulgari*'s appeal to *amicitia* marks an expansion of the definition of *amistà* articulated across *Vita nova*, as I described that definition in the first chapter. In the earlier work the sharing of language was also critical to developing a communion of understanding between Dante and his "primo amico" [first friend]. But the crucial difference arises in how we are to understand the position of that communion of two vis-à-vis the larger societies in which those two circulate. In other words, *De vulgari eloquentia* thinks differently about the value of *others* to the friendship the author proclaims with the one: against the piazza's exclusionary and competitive friendships, *De vulgari* instead posits friendships in and around the University that are collaborative, public-facing, and oriented towards outreach. As we saw in chapter 1, with his *primo amico* Dante anticipated a small and hierarchically ordered cohort, with strict gatekeeping measures in place to restrict all from its intimacies: the two friends (or at most six, if we include all the subjects – the men and their ladies – gestured to in *Guido, i' vorrei*) would enjoy their private *ragionar d'amore* [discourse about love] away from the commotion of civic concerns. Such gatekeeping was indeed so strict as to eventually exclude even the *primo amico* from apprehending the subtleties of the poet's insights, as he retreated further into his own isolation across the prose chronology laid out in *Vita nova*. Beyond isolation or estrangement, the claims to friendship in *Vita nova* suggest that the two are better thought of as competitors, sharpening one another's poetic intellect as iron against iron.[72] Much as we saw in the culture of *tenzone* exchange, which served as the backdrop to *Vita nova* and animated Dante's claims to Guido's friendship, the practices of rebuke, rivalry, and dispute were embedded in the very terms of late Duecento *amistà*. Dante's friendship with his *primo amico* was thus redolent with the antagonism of the piazza.

In *De vulgari*, by contrast, the fellowship called into being by proclaiming Cino's *amicitia* is an explicitly noncompetitive and public one, not only acknowledged on the pages of the text but also intending to institute a larger intellectual and civic movement led by the two *amici* within the learned culture of the field in which the treatise seeks to intervene.[73] Much as it was for Dante and Guido, the bond between Dante and Cino is founded on a common understanding of a particular kind of vernacular poetics. But here their commitment extends beyond mere private commerce and instead turns to an outward-facing advocacy project that allows others access to learned literary culture through its gates (however narrow and difficult to enter that gate might be). The treatise positions Cino and his friend at the forefront of an education and outreach program which might establish a solid ground for the *curia dispersa*.[74] If the treatise achieves its ultimate end, "Cynus et amicus eius" would lead the most elite poets to their own betterment: this elite (but not closed) group of disciples would become the *compagni*, in Brunetto's sense of the word, of Cino and his friend, committed to the project of founding a vernacular tradition that would emerge from the tradition of learning represented by the *doctores eloquentes*, and would be modeled on the literary example Cino and his friend have set, as the leaders of the field.

If in *Vita nova* the author intentionally obfuscates meaning – refusing to clarify the details of his own linguistic choices while also mocking "quelli che così rimano stoltamente" [poets who write in such a stupid manner] – in *De vulgari* Dante takes great pains to elucidate the stylistic features of the poetic exemplars whose work he seeks to promote.[75] This appears to have been the project of the later books, beginning with the unfinished second book, which lays out the form of the *canzone* in explicitly didactic terms.[76] Book 2 of *De vulgari* is essentially a training manual in which, as the author himself suggests, "illius artis ergasterium reseremus" [I will throw open the workshop of that art], welcoming novices into his studio to apprentice at his elbow.[77] The point, for the master-craftsman, is to train poets in the *canzone* form, "quem casu magis quam arte multi usurpare videntur" [which many clearly employ more at random than according to the rules].[78] In Book 2, the master sets out to train the apprentice in the *ars* of lyric construction, so as to draw him away from the herd of those who roughly dash off their *canzoni* by mere *casus*, chance or fortune.[79]

The metaphor of the master-craftsman at work in his studio concentrates the second book's focus on the labor of the poetic craft, a focus which the author will revisit shortly after, in his famous reference to the star-seeking eagle:

> Sed cautionem atque discretionem hanc accipere, sicut decet, hic opus et labor est, quoniam nunquam sine strenuitate ingenii et artis assiduitate scientiarumque habitu

fieri potest.... Et ideo confutetur eorum stultitia, qui, arte scientiaque immunes, de solo ingenio confidentes, ad summa summe canenda prorumpunt; et a tanta presumptuositate desistant; et si anseres natura vel desidia sunt, nolint astripetam aquilam imitari.

[But learning the necessary caution and discernment is the difficult part, requiring much effort, since these can never be achieved without exertion of the intellect, dedicated study of technique, and immersion in knowledge ... And this should suffice to refute the foolish claims of those who, devoid of technique and knowledge, relying on ingenuity alone, lay hands on the noblest topics, those that should be sung in the highest style. Let them lay such presumption aside; and, if nature or their own incompetence has made them geese, let them not try to emulate the star-seeking eagle.][80]

As in *Vita nova* 16, the poet again here lambastes the *stultitia* [foolishness] of rhymesters who cannot explain their own lyric choices, writing "casu magis quam arte," as he complained above. As before, mere ingenuity is insufficient for excellence. But where *Vita nova* quite decisively closes its gates to those who write *stoltamente*, the passage here implies that – with strong commitment, keen study, hard labor, and, of course, the proper training – a young poet can in fact follow the star-seeking eagle.

De vulgari plainly does not aim to open its gates to all comers; quite the contrary. The author continues to insist on a clearly defined *dignitas*, the worthiness of a poet to use the *vulgare illustre*, that he and Cino have laboriously acquired through their discerning choices of syntax, style, and meter. But unlike *Vita nova*, *De vulgari* seems to operate on the assumption that if such virtue is to be possessed by these two, it is also capable of being communicated to others. *De vulgari*'s educational program entails training (*habituare*) its reader in the *cautio* and *discretio* necessary to compose poetry in the *vulgare illustre*.[81] The authorial *nos* who opens the doors of his workshop to the apprentice holds up *Cynus et amicus eius* as the model for the strenuous labor necessary to achieve the correct degree of virtue.

Their mutual participation in the project of leading the new vernacular literary movement is such that *Cynus et amicus eius* are, for the first three-quarters of the treatise, never mentioned apart from one another. The conjunctive "et" and pronomial "eius" that join the two poets – one named, the other not – draws a more direct line of allegiance and intimacy than did the "primo" of the *Vita nova*.[82] It would be a stretch to apply Cicero's characterization of *vera amicitia* ("rerum humanarum et divinarum ... consensio") to Dante's friendship with Guido Cavalcanti. Even if the young Dante and his *primo amico* agreed in all matters – already a difficult proposition to accept – that is not to say that they shared a common project or goal, nor to deny that the ostensible agreement between them might conceal each friend's desire to raise his own prominence in the competitive field of vernacular literary culture in the *comune*. In other words, the hierarchical ordering of friends in *Vita nova* implied degrees of like-mindedness and accord, but not cooperation or collaboration.

In *De vulgari*, *amicitia* and *amicabilitas* are notions of individual attachment invested in questions of collaboration, outreach, and education, which were foreign to the concept of *amistà* signaled in the pages of *Vita nova*. Where *Vita nova*'s presentation of Guido's friendship implies a hierarchical pattern of intimacies arranged around the narrative's egocentric perspective, in *De vulgari* Cino and his friend are given precisely equal footing, dissolving the rivalries of the poetic agora into the disinterested *consensio* anticipated by Cicero's definition. In place of the egocentrism of *Vita nova* we find the impersonal authority of the treatise's author, who raises two third-person exemplars, *Cynus et amicus eius*, to positions of prominence in the intellectual environment in which the treatise seeks to intervene. The *amicitia* between *Cynus et amicus eius* is, unlike that of Dante and Guido, based not only on consensus on matters human and divine, but also on the mutual commitment to the linguistic-political-social project of which *De vulgari eloquentia* is both history and manifesto.

Unlike the various examples of *amistà* we saw take shape in the piazza of lyric exchange – which are grounded in reproach, antagonism, and contention – the *amicitia* the two poets enjoy in *De vulgari*'s presentation is one founded on the unified purpose of promulgating the *vulgare illustre*. What is more, *De vulgari* attempts to craft for the two protagonists of this literary movement a perfectly disinterested cooperative endeavor, where each would have his own distinct sphere of excellence: Cino as the master of *venus* [love], and *amicus eius* of *virtus* [moral righteousness]. The distinction drawn between their spheres of excellence is such that each one can benefit the other, driving his friend to greater heights in his friend's distinct sphere because of his excellence in his own. Dividing their expertise into two distinct arenas reinforces the claim to disinterested collaboration and non-competition, for each is afforded his own sphere over which to dominate. Theirs is envisioned as a model friendship that looks beyond their own *amicitia* to see how such shared commitments, ideals, and especially language could become a model, like that of Laelius and Scipio, and might admit others into its restrictive circle.

In sum, because it uses the collaboration of two like-minded individuals as the basis of an educational program invested in the public good, the concept of *amicitia* in *De vulgari eloquentia* reveals its distinct Ciceronian provenance, by contrast with *Vita nova*'s *amistà*. Cino's *amicitia* with the poet represents a chosen relationship that is reflective of and contributes to the moral character of each friend. It is collaborative, disinterested, and reciprocal without competition or conflict. It is invested in the good of the community at large and seeks to intercede in affairs of public concern. *Cynus et amicus eius* lead the literary field, and their friendship acts as exemplar of disinterested collaboration to the members of the dynamic, innovative, and often quarrelsome scholarly field to which the treatise is directed.

Amicitia as Self-Interested Sponsorship

This is, of course, only part of the picture. Dante represents himself in two ways in *De vulgari eloquentia*, bifurcating his authorial voice into the "two Dantes" that Ascoli and others have discussed.[83] Cino's friendship serves different strategic purposes to each of these "Dantes." On the one hand, Cino's friendship with the "humble exemplar" of vernacular excellence in *virtus*, the Dante known as *amicus eius*, is celebrated as perfectly disinterested *vera amicitia*, precisely because the two friends share a project, a *locutio*, and a mutual, non-competitive, disinterested commitment to moral excellence.

On the other hand, Dante has everything to gain from public acknowledgment of his friendship with Cino. At the time he wrote both his *De vulgari eloquentia* and his *Convivio*, Dante's personal and professional futures were extremely uncertain. He had been exiled from his native city; he had attempted to conspire with fellow exiles to re-enter Florence, but those attempts came to naught after the exiled White Guelphs were defeated at the Battle of the Lastra on 20 July 1304. Whether he had begun *De vulgari eloquentia* before the definitive rout of his fellow exiles remains an unsettled question. What is clear is that he wrote *De vulgari* from a precarious position – both in terms of his livelihood and his personal welfare – in which disinterested *amicitia* is nearly impossible: the self-sacrificing friendship the text envisions requires stable ground, not only in character but also in fortunes.

Writing from the instability of exile, Dante sought sponsors and guarantors who might provide him security, much like the security Brunetto Latini found in his well-resourced friend during his own exile in France. Brunetto refers to this "amico" as his "porto" [port], who provides him safe harbour in the storm of exile, principally in the form of a sponsorship that permitted him to pursue his translation and commentary of Cicero's *De inventione*, *La Rettorica*.[84] Throughout the *Rettorica*, Brunetto directs attention to his "porto" as the primary audience for the text's teachings, frequently interrupting his commentary to clarify some detail for his friend, and recognizing in this friend the daring, talent, and dedication necessary to undertake the training the *Rettorica* provides.[85]

Where Brunetto (in his telling, at least) had simply chanced upon a friend who would sustain him in his precarity, in the early years of exile Dante actively cast about for a "porto," searching in Arezzo, Casentino, Verona, and other locales for a patron or ally who would better position him to further his professional and personal ends.[86] Often publicly lamenting the poverty imposed upon him by exile, he would appeal to his networks of potential sponsors for assistance, in more or less explicit terms.[87] He details the abasement of his poverty and dependence in *Convivio* 1.3–1.4 – composed in the same uncertain period as *De vulgari* – in terms that directly recall Brunetto's. He describes himself as "peregrino, quasi mendicando" [like a stranger, almost like a beggar], an expression that highlights his shame in depending on others' charity. He recounts his earliest wanderings, exploiting Brunetto's metaphor of a ship seeking its "porto": "Veramente io sono stato legno sanza vela e sanza governo, portato a diversi porti e foci e liti dal vento secco che vapora la dolorosa povertade" [Truly I have been a ship without sail or rudder, brought to different ports, inlets, and shores by the dry wind that painful poverty blows].[88] Unlike Brunetto, who found a secure port in the "amico della sua cittade" [friend from his own city] that he happened upon in France, Dante depicts himself as blown about to "diversi porti," unable to find the steady protection of a single "amico," be he a patron, as in Brunetto's case, or a dependable ally who shares his interests and commitments.

As he wandered, he explains in *Convivio*, he presented himself to many potential friends and benefactors: "sono apparito alli occhi a molti che forse che per alcuna fama in altra forma m'aveano imaginato: nel cospetto de' quali non solamente mia persona invilio, ma di minor pregio si fece ogni opera, sì già fatta come quella che fosse a fare" [And I have appeared before the eyes of many who perhaps because of some report had imagined me in another form. In their sight not only was my person held cheap, but each of my works was less valued, those already completed as much as those yet to come].[89] His poverty, he claims, has prevented him from securing sponsorship even as he actively courts it, for when he has been able to present himself to a new patron, his contemptible appearance has diminished the "pregio" [value] of both his name and his works in the eyes of a potential benefactor. Exile and the resulting poverty have left his store of symbolic capital diminished.

The loss of "pregio" in the eyes of potential patrons, he concludes in *Convivio*, has left him with no other recourse but to reinvent himself as an even greater authority on the matters on which he dares to speak:

> Onde con ciò sia cosa che, come detto è di sopra, io mi sia quasi a tutti li Italici appresentato, per che fatto mi sono più vile forse che 'l vero non vuole non solamente a quelli a li quali mia fama era già corsa, ma eziandio a li altri, onde le mie cose sanza dubbio meno sono alleviate; conviemmi che con più alto stilo dea, ne la presente opera, un poco di gravezza, per la quale paia di maggiore autoritade.
>
> [Therefore since, as has been said above, I have presented myself to virtually everyone in Italy, by which I have perhaps made myself more base than truth warrants, not only to those to whom my fame had already spread but also to others, whereby my works as well as my person are without doubt made light of, it is fitting that I should add, with a loftier style, a little weight to the present work, so that it may seem to take on an air of greater authority.][90]

The humiliations of exile – and, especially, of mendicancy, "per che fatto mi sono più vile forse che 'l vero non vuole" – have only strengthened and refocused his ambitions, driving him towards more innovative work that could re-establish his "autoritade" and regain him his good name in literary society. It is notable that, by contrast with Brunetto's *Rettorica*, neither *Convivio* nor *De vulgari eloquentia* makes a direct appeal to any lord or patron, relying instead on the poet's self-fashioning as an authority in his own right.[91]

While he does not follow Brunetto in directly calling upon a patron in *De vulgari*, however, he does appeal to a friend's endorsement. Cino's *amicitia* represents a substitute for the kind of sponsorship Dante had been seeking, and which Brunetto discovered in his "amico" in France.[92] Like Dante, Cino also suffered a condemnation of exile, having been banished from his native city from 1303 to 1306.[93] But by contrast with Dante, Cino had already built significant networks of interlocutors outside of his native city, particularly during the last decade of the thirteenth century, while he had been a student and occasional teacher at the Bolognese Studium.[94] He was well known to the Bolognese literary establishment, as confirmed by his correspondence with a great number of interlocutors in the university city: Bernardo da Bologna, ser Cazamonte, Gherarduccio Garisendi, Picciòlo da Bologna, Tommaso da Faenza, and, crucially, Onesto degli Onesti.[95] During his years as a student at the Studium, Cino circulated a proposing sonnet, *Vinta e lassa era già l'anima mia*, which requests explication of a dream; it received no fewer than six replies from five different lyricists, an indication of his centrality and recognition within Bolognese literary society, even as a young man.[96]

Christopher Kleinhenz attributes Cino's ability to mediate between poetic schools and the individual poets who comprise them to his "extreme versatility as a poet," his stylistic and thematic dynamism. Because of this versatility, Kleinhenz says, Cino was able "to derive profit from and contribute directly to the several major literary currents of his age."[97] Much like the elder Onesto, Cino appears to have been an especially skillful networker, particularly beyond the bounds of his own native region.[98] Although in his exile he did not return to Bologna to profit from his former connections there, his centrality on the Bolognese scene would have been well known to Dante, who leans on Cino's name as his "varco," his "in," into the literary network.[99]

The strongest indication of Cino's central position within the Bolognese network appears in his exchanges with Onesto, who was one of the undisputed preeminent poets of late-Duecento Bologna and recognized as such by Dante throughout *De vulgari*. In his derisive but playful sonnet *«Mente» ed «umile» e più di mille sporte* (the first in a ten-sonnet exchange between the two poets), Onesto conspicuously elevates Cino's status by positioning him as spokesperson for the new poetics that would come to be known, following Dante's definition, as *stilnovismo*.[100] Mocking Cino and his companions for their style and lexicon, their "andar sognando" [sleepwalking] and "andar filosofando" [philosophizing], Onesto complains that these poets cannot even decide who their lord is, "o vita o morte" [either life or death]. Regardless, they have wearied ("avete stanco") whoever has heard their verses, where they debate with others and with themselves in the third person. Onesto's direct address in the second-person plural is ambiguous; in their correspondence he invariably refers to "Messer Cin" with the formal *voi*. But, notably, across the exchange Onesto treats Cino as part of a literary movement. Cino is not the unique proponent of *stilnovismo*, nor its originator: elsewhere Onesto overtly invokes Dante and Guido as Cino's allies in the new poetics.[101] Nevertheless, in their *tenzone* Onesto singles Cino out as the representative of and advocate for *stilnovismo* in Bologna in the late 1290s, at a time when both Guido and Dante found themselves deeply ensconced in their native city and its literary and political networks.

Onesto had died in early 1303, after the date of Dante's exile from Florence and likely around the time of Cino's from Pistoia. But after Onesto's death Cino retained his status among Bolognese poets, and Dante's elevation of Cino (and of Onesto, Guido Ghislieri, Fabruzzo de' Lambertazzi, Tommaso da Faenza, and others hailing from or working in Bologna) would have spurred the Bolognese poets to favour the work, presented, as it is, with "un poco di gravezza," much as Dante had intended to present his *Convivio*.[102] Ascoli has detailed the extraordinary measures Dante takes in *De vulgari* to promote his own *auctoritas* in the treatise, including the division of his authorial identity into two voices, one a "logical and detached" or "analytical" authority commenting on the history and condition of the *vulgare illustre*, and the other the "humble exemplar" of lyric practice.[103] But one of the most significant strategies for self-promotion used by the author in the treatise is his claim to his friendship with the well-established Cino, on whose reputation he stakes his own.

Asserting a mutual, disinterested friendship with Cino da Pistoia is one of *De vulgari*'s many self-defensive and self-promotional mechanisms. In his reading of *De vulgari*, Kleinhenz emphasizes the idiosyncrasy of Dante's pronouncements in the treatise: that the treatise is "*Dante's* art of poetry, *his own* personal catalogue of poets, *his own* preference as to meters, words, sounds, and subject matter."[104] Dante blankets this idiosyncrasy in objectivity, veiling the preferential nature of the judgments in the impersonal authority of the *nos*, who appears to have no personal stake in the questions at hand. This is, of course, part of the mechanism of the *nos*'s strategy of self-authorization and of self-promotion. But by aligning himself so inseparably with Cino, he also paints these idiosyncratic pronouncements as part of a common judgment, shared by at least two, but likely many more.[105] Cino, albeit silently, corroborates Dante's judgments, owing to their mutual commitment to vernacular excellence and their shared sense of *discretio*.

That their *amicitia* is not compromised of hope for individual profit, favour, or gain (Cicero's *utilitates* and *beneficia*) is staged in the author's insistence on concealing his name, hiding behind the moniker "amicus eius." Rather than directly elevate his own name, he promotes the name of the friend to whose reputation he has inseparably yoked his own. Barolini describes this yoke as making "semantically real the Aristotelian and Ciceronian idea of the friend as an 'other self' – the 'alter idem' of *De amicitia* 21.80. By defining his self as the friend of his friend, as 'amicus eius,' he is saying that to be 'his friend' is to be himself, to be Dante."[106] Beyond linking his personal and poetic identities with Cino's, he also aligns his fame and reputation with Cino's, notably placing Cino in the position of prominence – as if Cino's friend, Dante himself, is the mere mirror image of the named, well-esteemed poet. In doing so, he raises Cino's stature within the intellectual community, as primary named practitioner of the new poetics announced in the treatise.

De vulgari, in other words, enacts a publicity campaign on behalf of *Cynus Pistoriensis*, whose cachet is increased by the insistence of the treatise's seemingly impartial author, the *nos* who pretends to an objective perspective on the vernacular literary tradition he means to invent. The anonymous *amicus* – the "humble exemplar" of the new vernacular tradition – is partnered with a named, authoritative figure, one who has been recognized within the literary sphere in *tenzoni* with prominent Bolognese authors, and who stands as silent corroborator of and collaborator on the project.[107] Meanwhile, the author deliberately projects onto himself a sense of humility that might disarm any accusations of self-interest on his part. By virtue of the fact that this is a shared endeavor, the project moves further away from the isolation and presumption of the tower builders in Babel (and the exclusive coterie of *amici* in the magical little *vasel* of *Guido, i' vorrei*) and towards a cooperative exercise, laying the metaphorical foundations for a space that would eventually house the elite, wandering *curia*.

Because he represents his *amicitia* with Cino in the third person, Dante can depict it as perfectly collaborative, abstracted from the competition and backbiting that plague poetic and academic circles. The two can appear to be engaged in a project of mutual support and promotion, from which both partners will equally benefit. At the same time, the treatise's author likewise seeks strategically to accredit himself by publicly aligning himself with Cino and presenting himself as "Cino's friend." His use of the term *amicus* thus straddles the two contrasting positions of theoretical and practical *amicitia*: his claim to Cino's friendship is simultaneously disinterested and profitable, collaborative and self-promotional.

In her work on the shared resonance of Cino's work with Dante's, as evidenced by their correspondence in the early years of Dante's exile (1302–8), Leyla Livraghi contends that one cannot reduce Dante's friendship with Cino to "una mera questione di opportunismo," despite the fact, she concedes, that Cino may well have served as mediator between Dante and the Bolognese Studium.[108] Livraghi would count Cino's dependence on Sicilian models, his thoughts on the fungibility of love, and his sympathy – from personal experience – for the condition of exile among the causes for Dante's elevation of Cino to his position of prominence in *De vulgari*. She argues against interpreting their friendship in light of a cynical desire for self-promotion or self-stabilization. But reading the claim to *amicitia* as a self-interested and even opportunistic one does not mean reducing it to an *amicitia falsa*, as one might presume. If we look at the immediate successors of Dante and his interlocutors, the early humanists, the terms of friendship and sponsorship were deeply intertwined with one another. Much as Brunetto had relied on his "porto," an "amico della sua cittade," for subsistence as he composed his *Rettorica*, so the humanists would rely on their friends for personal and professional advantage, and they would apply the terms of friendship to their patrons and promoters. Opportunism and *amicitia* were not incompatible with one another; rather, the terms of friendship would take on an ever-greater flexibility as they were applied to a wide variety of relationships among the humanist *literati*.[109]

Abandoning *Amicitia*

In styling his identity as "amicus eius," friend of Cino da Pistoia, Dante straddles two opposing poles in theoretical accounts of *amicitia*: disinterestedness and self-interest. He deliberately models his friendship with Cino after that of Laelius and Scipio: equitable, generous, collaborative, mutually bettering. At the same time, he employs the term strategically to fashion the well-connected Cino as his partner and defender, counting on Cino's symbolic capital in the intellectual field of the University to underwrite his ambitious endeavor. For three-quarters of the treatise, he negotiates between these two contrasting shades of meaning, as he relies on his idealized Ciceronian friendship with his partner Cino to silently validate and endorse his enterprise, novel in its ambition to inaugurate a vernacular literary tradition of which he and Cino would be the first and best exemplars.

Dante's approach to *amicitia* changes near the end of *De vulgari eloquentia*. In 2.8 he abruptly abandons the epithet "amicus eius" and unites his divided poetic identities under the name "nos" – both treatise author and exemplary poet. He does so by pointedly acknowledging himself as the poet of the canzone *Donne ch'avete intelletto d'amore*: a canzone that marks the critical turning point in the narrative of *Vita nova*, where it inaugurates the poet's new *stile della loda*, and to which he will return in *Purgatorio* 24, as the exemplary poem of the *dolce stil novo* itself. In its "unam sententiam" [unified meaning] as he announces here, this canzone represents the poet's position as unique champion of both *virtus* and *venus*, taking primacy of place above his friend Cino as the singular paragon of vernacular excellence.[110]

We cannot be certain why he chose, in *De vulgari* 2.8, to "come out" as the poet who had been, for the first three-quarters of the treatise, cloaked behind the mantle of Cino's friendship. But when he does so, leaving off the epithet "amicus eius" and reclaiming the first-person plural "nos" for both his authorial positions, he effectively neuters the power of friendship to provide the kind of collaborative, non-competitive, disinterested partnership he had voiced throughout. Instead, he asserts his own interests with a renewed force, putting himself first as the singular exemplar of vernacular excellence, in both the arenas of *venus* and *virtus*.

When Dante discards the phrase "amicus eius" and discloses his identity as both "nos" and "amicus" in *De vulgari* 2.8 and following, he signals that he abandoned *De vulgari* and the disinterested friendship it purports to celebrate for a more practical embrace of his own authorial self-interest. In this shift, he pivots his strategy for self-fashioning, perhaps having realized that the tight allegiance with *Cynus Pistoriensis* was not going to yield the kind of network access he had sought. As he moves away from an alliance with Cino and the *doctores eloquentes* and enters the next phase of his post-exilic journey, he begins to assert himself as a unique authority figure worthy of individual sponsorship. In doing so, he turns his attentions away from the intellectual field and sets his sights on even broader audiences. In the most decisive turn of his literary career, he sheds any desire for collaboration to embark on the solitary enterprise of the *Commedia*, while also managing the need to defer to and serve the uncompromising authority of a patron.

As we will see in the following chapter, Dante's understanding of *amicitia* as commensurate with self-interest and sponsorship will take on new urgency and gravity in the environment of the court system. Where in *De vulgari* he relies on the *amicitia* of a colleague to sponsor a collaborative endeavor, in the patronage system he will be compelled to negotiate a new dilemma emerging when the terms of friendship are employed to the relationship with a patron of higher social status: hierarchy and equality. But he will maintain the possibility that friendship can be both true and self-interested, much as Brunetto had in his *Rettorica*, and he will defend that proposition pointedly, even provocatively and unabashedly, in the opening paragraphs of an epistle to his patron Cangrande della Scala, lord of Verona. It is to this text and to this social field that I turn my attention in the next chapter.

3
Hierarchy: The Court

As influential as Cicero's *De amicitia* was on the discourse of friendship, in the Middle Ages and in the early Renaissance, thinkers of this period diverged sharply over Cicero's view that equality was necessary to friendship.[1] For Cicero, in his devoted republicanism, friendship could be one of the great equalizing cultural forces. But for writers broadly accustomed to medieval assumptions of strictly hierarchical ordering in every facet of life – social, political, occupational, material, and metaphysical – inequality was a reality to negotiate with assiduous care. Inequality of social position undermined defining principles of friendship theory: how can two friends discover and nurture the kind of intense like-mindedness stipulated by classical friendship theory if their life experiences are sharply divergent? How can friends of unequal social or economic standing be assured of one another's loyalty in adverse circumstances? Doesn't inequality of fortunes mitigate, if not prevent altogether, the possibility of a purely disinterested generosity, to say nothing of the theoretical reciprocity of exchange between friends?

In four brief paragraphs that open the Epistle to Cangrande, Dante seeks to reconcile the presumed necessity of equality in medieval friendship theory with the realities of a strictly hierarchical social order. The rhetorical moves of these paragraphs present a more sophisticated resolution of the complicated *amicitia* between patron and client – a "friendship" deeply embedded in the shifting systems of social and political networks of the Northern Italian signorial courts – than we see elsewhere in the literature of the late Duecento and early Trecento. As I will demonstrate, the Epistle's argument hinges on two qualities that are central to friendship and antithetical to patronage: equality and reciprocity. In exchanges of goods, favours, and services between two unequal partners, how does the inferior satisfy a debt to his superior? How can reciprocity exist, where fortunes – both material and symbolic – differ so sharply? In its first four paragraphs, the Epistle to Cangrande offers a subtle negotiation around these conjoined questions within the realm of patronage.

To chart the Epistle's resolution to the dilemma of equality and reciprocity in friendships between patrons and their clients, I begin with a discussion of the discursive practices in relationships of inequality in the Duecento and Trecento. Surveying rhetorical manuals of the period, I identify patterns in the expressions of friendship between social equals and unequals in the *ars dictaminis*. Such conventional expressions testify to the strategic practices of letter-writers in the economy of patronage, dedication, and gift-exchange. Next I review the discursive modalities through which Cangrande's reputation as a great and magnanimous patron was constituted and maintained, in both direct and indirect address. Chroniclers, artists, and poets – both clients and not – contributed to and constructed narratives describing Cangrande's legendary magnificence and unrivaled eminence; an overview of these contemporary accounts establishes a sharp contrast with the Epistle's rhetorical moves. Unlike conventional frames that would insist on insurmountable inequalities of status between patron and client, the Epistle boldly claims that such inequalities can be bridged by symbolic – but not for that less real – affinities of taste, discernment, and honour. These arguments, I will show, initiate a theory of reciprocity that originates in a mutual recognition of patronage's debts, both symbolic and economic. I argue that the calculated improvisations seen in the Epistle accord new possibilities to dedication, as a practice that guarantees the gift's convertible value and the seals the giver's authority. The Epistle's resolution, furthermore, logically justifies the *Commedia*'s implicit claims for the possibilities of *amicitia Dei*, as a unique bond that can paradoxically be both rigidly hierarchical in its structure and yet radically inclusive in its reach.

Friendship in the Patronage Economy

The latter half of the thirteenth century saw the consolidation of interests – material, political, and sociocultural – into the hands of a few powerful *signori* who, over the next two centuries, would increasingly dominate the political landscape of Northern Italy. Already in 1300, during Dante's lifetime, at least half of Italian *comuni* had fallen to signorial rule.[2] In many *comuni* the struggle between *magnati* and *popolani* left a power vacuum into which a strongman found it easy to maneuver.[3] A *comune* might elect to turn power over to a single individual, who would act as *dictator* in the ancient sense: taking dominion of the affairs of the city through the *podestà*-ship or captaincy of the *Popolo* for a brief period of time, before retiring in honour.[4] Often *comuni* would gradually grant more authority to *podestà* and *capitani*, who eventually secured longer or even indefinite periods of rule.[5] Among communal civic leaders concerns over despotism and abuses of power were rampant – especially following the legendarily brutal regime of a tyrant like Ezzelino da Romano (1194–1259) – but *signori* and would-be *signori* strengthened strategic alliances with supporters (styled as "amici") through marriage, privilege, and patronage, winning enough political and military support to stabilize precarious regimes.[6]

As the market economy grew and flourished in the Tuscan commune, an active non-mercantile gift economy, premised on family wealth and nobility, began to shape literary production in the Northern courts, determining the success of authors and other artists. Patrons increasingly provided writers both the means for copying and distributing their manuscripts and financial support, even in the form of food and shelter, which, in this age of frequent political banishments, was essential for many public figures. Critiques and commendations of tyranny dominated the literary discourse coming out of these courtly environments, as did the general celebration of chivalric virtues.[7] Although literary patronage was not the only means for a vernacular author to successfully circulate his work in Italian urban centres, over the course of the fourteenth century *signori* increasingly sought to legitimate their precarious power by investing in artistic commissions that would elevate their esteem in the eyes of their subjects, and would promote their interests and image as legitimate rulers outside of the regions under their dominion.[8]

Unlike the networked literary communities of Florence and other republican *comuni*, the courts of the *signorie cittadine* functioned on a rigidly hierarchical model, with clusters of inner and outer circles competing for the favour of the *signore*. And yet even here, as the humanist letters of the century following would make clear, modes of friendly address would eventually become commonplace between clients and patrons, in which clients addressed themselves to their lords with humble expressions of loyalty and devotion, accompanying assertions of unique and abiding affection. The theoretical premise of a patron-client friendship is laid out in sections of books eight and nine of the *Nicomachean Ethics*, where Aristotle devotes paragraphs to defining and explaining the norms around friendship, exchange of services, debt, and benefaction.[9] The fifteenth-century humanists would apparently embrace these Aristotelian precepts, and conventional usage of the term "amicus" to define a patron would come to dominate the discourse of patronage in the Renaissance.[10] Petrarch, for example, addressed his early patron Cardinal Giovanni Colonna with the intimacy and warmth characteristic of classical friendship conventions.[11] Paul D. McLean's study of the discursive practices of Florentine patronage networks in the Italian Renaissance calculates the incidence of the term "amico" (among other keywords) across patronage letters; he finds the term in 39 per cent of the 1,146 letters he reviews, most commonly occurring in letters requesting benefices, recommendations, and release from prison.[12] Alongside servanthood, *amicizia* or *amicitia* became the most prevalent motif in patronage requests, as clients relied on the bonds of friendly obligation to prevail on their patrons for support.[13] The ambivalence and flexibility of the term permitted Florentine humanists to employ it within a wide variety of social frameworks, even those that would have violated the theoretical precepts of *vera amicitia* derived from the ancients.[14]

For the generation of writers preceding the humanists, however, assertions of friendship between client and patron were not yet commonplace. Where their letters did employ the language of friendship, clients did so with great care. The term "amicus" was often included among the customary forms of address in the *ars dictaminis*, but careful attention to its application reveals the delicate balance struck by letter writers who chose to use the term.[15] In the sample salutations in their rhetorical manuals, Bene da Firenze and Guido Fava (of the Studium in Bologna), as well as Bichilino da Spello (of the Studium in Padova), propose the term "amicus" as a conventional form of self-identification between relatives and associates, merchants and farmers, emperors and kings, among clerics in a variety of positions, and in many other circumstances. In most cases, it appears, calling a letter's recipient "amicus" was acceptable, whether or not social parity was present in the relationship. But the vast majority of occurrences of the term describe relationships among individuals who were comparable in status, even if not precisely equal.[16]

Even as rhetorical manuals of the later Duecento suggested that "amicus" could acceptably be used between individuals of unequal status, medieval *dictatores* remained preoccupied by inequality, particularly in their letters. The earliest letter-writing handbooks stipulated that all salutations should be composed with an eye to distinctions both in friendship and in rank.[17] While in their manuals rhetors recognized friendships of inequality as theoretically possible, the etiquette they proposed for patron-client relationships was determined by the inequality of the participants' respective standing, a social distance that was not overruled by any particular attachment, loyalty, confidence, or affective bond that they might have shared. The most revealing example of letter-writers' caution comes from the *Pomerium rethorice* of Bichilino da Spello (1304), which interrupts its discussion of the salutations between friends and companions to warn:

> Nota insuper quod talis locucio, ut dictum est in toto capitulo de amicis, quasi omnes status hominum comprehendit. Potest eciam sic amicabiliter loqui rex regi, miles militi, iudex iudici, medicus medico, clericus clerico, et quilibet alteri sibi pari, et eciam maior minori, si vult. Minor vero maiori, quantumcumque amicentur ad invicem, non sic amicabiliter, sed secundum status sui convenienciam loqui debet.
>
> [Furthermore, take note that such speech, as is said in this entire chapter about friends, comprises almost all ranks of men. Indeed, in such a friendly manner a king may speak to a king, a soldier to a soldier, a judge to a judge, a doctor to a doctor, a cleric to a cleric, and from anyone to another who is equal to him, and even from a superior to an inferior, if he wishes. But an inferior ought not address his superior in this way (that is, as "amicus"), however friendly they are with one another, but in a way appropriate to his own status.][18]

Bichilino leaves open the possibility that a superior would "break rank," so to speak, opting to turn to a friend with greater familiarity than the friend is due by virtue of his low station. But the same possibility is denied to the inferior, no matter how sincere the bond or how ardent the affection. The inferior must abide by status before all else and must remain mindful of it even as he freely performs the duties of a friend: offering companionship and conversation, and even, when necessary, gentle reproach. Under all circumstances, the inferior must attend to the social distance between himself and his friend, a clear constraint on the kind of free, open, and generous affect anticipated by the laudatory treatises on friendship circulating in the period. Given these constraints, it is perhaps surprising that clients of the period might adopt the discourse of *amicitia* at all in letters to their patrons.

As mentioned above, construing relationships of patronage as friendships raises two related problems within the understanding of friendship in late-medieval Italy: the issues of equality and reciprocity. Medieval writers found in Aristotle and Cicero an expectation that two partners would share equal status as the foundation on which bonds of loyalty, trust, and confidence could be built. If the partners were not already of equal status, friendship served as an equalizer, provided that the inferior attend to adequate gestures of respect and recompense, while the superior condescended to treat his inferior as an equal for the sake of the friendship.[19] Such friendships were, however, delicately balanced, requiring the generosity of the superior, the humility of the inferior, and the careful maintenance of the distinction between their roles. In a case of patronage, the humble client would only with great difficulty manage to negotiate his rhetorical modesty, as the letter-writing manuals of the period attest. Guido Fava, for one, stipulated in his *Summa dictaminis* that superiors should always be addressed as such, the marker of rank "dominus" invariably preceding the name of "amicus."[20] Maintaining the difference in status, in other words, had to precede attachment or affection, although it did not necessarily preclude it.

If a theoretical equality could be navigated with great subtlety and rhetorical care, reciprocity in patronage was nearly impossible. How could a client ever expect to make equal, and equally disinterested, restitution for the material gifts of patronage? Conventionally, of course, poets would express their gratitude for the gifts received in patronage by inserting dedications and passages of strategic praise within their works. And yet expressions of gratitude for favours received merely acknowledge the generosity of the patron; they do not – indeed, cannot – make restitution for the patron's gift. How does a client, presenting himself with the name of "friend," then, make a return on such a gift?

The exchange of gifts and services entailed in patronage generates the bond between patron and client, and it seems clear we should view such a bond in terms of Aristotle's "instrumental friendships." But if the law of friendship requires both equality and reciprocity, how can such demands be reasonably met and maintained in connection with the excess of generosity and the strict maintenance of hierarchy that together constitute patronage?

In their discussion of friendship among unequals in the medieval West, Constant Mews and Neville Chiavaroli turn to one "remarkable document" that takes seriously the thorny issues of friendship with one's patron and attempts to resolve them: the Epistle to Cangrande.[21] For Mews and Chiavaroli, the Epistle (addressed to the Veronese lord Cangrande della Scala by "Dantes Alagherii, florentinus natione non moribus") provides what they call "the most elaborate and eloquent defence of friendship between unequals."[22] While other medieval treatises or manuals may make claims about the possibility of these friendships or give advice for how to address one's superior in a friendly manner, the Epistle to Cangrande presents a logical justification for the friendship of men between whom stands a seemingly insurmountable social distance. Beyond what Mews and Chiavaroli have suggested, what is "remarkable" about this document is the author's choice to transcend mere rhetorical convention, giving a gratuitous defense of what was, as we have seen, an appropriate (if delicate) address for the *signore*. The writer of the Epistle pauses for some two and a half full paragraphs to give a full-throated defense for using a term that, if not yet broadly conventional, was at least already available to clients according to contemporary rhetorical handbooks. In doing so, the Epistle takes a formulaic expression and makes it a matter of contention. The letter highlights, in other words, the problems of equality and reciprocity that other medieval writers were content to evade.

The ingenuity of the Epistle's arguments on friendship, equality, and reciprocity has in part been overshadowed by the complicated history of its attribution, which has been debated vehemently for more than two centuries.[23] Centring primarily on the letter's dishomogeneous style and structure – in particular the author's use of the Latin *cursus* – but also surrounding the complexity of its transmission history and its dating (suggestions range from 1315 to 1321 and beyond), as well as a number of other interrelated concerns, scholars have questioned the authentic attribution of the letter to Dante himself, many proposing that all or part of the letter might have been composed by a later compiler or scribe.[24] The arguments on friendship are mostly limited to the first four epistolary paragraphs of the letter, which Bruno Nardi – despite his conviction that the remainder of the letter was spurious – convincingly defended as Dante's own.[25] Today, even some of the most vehement critics of the letter's attribution concede Nardi's point, and assign the epistolary paragraphs to Dante.[26] If indeed these paragraphs are Dante's own, the text would represent the poet's most explicit discussion of friendship across his oeuvre: Giorgio Brugnoli, in his commentary on the Epistle, goes so far as to consider these paragraphs a "trattato sull'amicizia" [treatise on friendship].[27]

For the record, I believe that Dante was the author of the four paragraphs under consideration here, and I will proceed by assuming that to be the case. But my argument here does not hinge on the case for attribution. My concern here is not to introduce a new reading of the Epistle's controversial doctrinal and expository paragraphs, nor to provide an exhaustive review of the authenticity debate. Neither do I wish to make a case for or against the attribution of the four epistolary paragraphs, in which Nardi and others so clearly see Dante's hand. Rather, I mean to highlight the subtlety of the theory of friendship spelled out in this Trecento "trattato sull'amicizia" [treatise on friendship]. Of interest to the present investigation is less the question of whether Dante authored these particular arguments and more how those arguments contribute to the late-medieval dispute over friendship with one's superiors. Whether or not Dante was the author of part, all, or none of the Epistle, the Epistle's take on friendship in its first four paragraphs demonstrates changes in the early-fourteenth-century use of the language of *amicitia.*[28] These changes expand on – and, in some respects, depart from – the theory of friendship presented in Dante's other works, including the *Commedia.* In particular, the Epistle strives to resolve the issues of equality and reciprocity, issues that were crucial not only within the hierarchical strictures of patronage but in all institutions of social life in late Duecento and early Trecento Italy.

Patronage, like any exchange, involves the strategic negotiation of material and symbolic hierarchies. In *Outline of a Theory of Practice* (and later in *The Logic of Practice*), Pierre Bourdieu likens the initiating of an exchange (issuing a challenge, making an insult or offense, giving a gift, and so on) to an act of aggression, domination, or even violence that is only transformed into a challenge by the manner of the recipient's riposte, retort, revenge, or return-gift.[29] For the recipient to regain honour and transmute aggression into exchange, an appropriately timed and measured answer must be made. But Bourdieu concedes that an equal answer is not expected in all cases of exchange:

> In the case where the offender [the donor or patron] is clearly superior to the offended [the recipient or client], only the fact of avoiding the challenge is held to be blameworthy, and the offended party is not required to triumph over the offender in order to be rehabilitated in the eyes of public opinion: the defeated man who has done his duty incurs no blame.… He only has to adopt an attitude of humility which, by emphasizing his weakness, highlights the arbitrary and immoderate character of the offence. This strategy is, of course, only admissible so long as, in the eyes of the group, the disparity between the two antagonists is unequivocal; it is a natural course for those individuals socially recognized as weak, clients (*yadh itsumuthen*, those who lean on), or members of a small family.[30]

Such are the conventions around patronage: clients are not expected to make a full return of the "challenge" of patronage but rather to embrace their postures of subservience in the face of the excesses of patronage. The client's public face, which could never equal the prestige of the donor, is restored by the client's humble acceptance of the patron's gift and celebratory gestures of thanksgiving.

By employing the language of friendship to raise and then mediate between the correlated problems of equality and reciprocity, the Epistle far exceeds what is expected of a client. In a series of tactical moves, the author redefines his position relative to the patron without creating further offense. At the same time, he insists on the patron's recognition of his own honour, recouping his symbolic capital within the exchange. In what follows, I will take the issues of equality and reciprocity in turn, walking through the Epistle's logical resolution for each in light of Bourdieu's theory of exchange and the game of honour. The Epistle, as we will see, is not merely a dedicatory letter from a client to a patron giving thanks and praise for the gifts of patronage. It is, rather, a reflection on the significance and possibilities inherent in the act of dedication itself, as a means to restoring the client's symbolic power.

Negotiating Inequality

In the Epistle's first four paragraphs, Dante defends his use of the appellation "amicus" for one so great as his patron, Cangrande della Scala, concerned he may otherwise "reatum presumptionis incurrere," be charged with the "crime of presumption," having presented himself to his patron in too familiar a fashion. But just how realistic or sincere is that concern? On the one hand, as I have shown, references to a superior as a friend had been embraced by rhetorical authorities, having been included in some manuals of the *ars dictaminis*. Viewed from this perspective, the author's concern over his presumption appears to be a strategic rhetorical position, as he embarks on an unnecessary philosophical justification of a term that was considered legitimate, albeit applied only cautiously.

On the other hand, the Epistle departs significantly from other modes of speaking about and to the particular patron to whom it is addressed, the young Veronese lord Cangrande della Scala (1291–1329).[31] Dante's use of a familiar and equalizing term like *amicus* signals a sharp departure from the deferential and elevated language Cangrande's other clients would use to speak of the lord. Before we turn to the Epistle's arguments in detail, we should begin by placing the letter into the broader context of contemporary writers' approaches to Cangrande and the Veronese court he oversaw, references that tended towards deference, subservience, and even sycophancy.

By the time of Cangrande's birth in 1291, the Della Scala had been increasing their power over the city of Verona for more than a generation, when Cangrande's great uncle Mastino I ascended to power, first as *podestà* (1259) and then *Capitano del popolo* (1262), following the infamous rule of the despot Ezzelino III da Romano.[32] After Mastino's assassination in 1277, Cangrande's father Alberto rose to power, continued consolidating control over Verona and the surrounding *contado* in the hands of the Della Scala family.[33] Alberto knighted his third son Cangrande when the boy was only 3 years old, thus initiating his lifelong career as a military leader.[34]

Cangrande was seventeen when he ascended to co-rulership of Verona with his elder brother Alboino, whom he would eventually succeed upon Alboino's death in 1311. At this time, Cangrande, a staunch supporter of the Ghibelline cause, had been tightly allied with the Emperor Henry VII, who bestowed upon him the title of Imperial Vicar over Verona and its surrounding lands. Upon Henry's death in 1313, Cangrande refused repeated papal demands that he renounce the title, and he was eventually excommunicated by Pope John XXII on 6 April 1318.[35] In addition to opposing papal authority and overreach, Cangrande doggedly pursued a program of significant expansion of Della Scala land holdings. During his eighteen-year reign as sole sovereign of Verona, Cangrande would complete the most ambitious land expansion that the Scaligeri would see, acquiring dominion over Vicenza (1311–1312), Feltre and Belluno (1321–1323), Padua (1328), and Treviso (1329).[36] The young lord died suddenly on 22 July 1329, mere days after his triumph over Treviso, when he was only 38 years old. Recent toxicological studies have confirmed that he was the victim of foxglove poisoning.[37]

Before rising to power, the Scaligero household had previously belonged to neither the political class nor the feudal nobility.[38] But the Scaligeri lords were skilled at self-promotion within the growing manufacturing economy of Verona; Silvana Anna Bianchi suggests that it is perhaps because of their lack of previous political and military credentials in the city that were able to maneuver themselves into a position of power.[39] As Philip Jones comments, "the Della Scala, model 'bourgeois' despots, commanded (purges apart) the support of leading feudal families and moved by degrees away from popular towards aristocratic associations and lifestyle, subordinating guilds, restricting councils to *amici*, and concentrating government in the hands of a magnate, bureaucratic, and courtier élite."[40] The Della Scala lords promoted their symbolic and material interests by a series of strategic exclusions and elevations.[41] During the early years of their rise to power, they asserted their lordship through networking efforts, beginning with their increased centrality in civic institutions like the *Domus mercatorum* and the guilds, followed by a targeted campaign to cultivate allies within the families of the Veronese ruling class.[42] They were among the earliest *signori* to embark on projects of civic beautification, restoring palaces, churches, and city walls.[43] The Scaligeri lords were experts at the ritual exhibition of symbolic power, displays that would in turn promote the growth of their economic capital and material power.[44]

The image of majesty (what the Epistle calls "magnalia") and liberality ("beneficia") seems to have been especially cultivated by Cangrande, over and above what his predecessors had sought.[45] As we will see in the praises detailed below, Cangrande's name was often coupled with terms like virtue, honour, courtesy, magnanimity, and largesse. By all accounts, lavish comforts greeted visitors to Cangrande's Verona. According to contemporary chroniclers, the young Veronese lord exhibited a deep and abiding fascination with the exotic goods of the East, much like the Hohenstaufen Emperor Frederick II before him.[46] Recent studies of Cangrande's tomb have uncovered a sumptuous collection of Oriental fabrics.[47] Andrea Placidi and Luisa Vergani both point out the presumably coincidental but nevertheless remarkable resemblance of his name to the title of the Tartar emperor in Marco Polo's *Il Milione*, the Gran Khan. Given the precariousness of his claim to the emperor's domain, Cangrande certainly would have wanted to cultivate imperial connections where he could.[48]

The rapid expansion of Cangrande's dominion, his prominence as a stalwart Ghibelline leader, and his mysterious and sudden death fueled the myths of his valor and virtue. And yet, despite what must have been ostentatious displays of wealth and military prowess correlated to imperial claims, many contemporary accounts celebrate the lord's indifference towards the accumulation of wealth.[49] Among both allies and enemies, Cangrande enjoyed a reputation for unparalleled magnanimity. The famous treatment of the young Cangrande in *Paradiso* 17 is just one entry in a long list of texts that extol the virtues of the lord and of his court: Cangrande's reputation was cultivated by the great number of court poets, artists, preachers, and intellectuals who gathered at the Scaligero palace – each, according to later legends, granted their own chambers decorated to inspire Cangrande's clients to great works.[50] Chroniclers of the period mention a host of names welcomed at the court: Immanuel Romano, a contemporary and admirer of Dante who wrote an account of Heaven and Hell in Hebrew that may have taken inspiration from the *Commedia*; Uguccione della Faggiuola, the mercenary captain and ally of Cangrande to whom Boccaccio believed Dante dedicated the *Inferno*; Spinetta Malaspina, whose family were early patrons of Dante, and who would develop a long partnership with Cangrande after residing with the Veronese captain; and Guido da Castello, who may, according to some accounts, have also hosted the exiled Dante either before or after meeting him at Cangrande's dining table. Each of those named in the chronicles had been exiled from his homeland amid political intrigues and found himself in need of support from the powerful young Scaligero lord.

Cangrande's court in Verona was, in fact, renowned as a haven for exiles. In an otherwise acerbic anecdote about Cangrande's patronage of Dante, Petrarch unironically calls the Veronese court and its lord "comune tunc afflictorum solamen ac profugium" [the common refuge and comfort of the afflicted at that time],[51] and the court was celebrated as a safe haven by clients, who loudly commemorated the lord's generosity as limitless and unreciprocable. One particularly vocal example is Immanuel Romano's *Bisbidis*, a *frottola* in celebration of Cangrande and his liberality. Immanuel, a Jewish poet living in a period of increasing instability for Jews in Christian Italy, had been generously welcomed by the lord in the early fourteenth century.[52] His *Bisbidis* sings the lord's praises as a magnanimous benefactor to the marginalized and the afflicted; Immanuel positions himself as an alien observer of the court, casting great distance between himself and the citizens of Verona.[53] Cultivating his distance from the courtiers and citizens allows Immanuel to portray them as bizarre, incomprehensible objects worthy of good-natured jest. Much like descriptions of the cosmopolitan court of Frederick II, Immanuel's portrait honours the Veronese court's tolerance of differences in everything from religion and culture to class and status and even species. Cangrande's court is displayed as a feast of freedoms – sexual, religious, linguistic, and economic – all overseen by a valorous and honourable lord, who is not, however, shown to participate in the freedoms his courtiers and others enjoy. The conclusion of the poem makes a ceremonious turn, emphasizing the praise of the patron whose generosity has given rise to Verona's grandeur:

> Qui son altri stati
> sì ben divisati,
> che tra li beati
> sen può ragionare.
> E questo è 'l signore
> di tanto valore,
> che 'l grande onore
> va in terra e per mare.
>
> [Here are other ranks
> well-dressed in their costumes,
> that you can talk about them
> being among the blessed.
> And this is the lord
> of such valor
> that his great honor
> spreads across land and sea.][54]

The single point that the comic poem seems to insist upon is Cangrande's liberality. In Immanuel's portrait, Cangrande aids indiscriminately the poor, the blind, the old, and the exiled, feeding and clothing them according to his "largo costume," his generous manner.[55] The emphasis on the poet's outsider status at the beginning of the poem contrasts sharply with the lord's eminence at its conclusion; in this way, Immanuel sustains the strict hierarchy, recognizing the distance between his own position and that of his patron.

The lord's dominance over an ever-expanding region of northern Italy positioned him as one of the most powerful *signori* of the first decades of the fourteenth century, one whose authority was increasingly difficult to question and whose character was earning him a reputation for both liberality and strength. Although the lord certainly had his critics – Albertino Mussato being the most prominent among these – none could dispute the increasing individual sway he held over the region, and many even celebrated it.[56] The city of Vicenza, for example, commemorated its liberation from Paduan control and its subjection to Cangrande's forces with a celebratory epigram: "Prona genu flexo Vicentia semper adoret/ victrices aquilas magnanimumque Canem" [May Vicenza, bowing with bent knee, always honour the victorious eagles and the magnanimous Cane].[57] Benvenuto dei Campesani likewise authored verses celebrating the lord's triumph over the Paduans, singing in similar terms his victory over the forces of tyranny ("et pulsos servili ex urbe tyrannos").[58] Nicolò de Rossi, who opposed Cangrande's advances over Treviso in 1324–5, nevertheless comments on the lord's "valor, senno e fortuna bona" [worth, wisdom, and good fortune], concluding (not without a sense of foreboding) that if all proceeds according to plan, "El sarà re d'Italia enançi un anno" [He will be king of Italy within the year].[59]

Even so critical a body of work as Mussato's, which explicitly condemns Cangrande as a despot, refrains from impeaching the lord's nobility or superiority. Although Mussato does not withhold critique of Cangrande's character (going so far as to call him "vir nefarius"), he does not challenge his sovereignty.[60] Indeed, Mussato's critiques of Cangrande rest on his drive to consolidate and command authority, which, Mussato claims, was instiled in the ruler at birth, nurtured through his rearing, and continued unabated even into his adulthood.[61] Late in his career, Mussato sought to align himself with Cangrande as a potential interlocutor or even counselor, and he occasionally offered praises of the lord's sense of justice or tendency towards mercy.[62] Whether praising Cangrande for his magnanimity or critiquing him for his despotism, Mussato nevertheless consistently retains the great distinction in their respective social standings, elevating Cangrande to a position of absolute dominance over all subjects in his realm, be they friends or foes.

Perhaps the most telling example from contemporary documents is the *sonetto caudato* Giovanni Quirini penned to the lord, requesting that Cangrande distribute new cantos of Dante's *Paradiso*.[63] The sonnet is revealing precisely for its adherence to customary modes of address to a patron. Before making his entreaty, Quirini sings Cangrande's praises in hyperbolic terms, artfully appealing to the lord's reputation for generosity in order to pressure him to accede to the poet's request:

> Segnor, ch'avete di pregio corona
> per l'universo e fama di prodeza
> di onor, di cortesia e di largeza
> e di iusticia, che meglior ancor sona,
> e di vertù vostra gentil persona
> ornata fulge e splende in grande alteza,
> sí ch'ogni nazion vi dotta e preza
> udendo ciò che di voi si ragiona.
>
> [Lord, who hold the crown of virtue,
> through the universe the fame of your valor
> and honour, your courtesy and largesse,

and of your justice, resounds ever greater;
and your gracious being, adorned with virtue,
glitters and glows to great heights,
such that every nation fears and honours you,
hearing what is said in your regard.][64]

Quirini's ingratiating hyperbole here falls well within conventional practice. He commends not only the virtues of the lord himself, but also the fame of those virtues, a second-order praise of praises that redoubles the lord's honour by extending it to those who praise him. Quirini's poem thus participates in the continued amplification of Cangrande's renown, maximizing the poet's prestige by calling attention to both the lord's honour and the honour of those who sing his praises.

Quirini strategically spends a full two quatrains of his sonnet foregrounding the lord's reputation for magnanimity and positioning himself as the humble (potential) beneficiary of that renowned generous spirit. In the sonnet, Quirini adopts the stance one expects of clients petitioning patrons: calling himself "un vostro fedel servitore" [your faithful servant], Quirini prostrates himself before the lord in order to make his petition. The lowering of the "servitore" at the feet of the sovereign was standard practice in addresses to the lord, as we saw above in the discussion of the *ars dictaminis*.[65] Adopting a position of inferiority and emphasizing the vast difference between his own humble status and his lord's immeasurable generosity, Quirini asserts his position in what Bourdieu calls "the game of honour," practices of exchange in which the symbolic capital of one player is staked against that of the other.[66] Quirini opens by extravagantly praising Cangrande's largesse, valor, virtue, and so on; by calling upon the lord's great magnificence, Quirini has challenged Cangrande to live up to the reputation for generosity that precedes him, staking that reputation on the request's fulfilment and so securing the petitioner of what he desires. Quirini's self-subjugation serves to elevate the lord, and his humility, he hopes, will gain the lord's favour.

The Game of Honour

As a client petitioning his lord, Quirini embodies a character that is, in many ways, the foil to Dante's in the opening paragraphs of the Epistle. Quirini, like others writing on Cangrande's liberality, seems content to maintain the social distance and status difference between the lord and his clients. The Epistle, by contrast, strategically elides those differences, defending its use of the term "amicus" to refer to a superior. The defense – purportedly occasioned by the fear of accusations of presumption – is, as I have indicated, largely gratuitous, turning what was becoming a formulaic mode of address between unequals into a matter of dispute. In treating the rote use of friendship terminology (his use of the term "amicus" to describe his superior in a petition) as a contentious claim, Dante occasions a discussion of inequality, a highly problematic construction needing careful navigation in the practices of friendship.

The Epistle artfully raises the contentious issue of inequality by first playing to convention. Just as the *ars dictaminis* prescribes, it opens with a salutation that positions author and recipient on opposing social planes:

> Magnifico atque victorioso domino domino Cani Grandi de la Scala sacratissimi Cesarei Principatus in urbe Verona et civitate Vicentie Vicario generali, devotissimus suus Dantes Alagherii florentinus natione non moribus, vitam orat per tempora diuturna felicem et gloriosi nominis perpetuum incrementum.[67]
>
> [To the magnificent and victorious lord, lord Cangrande della Scala, Vicar General of the Principate of the most holy Emperor in the city of Verona and the community of Vicenza, his most devoted servant Dante Alighieri, Florentine in birth but not in manners, prays for his happy life through many long years, and for the perpetual increase of the glory of his name.]

Much as Quirini had, the author describes the lord in hyperbolic terms, highlighting his magnanimity and military prowess, as well as his sacrosanct mission as Imperial Vicar. The hyperbole of the author's praise underscores his own subjection in the lord's regard, inscribed in his position as "devotissimus suus."[68] His posturing begins when he adopts a new self-identification, referring to himself for the only time in his corpus as "Dantes Alagherii florentinus natione non moribus." Rather than underscore the indignities of his exile – as Dante had in previous letters, identifying himself as "exul immeritus" [undeserving exile] – the new title instead vilifies the profligacy of his fellow Florentine citizens and highlights his own austere moral character.[69] While elevating himself above other Florentines as a man of stern morals, Dante simultaneously subjugates himself to the authority of the lord. By maintaining his status as "devotissimus" of the lord, the lord's humble devotee, the inscription establishes the conditions of possibility for the claims of the paragraphs to follow.

Dante revisits devotion at the end of the first full paragraph, reaffirming and clarifying his position as "devotissimus." Having described the means by which he confirmed rumors of the sumptuousness of Cangrande's court, he claims to have undergone a subsequent transformation of affect: "Quo factum est ut ex auditu solo cum quadam animi subiectione benivolus prius exstiterim, sed ex visu postmodum devotissimus et amicus" [And so, where first, by hearsay alone, with a certain subjection of mind I felt benevolence towards you, then, upon seeing, I became your most devoted subject and friend].[70] As Sabrina Ferrara has discussed, he uses four terms to define his relationship to the lord: *subiectio* (submission), *benevolentia* (benevolence), *devotio* (devotion), and *amicitia* (friendship).[71] Each of the terms here represents a step in a certain hierarchy of sentiment, a notable departure from what we saw with the "gradi dell'amistade" discussed in chapter 1. Where in the earlier work the "gradi" referred to the ranking of individuals according to degrees of proximity to the poet, here the author seems to adhere more closely to tradition, which thinks of friendship in steps or stages to be passed through over a length of time. But these four steps do not align along a single affective axis, so that one would pass from submission to benevolence, benevolence to devotion, devotion to friendship. Rather, there are two axes at work here: the temporal one – "prius," the time of rumor, and "postmodum," the time of witness – and the social one. The two temporalities are accompanied by two distinct pairs of terms: *subiectio/benevolentia*, in the time *prius*, and *devotio/amicitia* in the time *postmodum.*[72] The first set of terms derives from deliberate but impersonal, perhaps even dispassionate, admiration of another's virtue from afar: first, the author's voluntary submission to the office of the Imperial Vicar, a submission transferred to Cangrande following the death of Henry VII; second, his feeling of goodwill towards the person about whom he has heard rumors of such largesse. These are complemented by *devotio* and *amicitia*, which are only possible through a direct interpersonal knowledge, each of the other, in the time *postmodum*.

On the social axis, the pairs shift. *Subiectio* and *devotio* are attitudes held by an inferior in regards to the authority of his superior – one impersonal submission to the office and the other a personal devotion to the individual who holds that office. *Benevolentia* and *amicitia*, by contrast, are dispositions that do not depend on a differentiated social rank; they in fact tend towards equality and proximity between the two subjects. This proximity is premised on a moral, cultural, and intellectual affinity, which has the ability to unite two persons of unequal rank in spite of their difference of status. These affinities are not an equalizing measure that supersedes the distance between them, but rather a unifying measure that accompanies the social distance between them.

The Epistle makes this clear in terms that gesture towards the distinction between economic and symbolic capital. Drawing on the three Aristotelian modes of friendship – utility, pleasure, and virtue – Dante argues that even in cases of virtue-friendship men of unequal economic means can be bonded to one another through a shared sense of honour: "Et si ad veram ac per se amicitiam torqueatur intuitus, nonne illustrium summorumque principum plerunque viros fortuna obscuros, honestate preclaros, amicos fuisse constabit?" [And if attention is turned to true and perfect friendship, will it not be agreed that men, unknown for their fortune but famous for their sense of honour, have very often been friends of the most illustrious and supreme princes?].[73] Where material fortunes differ, the author claims, symbolic affinities may prevail. In this case, patron and client, distinct as they are in their respective "fortunae," are linked by their equal sense of honour ("honestate"), and by their mutual understanding of how the exchange of honour functions.

The idea of a shared sense of honour is crucial to Bourdieu's theory of exchange. In practices of exchange, which he calls "the game of honour," Bourdieu sees an underlying set of strategies that negotiate and restore one's place in relation to the honour of another.[74] In contrast to previous theorists of gift exchange and other practices in the game of honour, Bourdieu does not view such exchanges as ritualized, according to a reified and reifying model; rather, he compares exchange to activities like sports or games, activities that require training towards practical mastery, which ultimately appears as a "learned ignorance." Within this practical mastery appear strategic moves or improvisations, enabled by the deep inculcation of the structures of practice.[75]

The strategic improvisations of a social inferior in the game of honour can elevate the inferior to the symbolic status of the superior. Bourdieu asserts that an equality of honour may present itself alongside other material inequalities of which the popular consciousness remains aware.[76] But when both parties recognize their symbolic affinity, this recognition alters their respective positions within the social hierarchy. If a superior challenges an inferior and the inferior manages to reply, the inferior moves himself into a position of greater honour, drawing himself nearer the level of his superior by virtue of his symbolic affinity with the superior. Dante appears to be aware of this possibility, as he argues that he and his patron should be set apart from the vulgar, credulous crowds: "Sed habet imperitia vulgi sine discretione iudicium; et quemadmodum solem pedalis magnitudinis arbitratur, sic et circa mores vana credulitate decipitur. Nos autem, quibus optimum quod est in nobis noscere datum est, gregum vestigia sectari non decet, quin ymo suis erroribus obviare tenemur" [But the ignorance of the common folk makes its judgments without discernment; and just as they judge the sun to be the size of a foot, so about moral matters they are trapped by their vain credulity. We, however, to whom it is given to know the best that is in us, ought not follow in the footsteps of the herd, but are indeed bound to resist their errors].[77] The quality of mind that distinguishes the author and his patron (an elevated and unified *nos*, calling to mind the unified and socially isolated friendship of the stilnovist poets) is their *discretio*, an acculturated sense of discernment which they use to make clear judgments about everything from the size of the sun to appropriate moral customs.[78] This is the same quality that Dante had distinguished in his friend Cino da Pistoia, which elevated the two above the other practitioners of vernacular poetry in *De vulgari eloquentia*, as I discussed in chapter 2. Combined with their sense of honour (*honestas*), the "discretio" Dante shares with his lord Cangrande distinguishes them from the herd (*vulgus*, *grex*), the crowds who lack the proper sense of discernment in matters of judgment, morals, and taste.

Discretion, distinction, or discernment is, in the Epistle, both a marker of nobility and the foundation for the accrual of cultural capital. The two men share an intellectual and moral refinement, and this like-mindedness unites them as equals, without overriding the disparity in their social hierarchy. A shared sense of discernment is an equalizing measure; it permits the inferior to rise to the status of his superior within the field of culture, while maintaining their distinction in social status. The Epistle hails Cangrande as a refined reader of cultural and epistemological codes, one whose judgment is not bound to vulgar or popular opinion, which may insist on economic and social inequalities over and above symbolic affinities. Hailing Cangrande as a reader with *discretio* permits the author to assert his autonomy as a fellow producer in the economy of patronage.

In the final analysis, the author positions himself as simultaneously *devotissimus* (that is, Cangrande's inferior) *et amicus* (that is, his equal).[79] By positioning these words side by side the author is able to maintain the social distance between himself and his patron while systematically counterbalancing it with a theory of cultural affinity. The poet maintains their inequality of status, focusing on his role as the "devotissimus" servant of the lord, but affirms their equal sense of distinction – their symbolic capital – by distancing them from the herd.

What is at stake in the equalizing move the Epistle makes? Why would the poet assert himself in this way? The answer to this lies in the following paragraph, where the author raises the stakes of his claim to friendship with the lord beyond a shared sense of honour, to the restoration of his symbolic power through the dedication of an appropriate counter-gift.

Managing Reciprocity

With its judicious phrase "devotissimus et amicus," the Epistle resolves the problem of equality, creating and cultivating moral and intellectual proximities while strategically maintaining social distances. Yet the issue of reciprocity still hangs in the balance. Dante is painfully aware of this fact: if a client is to claim friendship with his lord and benefactor, he must also make equal restitution for the gifts of patronage. Only in making an equal return of the gift can the recipient of material support claim a friendship of the highest order with his benefactor.

The case of patronage, with its immoderate acts of generosity awarded to a recipient of limited economic means, severely restricts the possibilities of riposte: "the greatest gift," Bourdieu comments, "is at the same time the gift most likely to throw its recipient into dishonour by prohibiting any counter-gift."[80] In receiving patronage, one's honour is, in Bourdieu's scheme, gravely injured. But no one, least of all the patron, expects the client to make full recompense. The client of patronage has a duty to "adopt an attitude of humility,"[81] thanking the patron in deferential language that insists on the patron's superiority and magnanimity, as we saw in Quirini's sonnet and the writings of others among Cangrande's clientage. The client fulfils his duty but does not discharge his debt. To do so would mean to make a full return on the gift from a position of equality, which would reciprocate the immoderate generosity of the original gift. To claim such a reciprocity would be presumptuous indeed.

Reciprocity and recognition are critical issues for any relationship to be construed as a friendship. This is, after all, the distinction between mere good will and friendship.[82] In his earlier *Convivio*, also composed following his exile from

Florence, Dante acknowledges the necessity of reciprocity and recognition for friendship to arise and survive. Echoing Aristotelian precepts, *Convivio* 3.11 argues that only open and reciprocated benevolence can be called friendship: "Nella 'ntenzione d'Aristotile nell'ottavo dell'Etica, quelli si dice amico la cui amistà non è celata alla persona amata e a cui la persona amata è anche amica, sì che la benivolenza sia da ogni parte" [According to Aristotle's definition in the eighth book of the *Ethics*, one is called a friend whose friendship is not hidden from the person loved, and to whom the person loved is also a friend, so that good will is present on both sides].[83] Recognition and reciprocity are the very constitutive features of friendship – even in the case of the philosopher's love of wisdom, as is under discussion here in *Convivio*: for mere benevolence to turn into friendship, it must be both recognized and reciprocated.[84]

But fellow-feeling is not the only reciprocal good to be exchanged in a friendship. Exchange of *beneficia* – benefits or support, both material and immaterial – is equally critical to the establishment and maintenance of friendship. This is, perhaps surprisingly, to be anticipated even in friendships between unequals: husband and wife, lord and servant, patron and client, and so on. For such friendships to endure, they must locate their foundation in a fundamental likeness between the friends, a likeness that could coexist with the hierarchical foundation of such relationships. Dante defends such a proposition in *Convivio*, again closely adhering to Aristotelian precepts. Speaking of his desire to strengthen and preserve his love of Philosophy, his superior in beneficence and worth, Dante explains:

> [N]ell'amistade delle persone dissimili di stato conviene, a conservazione di quella, una proporzione essere intra loro, che la dissimilitudine a similitudine quasi reduca. Sì com'è intra lo signore e lo servo: ché, avegna che lo servo non possa simile beneficio rendere allo signore quando da lui è beneficiato, dee però rendere quello che migliore può con tanto di sollicitudine e di franchezza, che quello che è dissimile per sé si faccia simile per lo mostramento della buona volontade; la quale manifesta, l'amistade si ferma e si conserva.
>
> [In a friendship of persons of unequal rank there must exist, in order to preserve it, a relation between them that in some way transforms the unlikeness into likeness, as, for example, exists between a master and his servant. For although the servant cannot render a like benefit to his master when he receives a benefit from him, he must nevertheless render what best he can with so much solicitude and spontaneity that what in itself is dissimilar will make itself similar by the display of good will. Once (good will) is displayed, the friendship becomes strengthened and preserved.][85]

In order for master and servant to enjoy the rewards of friendship, the dissimilarity between their social stations must be overwritten by proportional exchange of goods. Clearly the servant cannot reciprocate precisely the *beneficia* – material and otherwise – that the master has bestowed on him, but in his effort to preserve the relationship, he bestows on his master what little he can, accompanied by a "mostramento della buona volontade." The affective performance of fellow-feeling that accompanies the servant's gift is enough to elevate the poor offering to equal the goods received from the master.

On its face, the argument Dante lays out in *Convivio* 3.1 appears to find its companion in the third paragraph of the Epistle to Cangrande:[86]

> Preferens ergo amicitiam vestram quasi thesaurum carissimum, providentia diligenti et accurata solicitudine illam servare desidero. Itaque, cum in dogmatibus moralis negotii amicitiam adequari et salvari analogo doceatur, ad retribuendum pro collatis beneficiis plus quam semel analogiam sequi michi votivum est; et propter hoc munuscula mea sepe multum conspexi et ab invicem segregavi nec non segregata percensui, digniusque gratiusque vobis inquirens. Neque ipsi preheminentie vestre congruum magis comperi quam Comedie sublimem canticam que decoratur titulo Paradisi; et illam sub presenti epistola, tanquam sub epigrammate proprio dedicatam, vobis ascribo, vobis offero, vobis denique recommendo.[87]

> [Considering, then, your friendship as a most cherished treasure, I want to preserve it with deliberate forethought and assiduous care. And so, since in the tenets of moral philosophy it is taught that friendship is equalized and preserved by means of analogy, I vow to strive for analogy, in order to make a return of all the benefits more than once bestowed upon me; and for this reason I have often looked over these little gifts of mine, and separated them one from the other and examined each one, looking for one more worthy of and more pleasing to you. And I have not found one more suited to your very preeminence than the sublime canticle of the *Commedia* that is adorned by the title *Paradiso*; and this, dedicated by the present letter as if under a special inscription, to you I inscribe, to you I offer, to you, in sum, I commend.]

Much like the servant who wishes to maintain friendship with his master, the author of the Epistle sets out to return the benefits that the lord has bestowed upon him. Recognizing the impossibility of the task, his "munuscula" unable to measure up to the "preheminentie" of the lord, the client makes what return he can, hoping that the dissimilar gift will rise to the occasion of its giving.

But the claims of the Epistle do more than follow the Aristotelian line of argument alluded to in *Convivio.* Dante aims to exceed the mere fact of a "mostramento de la buona volontade," which would render similar dissimilar gifts. Rather, he aims higher, to equalize (*adequari*) the two friends by seeking similarity (*analogo*) between them. He intends to give an analogous gift, which might be congruous (*congruum*) with the gift of patronage he has been given, and which, he hopes, will be suited to the dignity and grace of his patron.

In its aspirations to similarity and reciprocity, the Epistle positions Dante as the moral and intellectual equal of his esteemed patron, a bold claim the *Convivio* passage shies away from. *Convivio* 3.1 builds on the discussion of friendship with the poet's beloved, here Lady Philosophy. In her regard, the poet feels himself a servant of lowly station, who could never claim equality with or even similarity to his master. The lessons of such unequal friendships, characterized as they are by adoration of and subjection to either the master or the beloved lady, do not provide the theoretical apparatus that would permit the author to assert equal and equalizing friendship with one of the most powerful political lords of northern Italy. It is one thing to suggest, as *Convivio* does, that the servant's intention disguises – but does not erase – the dissimilarity between superior and inferior. It would be another to proclaim that superior and inferior are equally brothers in Christ – both recipients of divine grace and spiritual friendship (*caritas*) – but nonetheless preserving earthly hierarchies. It is quite another altogether to assert that the lord is a friend and an equal to the client he has supported. Such a delicate political assertion requires a strategic rhetorical performance. We see such a performance in the Epistle.

The level of strategic mastery on display in the Epistle contrasts tellingly with the account Bourdieu gives of the gameplay of gift exchange. Of the practical logics of gift exchange, Bourdieu writes:

> It is all a matter of *style*, which means in this case timing and choice of occasions.... Gift exchange is one of the social games that cannot be played unless the players refuse to acknowledge the objective truth of the game, the very truth that objective analysis brings to light, and unless they are predisposed to contribute, with their efforts, their marks of care and attention, and their time, to the production of collective misrecognition. Everything takes place as if the agents' strategies, and especially those that play on the tempo of action, or, in interaction, with the interval between actions, were organized with a view to disguising from themselves and from others the truth of their practice.[88]

Bourdieu suggests that the master of gift exchange actively disguises the objective truth of the game of gift exchange. The return-gift must be well timed (not too late, but especially not too soon) and well chosen, in line with but not identical to the initial gift.[89] But one who returns the gift ought to conceal – from oneself and others – one's obligations within the cycle of reciprocity, and one's strategic calculation of both timing and effort. This concealment is the "collective misrecognition" to which Bourdieu refers.

This is not, to borrow Bourdieu's word, the "style" of the Epistle's author. Rather than rely on the established conventions of gift exchange and dedication as a means to conceal his motivations, Dante strategically highlights his moves within the practice of exchange. Couching his claims in an explicit recognition of the economics of such exchanges (the patron's friendship as "thesaurum carissimum"),[90] he lays bare his understanding of the rules and objectives of the game of gift exchange. He refers to the principles of moral philosophy that underlie his motives, drawing specifically on Thomist language to justify his pursuit of equalizing friendship with his lord.[91] Unlike the servant in *Convivio*, who renders his counter-gift "con tanto di sollicitudine e di franchezza" [with so much solicitude and spontaneity], the Epistle's author searches for the most appropriate return-gift with "providentia diligenti et accurata solicitudine" [deliberate forethought and assiduous care]. The repetition of the word *solicitudo* in both passages draws attention to the difference in the term coupled with it: *franchezza* in the case of the servant, *providentia* in the case of the client. The servant gives spontaneously, with a boldness and freedom that cloaks the uncertainty of his gesture, hiding it not only from the lord but also from himself.[92] The client, by contrast, gives with caution and calculation, weighing carefully the relative worth of his *munuscula* until he has selected the one that might most appropriately correlate to the lord's magnificence.

The Epistle has settled on a subtly different strategy than what is anticipated either by contemporary rhetorical standards, by Aristotelian theory (as exemplified by the *Convivio* passage), or by Bourdieu's discussion of the agent's willing misconceptions of his role within the game. This departure is a strategic improvisation on the part of the Epistle's author, calling attention to the transactional nature of the exchange and the caution with which it must be undertaken. But if we take this difference as a tactical move in the gift-exchange game, what exactly is his grand design? In other words, to what end does the Epistle reveal its author's motives and objectives?

At stake in the Epistle's strategic moves is the distinction between the transactional largesse of the charitable patron and the unselfconscious generosity of friends. In a relationship of dissimilarity and inequality, reciprocity may be the goal, but it is not the expectation: lord and servant do not strive for similarity, each satisfied by the other's attempts to disguise their dissimilarity with affect and posturing. Under this guise, the lord maintains his prominence as the bearer of greater symbolic capital. His beneficence reaffirms the hierarchical structure of the relationship, precisely because there is no presumption of authentic reciprocity on the recipient's part. He accepts his inferior's humble gift with grace but does not in turn sacrifice any of the margin of his own standing.[93]

By contrast, giving between friends anticipates an equilibrium premised on the symbolic equality of the partners.[94] This is the stated goal of the Epistle: not merely to dissemble equality, papering over the disparity with good intentions, but instead to bring it about through directed action. Calling explicit attention to the "rulebook" of friendly behavior ("in dogmatibus moralis negotii"), the Epistle insists on the particular goal of "adequare," overcoming the inequality between the two friends. To surmount inequality, one must seek analogy not only in the form of giving but also in the content of the return-gift. Where the servant in the *Convivio*'s example could render his humble gift similar to the master's great one through his performance, the client in the Epistle must return like with like in order to render to his patron a gift that equals what he has received.

Equality-through-analogy is made possible through the mutual recognition and exchange of symbolic capital. Mutual recognition of the validity of such an exchange drives the possibility for the attainment of equality. The Epistle defends the practice of dedication as a legitimate means of converting and transferring symbolic capital. Its unique use of the sacral verb *dedicare* – a hapax in Dante's corpus (in both his Latin and vernacular works)[95] – implies a formal practice that appeals to divine sanction as sign and seal of the solemn undertaking. The object is a votive offering, given as ceremonial recompense for the benefits rendered in patronage. By arguing that the *Paradiso* is congruous ("congruum") with the benefits of patronage, the Epistle affirms that the capital bestowed on the poet in the form of the lord's patronage has been directly converted to the honour that the poem imparts to the patron, in the form of praises embedded in its verses. In the non-mercantile courtly economy, patronage invests material capital into recipients who will convert it into honour.

That the Epistle's author is cognizant of the convertibility of symbolic capital in such an exchange is made clear in the subsequent paragraph of the letter. He pre-empts a possible critique, continuing, "Illud quoque preterire silentio simpliciter inardescens non sinit affectus, quod in hac donatione plus dono quam domino et honouris et fame conferri videri potest" [My ardent affection also does not permit that I simply pass over in silence the fact that, in making this gift, it could seem that more honour and fame are conferred upon the gift than on the lord].[96] His concern here is that the act of dedication attributes greater symbolic capital to the object of his *donatione* than it does to the recipient of the return-gift. Such a concern betrays an understanding of the symbolic implications of the conversion of the *beneficia* of patronage into the patron's honour and fame.

Not wishing to imbue his gift with a greater worth than is due, the author cautiously claims that the honour imparted to the poem and the well-deserved praise of the patron are coextensive with one another and activated by the dedication. In a rhetorical question, he continues, "Quid mirum cum eius titulum iam presagiam de gloria vestri nominis ampliandum?" [And what wonder, when I already foresee that the renown of (this work) must be amplified by the glory of your name?].[97] The patron's glory and the renown of the work are inseparable from one another, one necessarily increased by the recognition of the other.

Such mutual recognition requires an active stance on the part of both participants. Aristotle clarifies, "Et amacio quidem, faccioni assimulatur, amari autem, ei quod est pati. Superexcellentibus utique circa actum, sequitur amare et amicabilia" [And indeed affection is to be likened to making, while being loved is like submitting to it. Love and friendly qualities surely follow for those who most excel in regard to its production].[98] In other words, the agent who produces love is more worthy of love than the one who passively undergoes it. With the gift of the *Paradiso*, Dante moves from one who receives or even undergoes friendship to an active participant in its production. The gift of the *Paradiso* thus partakes in the active practice of friendship, the encomium to Cangrande rendering actual the potential production of his patron's fame promised in the salutation of the letter ("gloriosi nominis perpetuum incrementum").

Bourdieu explains that the initial gift fulfils its intended meaning only when it is reciprocated. In the interval between gift and counter-gift, there remains a threat that the initial gift, "for lack of a response, [will] be stripped retrospectively of its intentional meaning (the subjective truth of the gift can, as has been seen, only be realized in the counter-gift which consecrates it as such)."[99] This is no less true in the case of patronage, where the client's "return" on the gift of the patron's generosity is what validates the act of that patronage. Patronage is consecrated and sealed when it is reciprocated with a dedication.[100]

But the act of giving back has more than just symbolic ramifications. Bourdieu notes that the counter-gift restores the client's honour and releases him from the debts incurred by the initial gift: "Until he has given back," Bourdieu explains, "the receiver is 'obliged,' expected to show his gratitude towards his benefactor or at least to show regard for him, go easy on him, pull his punches, lest he be accused of ingratitude and stand condemned by 'what people say,' which decides the meaning of his actions."[101] In clarifying his intentions to make a return on the gift of patronage through the solemn act of dedication, the author of the Epistle strategically positions himself as released from the obligation placed on him by the lord's patronage, imbuing him with the agency and authority to become an active "maker" of friendship, no longer merely its passive recipient.[102]

In contrast to *Convivio*, the Epistle argues that reciprocity of feeling does not suffice for the relationship to rise to the test of the highest form of friendship: all gifts must be reciprocated analogously to restore the equilibrium of friendship. A virtue-friendship cannot be assured if one is the recipient of another's charitable support, even if return-gifts have been granted with the most virtuous of intentions and the highest esteem. A handout, however charitably given, is a blight on the honour of the recipient, a mark of the recipient's need and a mode of domination or act of aggression on the part of the giver. In this sense, the client must find a way to make a return on the gift – if he is to claim equal friendship in the highest sense with his lord and protector. Thus the client will raise his own symbolic capital, ennobling himself and his gift in the process.

The Epistle actualizes what in *Convivio* had been mere theory, and, in doing so, departs from *Convivio*'s claim that the good intention of the inferior is enough to restore the balance between the gifts given. Because it has shifted its claims from the realm of theory to that of practice, the Epistle must disentangle the threads of the political and social realities that attenuate such a claim. The gift given must attend to the economy of generosity stipulated by patronage: that what is given is received with the proper measure of humility and thanksgiving. But in order to equalize the participants in this exchange, removing one from the position of domination and the other from subservience, the gift must then be returned with analogous gifts. In particular, the letter must make a claim for the proper proportional analogy between the gifts of patronage and the return-gift – the poem – reflecting on the exchange through Thomist language. Far from a mere conventional dedicatory letter, then, the Epistle becomes instead a reflection on the possibilities inherent in the practice of dedication itself.

The Epistle's commentary on the practice of dedication carries with it two critical conclusions: first, that the product of the patron's generosity (the poem) cannot be appropriated by the patron without the explicit dedication of the author – that, in other words, the poem is the author's to give and is not already the property of the patron who has sponsored its authorship. It removes the client from the symbolic protection of the patron and promotes his independence. Second, the Epistle concludes that dedication has real, convertible value in the practice of exchange. More than a gratuitous or ingratiating gesture, dedication releases a client from his obligations to his superior, restoring his honour by discharging his debt, and enabling his elevation in the social hierarchy to become the equal of his sponsor.

The Gratuitous Gift

Patronage, to Bourdieu, is a euphemism for aggression, domination, or violence: "symbolic violence, the gentle, invisible form of violence, which is never recognized as such, and is not so much undergone as chosen, the violence of credit, confidence, obligation, personal loyalty, hospitality, gifts, gratitude, piety – in short, all the virtues honoured by the code of honour – cannot fail to be seen as the most economical mode of domination."[103] Following from Bourdieu's analysis of patron-client exchanges, then, Cangrande's gifts are tantamount to territorial conquests: modes of domination in a symbolic mode that require the voluntary submission of their subjects.

The Epistle refuses to submit to the lord's domination in this way. Through the mediation of the language of friendship, Dante takes ownership of the product of the labor that had been facilitated by Cangrande's material assistance (in the form of shelter, work space, library access, and manuscript copying and circulation), asserts its value in the economy of symbolic capital, and offers it as recompense for the debt of patronage, from which the author secures his release. In the Epistle, Dante lays bare the economy of generosity at the base of the system of patronage. He does not criticize it, but he refuses to accede to its demands, and transmutes it from a relationship of domination to a reciprocal mode of equality. He strives to make an equal exchange for the goods he has received, "a present in which what counts is not so much what you give as the way you give it, the seemingly 'gratuitous' surrender not only of goods ... but of things that are even more personal and therefore more precious."[104] With its gratuitous gift, the Epistle releases the client from the bonds of patronage, thus elevating him within the field of sociability and making possible his authentic friendship, as equal, with the lord.

The Epistle's arguments resonate, in important ways, with those of the *Commedia*, in particular the *Paradiso*, where private attachments between the Lord and the members of his court will be both rigidly hierarchical and yet radically inclusive. Beyond providing a gratuitous gift that resolves the poet's debt within the economy of patronage, the Epistle's resolution also stands as a logical justification of the *Commedia*'s implicit claims for the friendship between humankind and God. This resolution – among several the *Commedia* seeks to offer in negotiating the dilemmas of friendship – will be the subject of the next chapter.

4
Difference: The Afterlife

I opened this study at the moment when the word *amico* first appears in the *Commedia*: Virgil's description of Beatrice's arrival in *Inferno* 2. In commissioning Virgil to rescue the bewildered pilgrim from the solitude of the dark wood, Beatrice makes plain her particular affection for him, in words that Virgil will comprehend: "l'amico mio, e non de la ventura," my friend, and no friend of fortune.[1] However plain this epithet may have been to Virgil and his pagan companions in Limbo, the exposition of *amistà*, *amicizia*, and *amicitia* over the past three chapters will have made clear that Beatrice's "amico" resonated, for Dante's contemporary audience, within a complex and nuanced register of meanings and practices that would have been largely illegible to a classical practitioner of friendship. If indeed Beatrice channels the classical notion of *vera amicitia* in her pronouncement, her labeling the pilgrim "amico mio" would be a unique instance in Dante's corpus, where classical *amicitia* would have reached its fullest reconciliation with Christian thought.

It is, of course, possible that the *Commedia* presents a vision of *amistà* quite unlike the articulations of friendship that we find elsewhere across Dante's corpus: that only here, on his journey to salvation, does the poet finally grasp the fullest meaning of *vera amicitia* as described by the ancients. In light of the dilemmas I have identified in the theories and practices of friendship among Dante and his interlocutors, however, I find the *lectio facilior* that would set Beatrice's friendship apart from all others unconvincing. While we may want to ascribe to Beatrice's "amico" a fluid transformation of *eros* to *amicitia*, and *amicitia* finally to *caritas*, or while we may wish to hear in it a smooth consolidation of classical authorities and Christian doctrine, we are instead – still here in the *Commedia* – left with the same complicated nexus of political, theological, and sociological meanings that need to be negotiated carefully, considering their polyphonous resonances. In other words, we need to hear also in her "amico" a negotiation with the dilemmas that the ethics and practices of friendship would have raised for Dante and for his contemporaries.

In this last chapter I will turn to the *Commedia* to investigate the practices of friendship as they appear in the three realms of Dante's afterlife. In doing so, I will take into account the dilemmas I have explored in the previous chapters, and I will examine a new one: difference and sameness. This dichotomy lies at the heart of Cicero's *De amicitia*, consistently held to be the most authoritative treatise on medieval friendship. Cicero's pronouncements on the love of true friends are often boiled down to a single pithy justification: one loves a friend "enim is qui est tamquam alter idem" [a friend is, quite simply, another self].[2] Defining a friend "alter idem" would become an immediate commonplace among Cicero's heirs. The phrase, often rendered in modern English as "a second self," implies the great likeness shared between two friends, so powerful as to overcome the necessary otherness of human subjectivity. Friendship, in Cicero's definition, has the unique capability to cross the boundaries that differentiate self from other, making, as he says immediately following, "unum ex duobus" [one out of two].[3] Many scholars who take up Cicero's definition to read the friendships between Dante and his companions in the *Commedia* and other works emphasize the likeness between these friends: their agreement on matters both human and divine; the alignment of their goals, commitments, and interests; their mutual support, judgment, generosity, and loyalty.

And yet Cicero's definition of friendship as a unifying force does not collapse the distinctions between the one and the other. Instead, his definition highlights otherness and difference in its paradoxical structure: the friend is "*alter* idem," both same and *other* at the same time. The paradoxical other-sameness of the friend, little explored in the medieval reception of Cicero's work, is not lost on the author of the *Commedia*, a poem which revels in the complex, multiform expressions of human identity and sociability. As I will show, Dante explores friendship in the *Commedia* through the paradox of difference and identity, exploiting friendship's other-sameness as a means to demonstrate the ethical positioning of one vis-à-vis the other in human society. He looks to friendship as a model for traversing, without erasing, the distinctions between individuals, ultimately using its structure as a reflection of the heavenly community, which is both many (other) and one (same).

Critically, Dante does not overlook the ethical dilemmas that the dyadic structure of classical friendship raises for sociability in the Christian afterlife. Instead, he confronts these dilemmas, plumbing their complexities and seeking to integrate them, where possible, with the social structures he envisions. Incorporating friendship into the fields of the afterlife proves to be a thorny exercise for the poet, as he seeks to straddle – and sometimes synthesize – opposing ethical positions. In doing the work of synthesis, he repeatedly alludes to the structures of friendship while also eschewing its name, a term which had appeared so prominently in his earlier works. Friendship's problematic heritage in Christian ethical thought is thus on full display in the *Commedia*'s verses, as the poet struggles to negotiate between the dilemmas identified in this study: inclusion and exclusion, collaboration and self-interest, hierarchy and equality, and likeness and difference.

In spite of this complexity, it has become a critical commonplace, especially in scholarship on *Inferno* 2 and on *Purgatorio*, to present friendship as an unambiguous moral value in Dante's afterlife.[4] In her recent monograph on Dante's notion of friendship, Filippa Modesto advocates for interpreting Beatrice's "amico" through the lens of a Christianized Ciceronianism: disinterested, reciprocal, intimate.[5] Other scholars point to the individual love between Dante and Beatrice as the apex of Christian friendship. Like Modesto, who suggests that Dante "transforms" classical *amicitia* into Christian friendship, Jerome Mazzaro argues that Dante reinvents his love for Beatrice through a "transformation" of *eros* to *amicitia*, marked by the passage of the "fiamma antica" to the duties of friendship.[6] Francesco Ciabattoni claims that a "new, special friendship with Beatrice occurs at the inception of Dante's journey so as to fulfil a specifically salvific function not fulfilled by any human relation explored in his earlier works."[7] Franco Masciandaro, further, sees in the *Commedia*'s representation of Beatrice "Dante's poetics … of *eros* transfigured into *caritas*, which are closely related to the poetics of friendship that informs the *Divine Comedy*."[8] Each of these scholars reads in Beatrice's "amico" a revision or innovation that marks a sharp departure from previous articulations of the term, one that would blur the distinctions between the three principal types of love: *eros*, *amicitia*, and *caritas*.

Beyond Beatrice, scholars identify an array of characters as particular "friends" of the pilgrim, placed in the poem to aid him on his journey. Guy Raffa's analysis of the "complex interpersonal bond" between Dante and Virgil presents in Ciceronian terms the "beautiful friendship" shared between the two poet-pilgrims in their explorations of the second realm.[9] Scholars such as Piero Boitani, Manuele Gragnolati, Franco Masciandaro, and many authors of individual *lecturae dantis* have recognized encounters with multiple characters in the second canticle as indicative of the necessity of friendship for spiritual growth and support: Casella, Belacqua, Nino Visconti, Forese Donati, and others who greet the pilgrim with a distinct affection.[10] These scholars lean on the purgatorial encounters with friends to remark on the necessity of *amistà* or *amicizia* to the pilgrim's progress.

And yet few of these scholars (with the exceptions of Teodolinda Barolini and Francesco Ciabattoni, who are invested in the "semantics" and "rhetoric" of friendship, respectively) remark on the comparative absence of the terms *amistà* and *amicizia* in the language of Dante's masterwork: for a work that so many scholars have interpreted as steeped in the relationships and gestures of friendship, the term "amico" itself, which we have seen so present in Dante's lyric and epistolary corpora, appears with surprising rarity in discussions of friendship among saved souls.

Of course, there are crucial exceptions to the relative silencing of *amicizia* and *amistà* as terms for virtuous individual relationships: most notably, Beatrice's reported "amico" in *Inferno* 2, to which I will return, and Virgil's doubled "amico" in his conversation with Statius in *Purgatorio* 22. That Virgil presents his affection for Statius as *amicizia* has been interpreted as a model of a new Christian mode of friendship, illuminated by Statius's conversion through his (mis)reading of Virgil's verses. Modesto, for one, claims that their *amicizia* "transcends classical friendship" because of Virgil's pivotal role in Statius's conversion and eventual salvation.[11] But such a reading imposes onto the encounter a Christian articulation that is not present in the actual words exchanged between the two ancient poets. What I find most telling in the passage is just how precisely Virgil employs his terms: in strict Aristotelian fashion, Virgil claims that what he had long felt for Statius, upon hearing of his affections (called by the generic terms "amore" and "affezion") in Limbo, was "benvoglienza" [benevolence], that kindly feeling one experiences when admiring another from afar.[12] But not until their meeting in *Purgatorio* can Statius become Virgil's "amico," welcoming Statius into his intimacy as companion in a search for truth:

> Ma dimmi, e come amico mi perdona
> se troppa sicurtà m'allarga il freno,
> e come amico omai meco ragiona.

> [But tell me, and as a friend forgive me if too much confidence loosens my rein, and as a friend speak with me now.][13]

In his parenthesis to Statius, Virgil asserts their new friendship with his adverbial "omai," friendship becoming the final conclusion of their longstanding blind affections. The *amicizia* Virgil claims with Statius here is one of preference and particularity, Statius becoming elevated in Virgil's estimation because of his previous kindnesses and the generosity of his conversation here. Virgil's address to Statius, and especially his use of the appellation "amico" – exceptional in the *Commedia* for its Greco-Roman usage – conceives of friendship according to the ancient world view from which his pagan perspective derives. Indeed, the only two times that the term "amico" appears as an appellation in the text are both in the mouth of the pagan Virgil, here and in Beatrice's speech reported by Virgil to the pilgrim at the beginning of his journey.[14]

If it is friendship that the penitents in Dante's Purgatory must cultivate, and friendship that the blessed in Paradise indeed celebrate, then why would it be so scarcely named? Why have Beatrice proclaim the name of friendship only at the very beginning of the journey? And why then only in speech that is reported secondhand to the pilgrim, as Virgil recounts his encounter with her? Why does the word not appear in any direct speech to the pilgrim throughout his journey through the afterlife? If Beatrice's "amico" represents the pinnacle of human social striving, then why reserve the name exclusively for her?

In the previous chapters, I have shown how the value of *amistà* raised ethical dilemmas in each of the various sociohistorical milieux in which Dante and his Italian contemporaries circulated and exchanged texts, judgments, dedications, honours. In this last chapter, as we turn to the communities of the afterlife, we must read with an equally critical eye the complex social practices of the dead. Throughout this book, I have applied Bourdieu's concept of "fields" to analyse the specific strategies practiced by different players in a particular milieu of literary society: the piazza, the university, and the court. In the realms of the afterlife, only Purgatory can be treated as a proper "field" according to the terms Bourdieu has laid out: only Purgatory has a distinct goal or outcome, as well as sets of strategies and practices to achieve that goal. Only Purgatory has time, rhythms, cadences, movement, directionality. But even if the two timeless realms of Dante's afterlife cannot strictly be considered "fields," they nevertheless have precise social systems that structure the interactions, movements, and practices of their respective inhabitants. Thus, in *Inferno* we find a series of individuals estranged from their neighbours, even as they are clustered together with them in their communal punishments, which will also perdure beyond the end of history. In *Paradiso* we find a community of brethren united in their collective enjoyment of beatitude in an eternal present outside of time (while also awaiting the complete fulfilment of that delight through the resurrection of the body).[15] The parameters and values of private attachments will vary according to the specific social sphere in which these individual relationships are embedded.

In what follows I will examine how each realm of Dante's afterlife confronts the dilemmas emerging from theoretical approaches to friendship – by which I mean elective, preferential, and reciprocal attachments between individuals – that have been raised in the previous chapters of this book. The practices of friendship articulated in these three distinct realms straddle – but do not resolve – the dilemmas Dante has grappled with elsewhere in his works. Questions of inclusion and exclusion will loom large over *Inferno*, as the willfulness of sinners deprives them of productive social relationships with even their closest neighbours and removes them from the exclusive and exclusionary sphere of God's friendship. In *Inferno*, social practices favour difference over identification and disengagement over confrontation, preferences that will remove the souls from God's friendship, which is inclusive within its strict barriers, but is uncompromising in its exclusion of the damned.[16]

In *Purgatorio* – the so-called "canticle of friendship" – the penitents will use the dyadic structure of friendship as a steppingstone towards the radical inclusivity of *carità*: private, voluntary attachments provide the opportunity to practice the alignment of the individual will with the will of God.[17] Purgatorial friendship, which is aimed at virtue and community engagement, must thus be private and individualizing while also training souls towards inclusive modes of attachment. Friendship practices in *Purgatorio* are also goal-directed and strategic, much like the practices of friendship in the world below – debate, exchange, cooperation, dedication. Here, practices of collaboration and exchange straddle self-interest and mutual support, as each penitent moves towards his or her own moral betterment, but without the competitive rancor that develops in arenas that traffic in limited, diminishing goods. By identifying with one's companions, the penitents learn to practice the unifying love that will unite them in Paradise, but they maintain their individual focus, permitting them to pursue distinct outcomes while also offering genuine support to their peers.

In *Paradiso*, by contrast, friendships – while still productive of delight and a source of beatitude – will be rendered superfluous, eclipsed by the individual's singular attachment to God, through which all other bonds are reflected and made coherent. Private attachments persist, but in transmuted form, and the poet is careful not to conflate them with *amistadi*. Friendship among the blessed souls in the court of heaven exists as a reflection of the vertical relationship of the individual soul to the Lord; that it is reflected from divine *carità* does not diminish its strength, but only enhances and multiplies it, so that paradisiacal friendship may become both individual and collective, assimilative and differentiating.

The dilemmas emerging from friendship in the social fields of the Earthly City – inclusive and exclusive forms of attachment, cooperation and self-interestedness, equality and hierarchy, alterity and identity – take on new moral weight in the realms of damnation and salvation. The *Commedia* seeks to conjoin opposing poles, representing private human attachments as simultaneously inclusive and exclusive, collaborative while still strategic, hierarchical and yet equalizing, unifying without eliding difference. Beyond a mere integration of Ciceronian theory into a Christian mold, the modes of personal attachment presented in the *Commedia* instead represent careful negotiations around and through the dilemmas of friendship as they existed in Dante's era. Voluntary, private attachments do the work of negotiating between conflicting ethical demands under new names, abandoning the terms of *amistà* and *amicizia* in favour of a different language – that of *fratellanza* and *carità* – that might better illustrate the new moral configuration of individual social relationships. Sociability in the three realms of the afterlife does not, therefore, overlook or resolve the dilemmas friendship presented to Dante and his contemporaries, but instead strives to mediate between contradictory ethical standpoints, holding both positions, simultaneously, to be valid and true.

Inferno: Against the Other

In a passage from the *Nicomachean Ethics* well known to Dante – and paraphrased in *Convivio* 4.25 – Aristotle asserts, "Sine amicis enim nullus utique eligeret vivere" [for without friends undoubtedly no one would choose to live].[18] If it is indeed true that to live without friends is a violation of our very human nature as social creatures, we might well wonder what the pilgrim made of the choices of the sinners in hell when it comes to friendship. As we might expect, among the damned in Dante's hell, friendship finds no refuge. The inhabitants of hell remain in various conditions of estrangement from their peers and from themselves; they can find no communion with others even when crowded together or coupled with them.[19] Keeping in mind Aristotle's truism, that no one would willingly choose to live without friends, we might ask ourselves whether the alienation of the damned is cause or effect of their sin. Is their isolation a consequence of the habits of body and mind that led to their damnation, or have they, in violation of Aristotle's dictum, willfully chosen to live without friends?

Estrangement haunts all habits of the damned in hell, from the earliest sight of the group of sinners on the shores of the Acheron. Even here, as the numberless crowds of souls await Charon's ferry, individuation marks the sinners apart from one another. When the sinners appear before the pilgrim for the first time, they clamor to cross the river, their fear of punishment giving way to a desire to succumb to old habits. They famously appear to the pilgrim as leaves seeking the autumnal ground:

> Come d'autunno si levan le foglie
> l'una appresso de l'altra, fin che 'l ramo
> vede a la terra tutte le sue spoglie:
> similemente il mal seme d'Adamo
> gittansi di quel lito ad una ad una
> per cenni, come augel per suo richiamo.

[As in autumn the leaves remove themselves one after the other, until the branch sees all its raiment on the ground: so the evil seed of Adam throw themselves from that shore one by one, when beckoned to, each like a falcon to its lure.][20]

Like the falling leaves in Dante's adaptation of the Homeric-Virgilian simile, the sinners descend to the shore as individuals, having freely determined the particular circumstances of their afterlives. Notably, just as the leaves fall "l'una appresso de l'altra," the damned distinguish themselves from one another "ad una ad una," one by one, as they course towards Charon's ferry. Robert Harrison reads the simile as a Christian commentary on free will and individual choice. He argues that Dante employs the Virgilian simile to distinguish the freely chosen, self-determined fates of each of the "mal seme d'Adamo" from the recognition of our collective mortality, as Virgil would have it.[21] More importantly for our purposes here is the sinners' continued insistence on this individualism and self-determination, their inability to overcome their estrangement from their fellows, even when forced to confront their common mortality in the gathering crowd of dead souls. They refuse to see themselves as the abundant leaves of Virgil's account, which descend together to a collective fate on the frozen ground. Rather, the "mal seme d'Adamo," who gather on the shore as a singular mass, nevertheless disperse themselves "ad una ad una," refusing in their egocentrism to recognize their communal damnation. In other words, they favour alterity over identification, unknowability over recognition, and estrangement over communion.

Indeed, all the sinners we meet in Dante's hell adopt a posture that highlights difference over the recognition of their common faults and fates. Nevertheless, among the isolated damned we find a startling number of companions and groups, whose estrangement from those with whom they are most closely joined reveals how starkly they have rejected the principles of friendship, whether personal or civic, voluntary or natural.[22] Paolo and Francesca, Farinata and Cavalcante, Ulysses and Diomedes, Master Adam and Sinon, Ugolino and Ruggieri – each pair represents a missed opportunity for connection and mutual recognition.

One of the most commented of these missed opportunities is that of Paolo and Francesca, who, despite their togetherness on the winds, nevertheless display their rejection of the authentic recognition of self in other. Scholars are divided on the nature of Paolo and Francesca's intersubjective understanding.[23] In his reading of their "perversion" of mutuality, Masciandaro sees in their coupling "not a true union in love, or a communion ... as we note that both Paolo's silence throughout the episode and his inseparability from Francesca speak of a total suppression of their reciprocal and always problematic, infinite 'otherness.'"[24] Masciandaro finds in their commingling an erasure of difference, one that suppresses the self in its attempt to bind with the other. To Masciandaro's observations I would add that the "melding" or "inseparability" of this pair is only a matter of performance. The silent, weeping figure of Paolo, identified only in the text as "l'altro" [the other], testifies to the chasm that separates their two identities, disguised behind a false union that outwardly signals reciprocity but in fact suggests nothing of mutual recognition. They separately perform the two verbs Francesca promises to enact for the pilgrim: she speaks, while Paolo weeps, betraying their inability to mirror the self in the other and to find solace in the sharing of pain.[25] In their refusal to speak and weep with and alongside one another, the two lovers display the dominance of self-interest over compassion or commiseration, which ultimately eliminates any possibility of achieving the peace that Francesca so desperately craves.

The language of peace and rest dominates the fifth canto of *Inferno*, already appearing in Francesca's first words to the pilgrim: "se fosse amico il re de l'universo, / noi pregheremmo lui de la tua pace" [if the king of the universe were friendly we would pray to him for your peace].[26] Francesca offers to pray for the pilgrim's peace – the quality she most yearns for in the midst of the "bufera infernal" [infernal whirlwind] – but she claims that she is prevented from doing so, because the king of the universe is not "amico" to her. Having fallen out of favour with God, she feels unable to offer the pilgrim her compassion: she fears that any prayers on his behalf would go unanswered, as her own have been.[27]

Francesca is not wrong to count herself (and all of the damned) outside the circle of God's friendship. The friendship with God from which the damned are excluded is, in fact, the dominant relationship that retains the language of *amistà* or *amistade* in the *Commedia*. From the soteriological perspective of the *Commedia*, *amistà* – perhaps surprisingly – persists as a tool of exclusion, hierarchy, and preference. The "anime che Dio s'ha fatte amiche" [the souls whom God has made his friends], as Dante will describe the blessed in his examination on hope in *Paradiso* 25, are distinguished from the isolated damned by God's preference for the former and exclusion of the latter.[28] *Amistà* sets the *anime amiche* apart from the herd, elevating and isolating in a manner similar to that described in the wishful sonnet *Guido, i' vorrei*, which I discussed above in chapter 1 and to which I will return shortly. In the *Commedia*, the language of friendship is not, as we might have expected, used to describe the social bonds that aid souls through their purgatorial penitence, nor those that persist between the community of the blessed. It is not, in other words, a term that implies the affinity, camaraderie, or affection that unites the social fields of the two realms of blessedness. Rather, the term is employed as a means of articulating borders, of marginalizing or expelling those who, overly invested in and committed to ego, willfully rebel against divine law. Those who remain excluded from God's *amistà* are the objects of righteous disdain: "Or che di là dal mal fiume dimora, più muover non mi può" [Now that she dwells beyond the evil river, she can move me no longer], Cato coldly claims of his once beloved Marcia, echoing Beatrice's words to Virgil in *Inferno* 2, "la vostra miseria non mi tange" [your misery does not touch me].[29] Exclusion from God's friendship warrants the damned no sympathy, only scorn. The language of *amistà* is retained in the societies of the afterlife only to exclude some from the realm of salvation.[30]

The estrangement of the damned – their refusal to recognize the self in the other – is both cause and consequence of their exclusion from God's *amistà*. Such a refusal is most emphatically performed in the final dramatic encounter of the *Inferno*: that of Ugolino and the Archbishop. In Ugolino and Ruggieri Dante offers a perversion of neighbourly relations: the companions come to represent the infernal city's answer to fraternity and friendship.[31] Ugolino's self-identification as "tal vicino" [such a neighbour] to Ruggieri is rich in infernal irony: Ugolino emphasizes the grotesque nature of his association to Ruggieri by his conscious parody of neighbourliness.[32] If Farinata – in his overweening, chest-puffing posture as he rises from his tomb, holding even hell in disdain ("com'avesse l'inferno a gran dispitto")[33] – inverts the motion of love as he leans away from both pilgrim and tomb-mate Cavalcante in his pride, then Ugolino parodies it, mimicking the divine *piegare* of love described by Virgil in *Purgatorio* 18.[34] Ugolino bends down and over his victim, clutching him in a perverse embrace and raining hatred down, as the pilgrim witnesses, "sovra colui che tu ti mangi" [over him you are eating].[35]

And yet the relationship with his co-traitor is, of course, not even the primary missed opportunity for the radical identification of self with other that Ugolino had been privy to. The bonds that break down in Ugolino's example are not only civic; the rejection of civic union figured in the gruesome coupling of Ugolino and his sworn enemy is but the precursor to the repudiation of the most basic bond of human life: the familial.[36] Ugolino's response to his sons in the tower represents an even more abject rejection of the most basic definition of friendship: to see in the friend an *alter idem*.

As we know from comments in both *Vita nova* and *Convivio*, Dante considered familial bonds to be a form of friendship – not a voluntary one, to be sure, but a natural friendship in which one could elect to participate with greater or lesser degrees of affection.[37] Certainly the responses of the children to their common plight in the tower is a plea for the communion offered by paternal love.[38] In his bestial cruelty, however, Ugolino inverts the Gospel: the children ask the father for bread, and he returns it with stone. The Scriptural echo may well refer to either Matthew 7:7–10 or, as Robert Hollander has insisted, Luke 11.5–13.[39] Hollander's suggestion raises the question of friendship in Ugolino's account, identifying the allusion with the "parable of the importunate friend," who persists in knocking at his friend's locked door to ask for bread in the middle of the night. The man's initially selfish rejection of his friend's request is eventually overcome by his friend's insistence. So, too, Hollander says, should Ugolino have been overcome by his sons' importunity, which persists in seeking bread from a father who has offered stone.

Ugolino's own response appears especially cruel when viewed in the light of friendship's other-sameness. In his sons' expressions he sees his own pain mirrored ("e io scorsi / per quattro visi il mio aspetto stesso"), but he refuses to see that perception through to action.[40] "Io non piangëa, sì dentro impetrai" [I was not weeping, I so turned to stone within], he recounts, a verse which he follows immediately with a recognition of the boys' tears ("piangevan elli").[41] In other words, as his sons weep, he withholds his tears, refusing their attempts to mirror their own pain in his.[42] He has rejected their offer of companionship, mistaking it for a literal offer of the flesh.

His final words contrast his blindness in the tower with the pilgrim's witness to his current pain:

> e come tu mi vedi,
> vid' io cascar li tre ad uno ad uno
> tra 'l quinto dì e 'l sesto; ond' io mi diedi,
> già cieco, a brancolar sovra ciascuno,
> e due dì li chiamai, poi che fur morti.
> Poscia, più che 'l dolor, poté 'l digiuno.

[and as you see me, I saw the three fall one by one between the fifth day and the sixth; and I, already blind, took to groping over each of them, and for two days I called them, after they were dead. Then fasting had more power than grief.][43]

Much as the leaves fell from the autumnal branch "l'una appresso de l'altra," and the souls flocked singly to Charon's shores "ad una ad una," Ugolino watches his sons succumb to death "ad uno ad uno," individuated, alone, spiritually unaccompanied, and abandoned by the father whose friendship they had persistently sought. The father, "già cieco," passes his unseeing, directionless hands over each body in turn, uselessly individuating them and calling them by name, offering his voice only after they can no longer hear it.

Ugolino's famously ambiguous and horrific final act is rendered possible by his "digiuno," he says: a literal and spiritual hunger that blinds him to the unity promised at the divine banquet of the Eucharist.[44] In the *Purgatorio* we see an alternate version of Ugolino's hunger: the pilgrim's craving to understand the *caritas* of the heavenly cloister. Virgil concludes his discourse on charity with this paradox:

"ché, per quanti si dice più lì 'nostro,'
tanto possiede più di ben ciascuno,
e più di caritade arde in quel chiostro."
"Io son d'esser contento più digiuno,"
diss' io, "che se mi fosse pria taciuto,
e più di dubbio ne la mente aduno."

["for the more say 'our' up there, the more good each one possesses, and the more charity burns in that cloister." "I am hungrier to be contented," I said, "than if you had been silent earlier, and I am gathering more doubt in my mind."][45]

Virgil describes the phenomenon of love in Paradise, which multiplies as it is distributed like Christ's loaves and fishes: this is the *agape*, the sacred, communal banquet of the Eucharist.[46] Upon hearing of it, Dante is filled with a new hunger, a *digiuno* that cannot but show in silhouette the *digiuno* with which Ugolino returns to his "fiero pasto" [savage meal].[47] Here, where Virgil explains the central premise of paradisiacal love, Dante recalls the final words of Ugolino, whose "neighbourliness" parodies divine love. In both cases the rhyme words echo: *ad uno / ciascuno / digiuno* in *Inferno*, and *ciascuno / digiuno / aduno* in *Purgatorio*. Aside from the identical rhyme, though, we should also note the substitution of one homophone for another: *ad uno ad uno* in *Inferno*, implying the individuation of one from many, and the verb *adunare* in *Purgatorio*, the gathering of the many into one.

It is in the transition from the infernal *ad uno* to the blessed *adunare* that we can understand the fundamental divide between damnation and salvation. Like Ugolino, Francesca, and the "mal seme d'Adamo," the sinners in hell refuse the mirroring of the self in the other that friendship proffers. Clinging to individual identity over communal identification, the denizens of hell favour difference and isolation in violation of their natural human capacity for friendship. This is, fundamentally, the state of all repentant sinners, who must unlearn their patterns of estrangement if they wish to reach the *adunare* of the community of saints. The penance of Purgatory thus must present the dead with opportunities to practice the discovery of self through reflection in the other. They do so through their encounters with friends.

Purgatorio: Beside the Other

As I mentioned in the introduction to this chapter, Purgatory most clearly maps onto the notion of a *champ* as Bourdieu theorized, in particular because of the realm's relationship to the earth and especially to time. The experiences of the penitents in Purgatory take place in time; their interactions have their own sequences and tempos, depending on each terrace's mandates. Time structures not only the global mechanism of the mountain's treatment of evil, but also the specific, alterable, and contingent remedy for the vices of each individual penitent.[48] Each terrace of the mountain, furthermore, positions the penitents within a new social group, with its own objectives and practices. In each of these they must undo their patterns of estrangement, reconstituting their social bonds through liturgical performances.[49] Synchronized, they move past tantalizing trees and through murky smoke; they kiss chastely and clasp hands, calling out to one another in unison; they race quickly and bow down alongside one another. They also pray and sing in harmony, calling out verses from the Psalms and the liturgy.[50] In effect, Purgatory trains its penitents to be good neighbours in the new city. Where in Hell civic bonds collapsed under the weight of sin, in Purgatory the hard-bought bliss of atonement unites the community of the penitents under a new law.[51]

When we think of the terraces of Purgatory collectively as a *champ*, then the series of purgations to which the penitents subject themselves comprise a set of practices over which each needs to develop a "mastery" – not a cognitive or intellectual understanding of the terrace's "principles" or "rules" but an embodied "sense" of its logic.[52] Bourdieu describes this "sense" as "a permanent disposition, embedded in the agents' very bodies in the form of mental dispositions, schemes of perception and thought, extremely general in their application … and also, at a deeper level, in the form of bodily postures and stances, ways of standing, sitting, looking, speaking, or walking."[53] Such practices are so deeply integrated into the agent's character that they occur beneath any level of conscious choice. And yet they are not ritualized in the rigid, prescribed, context-dependent terms of liturgy or ceremony, for when confronted with a new circumstance or acquaintance the agent with mastery remains composed and able to improvise strategies appropriate to the occasion. Bourdieu calls this mastery the "sense of honour"; for the penitents in Purgatory we might well call it the "sense of virtue."

That virtue, unlike honour or fame, is not the object of a zero-sum game suggests the limits of Bourdieu's model of fields and practical mastery for reading

Purgatorio. The kind of competitive jostling for position that Bourdieu describes when he discusses the "sense of honour" depends on limited forms of capital that diminish when shared. But as we know from Virgil's discourse on diminishing goods in *Purgatorio* 15, the penitential practices of Purgatory reorient the souls away from "cose terrene" [earthly things] – forms of capital that, when distributed, make each possessor poorer – towards a good that "distributo/ in più posseditor, faccia più ricchi" [distributed among many possessors, can make them richer].[54] Virtue is just such a non-diminishing good. But because we have seen how antagonism, competition, and self-interest can all accompany friendship in social fields that traffic in status, honour, or fame – fields like the piazza, the university, and the court – we are better able to understand how exactly Dante reorients friendship here, confronting the central dilemmas that arose in social fields "dove per compagnia parte si scema" [where sharing lessens each one's portion].[55] Here, by contrast, friends can perform that theoretical "honesta certatio" [honourable competition] that Cicero had envisioned, without fear that, as one climbs higher, the other must fall.

Practices in Purgatory help one attain the "sense of virtue." These practices are the postures, gestures, and expressions of the penitents, described by Heather Webb in her work on the body's relationship to ethical training in *Purgatorio*.[56] The penitents, Webb argues, develop a sort of muscle memory around correct behavioral patterns, which shape and are shaped by the dispositions of the individual's will. Starting from Webb's analysis of gesture, we might continue to suggest that the more one adopts a posture or practices a gesture in Purgatory, the more one trains what Bourdieu would call one's "habitus" – the collected set of embodied dispositions that predispose both body and mind towards repetition – away from a vicious practice and towards a virtuous one.

In her analysis of the terrace of envy, Webb emphasizes the curative aspect of the punishment made evident in the postures of the penitents. For our purposes, the terrace of envy provides a further opportunity to examine the relationship between embodied purgatorial practices and the "sense of virtue," particularly in relation to this chapter's first framing question, on the function of private human attachments after the first life ends. On this second terrace of Dante's seven, the souls endure debilitating blindness to purge themselves of their competitive resentment of one another's good fortune. The vivid description of the wire that binds the eyes of the envious drives the reader's focus towards that aspect of their torment. But Webb observes that the penitents also purge themselves of envy by leaning on one another for support, a posture that they did not readily assume during their lifetimes, consumed as they were with a desire for the downfall of their neighbours.[57] Citing the description of the penitents as they lean piteously against one another and the rock that supports them (*Purgatorio* 13.58–66), Webb points out that the envious are forced to "suffer" (*sofferire*) their neighbours' presence, sustaining the weight of the neighbour's body with their own shoulders.[58]

Adopting this posture trains each penitent's disposition towards virtue, so that they develop what I would call a "sense" for it.

But to understand the relationship between the "sense of virtue" embodied in this *sofferire* and the role of human attachments in Purgatory, we must also ask ourselves what exactly is the virtue that this leaning, supporting posture intends to inculcate.[59] The poet describes it with the generic category "amor," an especially capacious (and therefore obscure) term. The penitents – whipped by cords "tratte d'amor" [braided of love] – are exhorted by the disembodied voices of spirits who, inviting the penitents to the "mensa d'amor" [the table of love], aim to undo the penitents' habitual disposition to envy.[60] As we saw above in chapter 1, Dante's immediate predecessors would have termed envy's contrasting virtue not *amor* but *amicizia* or *amistà.* We saw the opposition between *invidia* and *amistà* in the works of vernacular authorities like Brunetto Latini and Guittone d'Arezzo, the latter of whom calls friendship the "medicina" of envy.[61] That the word chosen here is the nonspecific *amor* rather than the precise *amistà* should be noted.[62] The *Commedia*'s early commentators appear to be at pains to define with any precision what the poem means by its generic reference to "amor." In their commentaries Jacopo della Lana, Pietro Alighieri, the Ottimo Commento, and Benvenuto da Imola call the kind of love cultivated here by a variety of terms: "carità al prossimo," "caritade verso il prossimo," "karitatem proximi," "dilectionem proximi," "amore," "pietade," "caritade," "amore di carità," "dilectionis et caritatis," and others, all variously defined as charity or love, and sometimes specified as love of neighbour.[63]

The terrace's exemplars of *amor* do not clarify the question of what exactly this love entails. Each seems to embody a different kind of disposition to the neighbour. Unusually for Dante's terraces, two of the three exemplars are Biblical: the first, as in all cases, is Mary, who notes with compassion the lack of wine among the guests – neighbours and friends – at the wedding in Cana. The third derives from a commandment issued directly by Christ himself in the Sermon on the Mount, in which he charges his followers, "Amate da cui male aveste" [Love those from whom you have had evil].[64] This is the most radical form of the Christian commandment towards "amore del prossimo," loving one's neighbour even if that neighbour is your enemy.[65]

But the most telling example is the second of the three: a classical reference, as is typical for the terraces, but also unusual in making obscure reference not to one individual exemplar of virtue but to two, here Orestes and Pylades, whose self-sacrificing acts of friendship are mutually recalled in the same verse, "I' sono Oreste" [I am Orestes].[66] As Cicero noted in *De amicitia* 7.24 and *De finibus* 5.22.63, a friend and contemporary of his had written a play that staged one of the most legendary acts of *vera amicitia.* In the scene both Orestes and his dearest and most devoted friend Pylades profess to be the man condemned to death by the king, proclaiming "Ego sum Orestes." Their mutual act of self-sacrifice, each refusing to watch idly as his friend would be put to death, was received, Cicero recounts, with uproarious applause from the crowds of spectators. The two men, indistinguishable from one another in their proclamation, together become what we might consider a single exemplar of the mutual self-sacrifice that the truest form of Ciceronian friendship makes possible.[67]

What is telling about the love between Orestes and Pylades is its specificity, which stands in sharp contrast to the two Biblical cases: where the Biblical models embody a "carità" or "amor" that is all-encompassing and non-specific, the classical example depicts a directed, unique, and exclusive love between two individuals. In their act of radical self-sacrifice, each man sets aside his distinct identity – the distinction between them as selves – for the sake of the other. The love between them is not a mere "amore del prossimo" but a friendship that begins with the radical mirroring of the self in the other. The Orestes-Pylades example anticipates the "mutual indwelling" of paradisiacal being: the "inluiarsi" of the souls in God, and the "intuarsi" of one individual blessed soul with its companions.[68] As in the Orestes-Pylades exemplar, the souls in Paradise will likewise retain their individual identities, while also effacing the boundary that separates one mind, one body, or one will from another. The classical example suggests that in Paradise distinct identities might need to be set aside for the sake of a non-possessive, binding, even co-penetrative love. These two forms of love – the communal love of one for all and the specific love of each for each – are both practiced here on the terrace of envy. Both are set forth as models to which the penitents, and the readers who learn from their example, must strive.

Beyond its telling individualism and specificity, however, it is also startling to note that the mention of Orestes and Pylades, this supreme classical example of friendship, makes no mention of the terms *amistà* or *amicizia* in its account of the friends' mutual self-sacrifice. Indeed, the entire terrace – which is structured on the premise of cultivating the virtue that would combat *invidia*, traditionally *amicitia* – avoids using the term at all, a term which had been so pervasive in Dante's earlier works. That this paradigmatic exemplar of Cicero's "unum ex duobus," "alter idem" model retains friendship's structure (in idealized form) while avoiding its terminology should tell us something about the ambivalence of the term *amico* in contemporary discourse and the unresolved contradictions the poet saw in the term itself. Orestes and Pylades are removed from the sphere of individualized, classical *amicitia* into a communitarian, self-sacrificing *amore del prossimo*, which straddles individual identity and communal identification. Gesturing to their example while rejecting the conventional terms traditionally associated with it thus provokes the reader to a deeper meditation on the contradiction between "alter" and "idem," between other and same.

Such a shedding of old differentiating identities for new forms of radical identification with the other is evident in the first words spoken by an envious penitent in *Purgatorio* 13. Responding to his request to speak with an Italian, Sapia gently admonishes the pilgrim for misunderstanding civic identity in the afterlife: "O frate mio," she says, "ciascuna è cittadina / d'una vera città" [O my brother, each of us is a citizen of one true city].[69] In correcting the pilgrim's commitment to earthly attachments, Sapia uses the term nearly all the penitents choose when they address the pilgrim: *frate*, here coupled with the possessive *mio*.[70] Sapia's hailing of the pilgrim as "brother" – along with the notable absence of the terms of *amistà* and *amicizia* in the Orestes-Pylades example – signals a key transmutation that this new kind of *alter idem* model will usher in. Social interactions in the field of Purgatory abandon the conventional language of *amicizia* or *amistà* in favour of a kind of *fratellanza elettiva*, an elective relationship that will train the individual will towards the radical identification of self and other performed by Orestes and Pylades in their self-sacrificing act.[71] Despite its emphasis on friends and friendships, *Purgatorio* (indeed nearly all of the *Commedia*) will virtually abandon the old terms of classical *amicitia*, which as we've seen in the previous chapters have become redolent of hierarchy, preference, ritual, competition, rivalry, self-interest, possession, exclusion, even duplicity. This is, of course, the contrast between human *amistà* – which, as we know from Dante's handling of lyric exchanges, is a mode which individuates and excludes – and divine *carità*, which redoubles as it is shared, a multiplication that Virgil expounds as they depart from the terrace of envy in *Purgatorio* 15.

The penitents on the terrace of envy practice, and eventually master, their "sense" of self-sacrificing, non-possessive *carità*, which unlike the strictly dyadic structure of classical friendship targets simultaneously the individual and the collective.[72] The leaning, supportive posture of the envious penitents undoes the disposition towards one's neighbour that we saw reflected in interactions in a competitive environment like the university, where the honour of one is limited or diminished by the honour of his colleagues. If in academic fields self-interest often impedes genuine support, here on the terrace of envy the penitents find themselves seeking their own well-being while also acting as pillar and succor for their neighbours. The posture they adopt offers a unique opportunity for non-competitive collaboration: because virtue is not a limited good, they are able to act in their own interest and in the interest of their neighbours in the same actions and at the same time. The "pena" [suffering] of the neighbour's physical proximity and presence is eventually trained into the "sollazzo" [solace] of companionship, as the envious penitents practice their new embodied dispositions towards their neighbours.[73] The virtue practiced here is pointedly not *amistà*, which remains unmentioned, perhaps because of its connection to competition, antagonism, and self-interest. Here instead the words are *fratellanza*, *amor*, and *carità*, terms that indicate a similarly structured relationship but which, when considered carefully, point to a specific disposition of the self towards the other, a non-possessive posture that can be equally practiced in this life and the next.

If *amistà* as it had been understood throughout Dante's *opere minori* is not the correct disposition among the penitents in Purgatory, then, why does the so-called "canticle of friendship" so insist on the presence of friends? The aim of Purgatory, after all, is to cleanse the individual of sin and to prepare each penitent for the collective embrace enjoyed by the saints in Paradise. It might well be argued that this individual work could or should only be accomplished alone. John Took, for one, stresses the pilgrim's private experience of penance in *Purgatorio*, noting, "for all his breaking bread with those he meets along the way (the meaning of the term 'companion'), it is none the less the resolution of his own humanity, the restructuring of his own affective existence, that occupies the mind of the pilgrim-poet as he makes his, properly speaking, still solitary ascent."[74] And yet the value of one's elective, private attachments to this affective restructuring cannot be underestimated, as we see in the repeated encounters with friends throughout the pilgrim's purgatorial journey: Casella greeting the pilgrim by singing one of Dante's own lyrics (*Purg.* 2); Belacqua and the pilgrim exchanging teasing quips (*Purg.* 3); Nino Visconti moving towards him in irrepressible joy (*Purg.* 8); Forese and Dante swapping news of old Florentine compatriots (*Purg.* 23–4); Matelda affectionately welcoming him in Earthly Paradise, joining him as both object of erotic desire and compassionate companion (*Purg.* 28). Allusions to friends, allies, and patrons abound, from Giotto and Guido Cavalcanti (*Purg.* 11), to Guido da Castello and Gherardo da Camino (*Purg.* 16), as well as the Malaspina family (*Purg.* 8). Attempted embraces – which most often fail or are interrupted – accompany greetings of compassion and care. Friends are everywhere in Purgatory.

Preparing to join the paradisiacal collective involves a dialectical process: on the one hand, each individual soul must make a solitary journey of reckoning with his or her own private misalignment of will. On the other hand, the souls together must learn to unite their wills as a community, in companionship with one another.[75] In neither of these endeavors – the personal or the collective – does the dyadic structure of private friendship we have seen in the previous chapters seem to serve an essential strategic purpose. We know that dyadic friendship makes available the possibilities of radical mirroring of self in the other, as in the case of Orestes and Pylades. But private *amistadi* can also, as Cato's rebuke of the "negligenza" [negligence] of the "spiriti lenti" [laggard spirits] lingering on the mountain's shores seems to show, distract with their sweetness from the penitents' arduous task of self-reflection.[76] Dyadic friendship risks drawing two friends away from the rest of their community, separating them from their companions as they delight in private, intimate conversations and recollections.

The danger of friendship's potential to exclude is one Dante of course knew well, as we saw in relation to the dream-vision of *Guido, i' vorrei che tu e Lapo ed io*, discussed in chapter 1.[77] Indeed, the "vasello snelletto e leggero" [vessel so swift and light] that carries Dante's friend Casella and his shipmates across the seas to the penitential mountain cannot but recall this other *vasel*, from Dante's early encomium to friendship.[78] The earlier sonnet yearns that Dante, Guido, and Lapo – much like the penitents at the mouth of the Tiber – would be "messi in un vasel" [set upon a ship] which would set out to sea, "sì che fortuna od altro tempo rio/non ci potesse dare impedimento" [so neither thunderstorms nor cloudy skies might ever have the power to hold us back]. The elite group of friends would exercise their virtue in rational activity; that is, in dialogue with one another (Dante's "ragionar" [talk] in verse 10), a conversation that in the sonnet is concentrated fixedly on the matter of love. The poem, styled as a *plazer*, crafts a scenario of separation from the world and its cares: Dante desires that he and his friends sail away from the political and social strife of the city in a magical boat on a peaceful sea, enjoying a unity among themselves that Barolini characterizes as a "distant preview" of Trinitarian wholeness.[79]

But the exclusionary thrust of the sonnet's vision of social life stands in sharp opposition to Virgil's description of the multiplying love of Paradise in *Purgatorio* 15, which I cited above in relationship to Ugolino's failings: "per quanti si dice più lì 'nostro'/ tanto possiede più di ben ciascuno,/ e più di caritade arde in quel chiostro" [for the more say "our" up there, the more good each one possesses, and the more charity burns in that cloister].[80] As I argued in chapter 1, *Guido, i' vorrei* encapsulates both the exclusive desire at the base of friendship and the pitfalls associated with the realization of such a desire. The sonnet's wish for exclusive and intimate friendship depends on an impossible escape from the human social realm and its vicissitudes. Such an impulse renders the sonnet's vision of friendship paradoxically antisocial, driving the small clique of friends away from their larger society. This sort of friendship seeks to individuate and elevate, not to integrate.

The kind of isolation celebrated by *Guido, i' vorrei* is irreconcilable with the sense of sociability and community the penitents must develop. The pilgrim learns this early in his ascent as Cato condemns Casella's song as a pleasurable but dangerous distraction, interrupting the negligent souls as they listen "come a nessun toccasse altro la mente" [as if nothing else touched anyone's mind].[81] The song dangerously diverts the pilgrim and the new arrivals to the mountain not only in its content, as many have discussed, but also in its form. The episode contrasts the solitary voice of the lone singer – individuated from and celebrated by the crowd – with the choral, communal voices of the penitents who had banded together to sing the psalm as they approached the mountain. Cato's admonishment draws the souls back from nostalgia for the delights of the world, which, the episode suggests, include the exclusions of private *amistadi*. Here in Purgatory, exclusionary *amistà* must be set aside in favour of a sociability that integrates the penitents into a single community.

We might at this stage in the journey assume that the *vasello* ferrying Casella and his shipmates to the shore is a corrective of the sonnet's *vasel* that sweeps the trio away on the placid and endless seas of friendly discourse, the canticle dismissing the pleasures of friendship as a diversion from the labors of penitence. And yet, surprisingly, the metaphor of the ship of friendship returns once again higher up the mountain, this time in an exchange with another Florentine friend, a poet of a different register: Forese Donati. Before his death in 1296, Forese had traded with the young Dante a series of vulgar, offensive sonnets, a backstory that has been much discussed in scholarly treatment of the two poets' later encounter on the mountain.[82]

What is more relevant for the present purposes is not the past performance of their friendship, but how friendship is performed in their dialogue here. Whereas *Guido, i' vorrei* removes the group of young poets from the vicissitudes of Florentine urban life, the verses of *Purgatorio* 23 and 24 immerse Dante and Forese in reflection on it.[83] Forese recalls his wife, become beloved in his memory; his family and the misery wrought on Florence through their political machinations; the scandalous dress of the "svergognate" of the city (*Purg.* 23.106).[84] The pilgrim, in turn, recalls his own sinful behavior, specifically his obscure sinful past with Forese; the beginning of his journey in the dark wood; and its goal, reunion with Beatrice.[85] Their reflections are local, particular, and historically specific: in their conversation they conjure a Florence where both friendship and vice can flourish, but they do so without nostalgia for a bygone past, whether personal or civic, and with an eye to their current setting, the terrace of gluttony.

Rather than linger in wistful recollections, the pilgrim and his friend hasten their steps, Forese with his eyes to his companions and their communal cleansing, Dante with his own fixed on his salvation in Beatrice. Their companionship makes the movement all the easier:

> Né 'l dir l'andar, né l'andar lui più lento
> facea, ma ragionando andavam forte,
> sì come nave pinta da buon vento.

> [Speech did not slow our walking, nor walking our speech, but we hastened on while speaking, like a ship driven by a good wind.][86]

Both men walk briskly towards their goals, each driven forward by his delight in his friend's company and conversation. They move along "forte," their *ragionar* ferrying them forward, as if in a ship carried along by a "buon vento" towards its destination.[87]

It is here in Purgatory that Dante and Forese seem to have finally realized that dream of perfect companionship wished for in *Guido, i' vorrei*: that is, a ship, blown by a strong wind that allows them to delight in their *ragionamenti*. But the purgatorial ship (no longer a "vasel," as before, but a "nave") that carries the two pilgrims towards their respective goals moves purposefully, and for a period of delimited time, in contrast to the "ragionar sempre" celebrated in the earlier poem. It is the boundless, whimsical discussion – this literal and figurative getting-carried-away, as both ship and conversation drift aimlessly – that submission to the mountain's structures of penitence will correct. This is the crucial difference between the ship that the young Dante wishes to share with Guido and the one that he now shares with Forese in his middle age: while Guido's "vasel" moves aimlessly, directed by nothing save the caprice of its passengers ("ch'ad ogni vento / per mare andasse al voler vostro e mio"), Forese's "nave" finds itself with a strong tailwind ("pinta da buon vento"), rushed swiftly along the mountainside towards its proper port. The matching rhymes in "-ento" highlight the corrective that the speedy "nave" represents to the slow wanderings of the youthful "vasel." Where the former was free to follow its whims in endless, directionless motion, this ship hastens to its coveted destination – which is not only Paradise, not only God, but also the communion of the blessed who will welcome the newly purged soul.

As we saw in chapter 2, Dante and his literary contemporaries recognized the functional advantages of friendship: promoting collaboration, stimulating (healthy) competition, providing sponsorship. Here we see a similarly instrumental version of friendship, where personal attachments like the one shared between the pilgrim and Forese are directed towards achieving the individual moral betterment essential to the purgatorial process. The mountain conditions the penitents to restructure what Bourdieu would call the "system of objective relations" with their compatriots, relearning how to live alongside one another, first each with each, then each with all. Bourdieu explains: "Native experience of the social world never apprehends the system of objective relations other than *in profiles*, that is, in the form of relations which present themselves only one by one, and hence successively."[88] In other words, the individual agent does not understand the objective principles of sociality in the field at large except through unique encounters with other individuals in a given field. In these particular encounters one develops one's *habitus*, the system of thoughts and perceptions that allows the agent to develop a degree of social mastery. Such is the case with individual friendships in *Purgatorio*, which train the penitent towards the universal participation in *carità* in which each will delight in Paradise. At its heart, Purgatory seeks to restore the community that has been fractured by sin. The purgatorial mountain is, effectively, the starting point for the new Church – the new Body of Christ – that will become the paradisiacal collective upon entering Heaven. The drive to collective contemplation and enjoyment of God's love is impeded by the splintering, individualistic nature of sin, and it is this obstruction that Purgatory seeks to remove.

We might see the collective practices of Purgatory as a diminishment of the individual. But the collective impetus of purgatorial practices is, counterintuitively, a reinforcement of the individual through the distinct mirroring of the one in the other.[89] Far from being impeded by the dyadic structure of friendship, Purgatory's two-pronged assault on misguided will – one individual, the other communal – is facilitated by friendship, which uniquely bridges individual and communal forms of love.

Unlike the exclusionary portrait of friendship Dante developed in his early lyric, purgatorial friendship anticipates, at the level of the individual, the kind of love that the penitent must learn to cultivate for each member of the entire community. Recognizing in a companion the *alter idem* that friendship aims to uncover (à la Orestes and Pylades) permits each penitent to imagine the possibility of an "other same" in any of his or her compatriots within the particular social field of that terrace. Each instance of individual recognition of the self in the other trains the penitent towards mastery of a new kind of civic friendship, one that begins from two individuals and then radiates out to eventually encompass the whole *polis*. This phenomenon is what Janet Soskice, writing widely on Christian friendship, calls "an anthropology of the at-least-two": that friendship in and with God does not seek in the other a reflection of the self, but rather celebrates the distinctiveness of the other. Because Christian friendship is not grounded in love of self but in celebration of other, it is able to accommodate each within its reach.

In the encounters with Forese and other friends of the pilgrim, *Purgatorio* provides us with an extended reflection on what Soskice sees in Christian friendship more broadly: that the community the penitents build initiates between two companions and then radiates out to accommodate a third, a fourth, and so on.[90] For such a radiating vision of civic friendship to be possible, the friends must learn to keep their focus trained on their respective, individual objectives, much as Dante and Forese do by refraining from nostalgic recollection and keeping their minds focused on purgation and healing. If we are considering Dante's friendship with Forese in relation to Soskice's more general model, the key function of that friendship is the eschatological element she perceives in her "anthropology of the at-least two":

> [W]ithin an anthropology of the-at-least-two, the friend is not a blank sheet for the free play of my emotions or a mirror for my virtues. Nor are the friends aligned in Cicero's symmetrical and essentially static perfection; rather, I am becoming myself in and through who I am for others and who they are for me. Friendship is in this sense an eschatological relationship, for it has as much to do with what I may become as what I now am.[91]

Soskice's definition gestures towards what was lacking in *De vulgari*'s claim to friendship with Cino: there, Dante signals their collaboration, their *consensio*, but not how friendship might nurture distinctiveness and particularity. By contrast, one hears in Soskice's description an echo of the words of the pilgrim, who grieves as he recalls with Forese "qual fosti meco, e qual io teco fui." By recognizing distinctly who Forese was and is, the pilgrim is able to see more precisely who he himself was and is; that (self-)recognition will be necessary for him to complete his passage through the penitential terraces. But the two friends do not dwell on what they had been to one another; rather, here on the terrace of gluttony, they rely on their distinct experiences of one another's dynamic and developing sense of self to become what the purgatorial process has ordained for each of them (as, indeed, the envious had leaned on one another more literally as they learned to *sofferire* the presence of their neighbours). One leaning on the other, they look together towards a future in which each can celebrate "qual sarai meco, e qual io teco sarò."

The dynamism of Dante's friendship with Forese extends the terms of the kind of mutually beneficial friendship he had projected in his references to Guido's *amistà* in *Guido, i' vorrei* and Cino's *amicitia* in *De vulgari eloquentia.* Even as the canticle eschews the language of classical *amicitia* as it had been known to the pagan authorities, it is nevertheless here that the friends' collaborative moral development distinguishes it as a "true friendship" in the Ciceronian-Aristotelian sense: it simultaneously seeks each of the three ends towards which perfect friendship aims. It is an exercise of mutual virtue, as the two friends assist in one another's attainment of salvation. It is pleasurable, as the two delight in one another's company and conversation, using this delight to propel themselves forward towards their respective goals. And it is instrumental, each man leaning on his friend's support to aid his achievement. Unlike earlier relationships with Guido or Cino, where such instrumental aims could not escape self-interest, here each of the two friends finds in the other the ability to assist his friend without neglecting his own interests, to cooperate without competing, to better the other as he betters himself. Their ends are not identical: Forese must train himself to find nourishment in the spirit, and the pilgrim must attain sovereignty over his own will, that he might assure himself an eventual place in Paradise. Their objectives do not compete with one another, precisely because of the principle of non-competition described by Virgil in his discourse on earthly and heavenly goods (*Purgatorio* 15.46–78). Forese and the pilgrim each reorient their individual goals away from those "cose terrene" [earthly things] towards a good that "distributo/ in più posseditor, faccia più ricchi" [distributed among many possessors, can make them richer].[92] And because the respective goals towards which they advance are not ones "dove per compagnia parte si scema" [where sharing lessens each one's portion],[93] the friends are able to support one another's mutual progress without concern for jealously guarding his own self-interest. By doing so, they simultaneously rejoice in their private friendship while avoiding the dangers of opportunism, competition, and distraction. In his friend's company, each grows more into himself, while affirming what is common between them – their mastery of virtue. Such friendship – be it civic or personal, natural or volitional – is not assimilative even if it is unitive: it brings two distinct individuals together, bonding them one to the other not despite but because of their differences. In one's friendship with another – a close personal friend, a neighbour, or a fellow citizen – one is recognized and celebrated as both *alter* and *idem*.

Paradiso: Beyond the Other

If the social field of hell is static, dominated by disengagement and exclusion, and that of Purgatory is dynamic, as friends use their relationships to affirm their personal identities and to sustain their companions' moral growth, what can we make of the sociability of the saints? The blessed have, in theory at least, successfully moved beyond the becoming that characterizes purgatorial friendship, as each one leans on neighbours to support the other's engagement and success, as well as one's own. Having attained mastery of the "sense of virtue" that the penitents of Purgatory strive towards, the souls of the blessed, we might imagine, no longer have need of preferential friendships. Indeed, the fellowship of the paradisiacal community, unlike infernal and purgatorial bonds, transcends the question of election in attachments. This is not to say that blessedness surpasses individuality or erases the individual's volition; this is clearly not the case, as Manuele Gragnolati and Heather Webb have both made clear.[94] Rather, what is critical to heavenly sociality is that the bonds of the blessed are not premised on the election of one individual or (and, implicitly, over) another. That they embody a collective is predicated on their mutual love of and conformity with the divine. As souls pass the threshold of Purgatory to join the heavenly ranks, they freely relinquish the autonomy that was only just restored to them at the end of their purgatorial journeys, using their newfound freedom to align individual will with the force of divine *carità*.[95] Ultimately, the blessed enter into a community in which, as I aim to show here, the strict substance of relationships will be the bond that exists between individual soul and God. There will be no essential horizontal component to these attachments that would exist independently of the vertical bond of God's *carità*.[96] And yet horizontal bonds persist as particular instances of that essential bond. The bonds between heaven's inhabitants consist of the specular diffusion of that vertical bond common to all. Paradisiacal love is not contingent on the love of neighbour – even if it is coextensive with it – and it is no longer susceptible to the pitfalls and vulnerabilities of the kind of individual, elective love that is characteristic of human friendship.[97]

It is another member of the Donati family who explains the issues surrounding verticality, hierarchy, and multiplicity in the social architecture of Heaven. The pilgrim's meeting with Piccarda in the heaven of the moon (*Paradiso* 3) lacks the exuberance we might have expected, given the concern for her the pilgrim expresses to her brother Forese in *Purgatorio* 24.[98] That the pilgrim does not embrace Piccarda warmly might surprise the reader after the emotional encounter with her brother; shouldn't a reunion with a beloved member of the Donati clan, now among the blessed souls of Paradise, be all the more celebratory? Yet their reunion is instead rather restrained, and Piccarda's first words to the pilgrim have none of the pathos of the recognition scenes the reader of *Purgatorio* knows so well. Responding to the pilgrim's request, Piccarda begins:

La nostra carità non serra porte
a giusta voglia, se non come quella
che vuol simile a sé tutta sua corte.

[Our charity does not lock its doors to a just desire, but follows his love who wishes all his court to be like himself.][99]

Invoking both justice and *carità*, the third canticle's two guiding principles, Piccarda replies to the pilgrim's request to know her identity not in the name of a particular, personal attachment emerging from their earthly connection to one another, but in the terms of a boundless heavenly charity. In other words, she offers her reply not for love of the pilgrim, but for the *carità* of the blessed, which adheres so closely to divine will that the court of Heaven ("tutta sua corte") reflects the likeness of its Lord as in a mirror.

Divine *carità*, as opposed to human *amistà*, is a collective love. Aquinas, defining charity as "a friendship of man and God," explains:

[A]micitia se extendit ad aliquem duplicitur. Uno modo respectu suiipsius, et sic amicitia nunquam est nisi ad amicum. Alio modo se extendit ad aliquem respectu alterius personae, sicut si aliquis habet amicitiam ad aliquem hominem, ratione eius diligent omnes ad illum hominem pertinentes, sive filios sive servos sive qualitercumque ei attinentes. Et tanta potest esse dilectio amici, quod propter amicum amantur hi qui ad ipsum pertinent etiam si nos offendant vel odiant. Et hoc modo amicitia caritatis se extendit etiam ad inimicos, quos diligimus ex caritate in ordine ad Deum, ad quam principaliter habetur amicitia caritatis.

[Friendship goes out to another in two ways. When he is loved in himself, and such friendship is only for a friend; and when he is loved because of another person, as when for the sake of a friend you love those belonging to him, be they children, servants or anyone connected with him at all, even if they hurt or hate us, so much do we love him. In this way the friendship of charity extends even to our enemies, for we love them for the sake of God who is the principal in our loving.][100]

Aquinas lays out two directions that the love of *amicitia* extends: either its movement is direct, in forms of private attachment between two individuals (that is, one is "loved in himself," "respectu suiipsius"), or it is diffused, as when an individual is loved because of our love of another.[101] Charity, which Aquinas pointedly calls "amicitia caritatis," proceeds according to diffuse reflection; that is, it extends to all, including "ad inimicos," who are loved through the reflection of our love for God, "ad quam principaliter habetur amicitia caritatis." This obligation to love inclusively and diffusely is among the lessons of the purgation of envy that we saw above. There, the penitents are reminded of the commandment "Amate da cui male aveste" (*Purg.* 13.36) as a means to cultivate "amor" and to insulate themselves against their habituated envy.[102]

It is perhaps more accurate to describe *carità* as a bond between God and humankind in which one participates than an individual sentiment, like *amistà.* Aquinas later specifies that *caritas* can have only one object, which is God. Responding to the theoretical objection that charity cannot be a single virtue because it has two objects (God and neighbour), Aquinas writes, "Ad primum ergo dicendum quod ratio illa directe procederet si Deus et proximum ex aequo essent caritatis objecta. Hoc autem non est verum, sed Deus est principale objectum caritatis, proximum autem ex caritate diligitur propter Deum" [The objection would be to the point if God and neighbour were equally the objects of charity. But this is not so. God is the principal object of charity and it is for his sake we love one another].[103] Thus properly aligned bonds of charity are directed to God as object, and it is only by means of this personal mastery – Bourdieu's term for the successful integration of a particular set of dispositions and perceptions – that the love of charity can be diffused to reach one's companions in Paradise. In discussing love in *Purgatorio* 15, Virgil anticipates the language of specularity, light, and diffusion, explaining the indivisible nature of divine love in Thomistic terms:

> Quello infinito e ineffabil bene
> che là sù è, così corre ad amore
> com'a lucido corpo raggio vene.
> Tanto si dà quanto si trova d'ardore;
> sì che, quantunque carità si stende,
> cresce sovr'essa l'etterno valore.
> E quanta gente più là sù intende,
> più v'è da bene amare, e più vi s'ama,
> e come specchio l'uno a l'altro rende.

> [That infinite and ineffable Good which is up there, runs to love just as a ray comes to a shining body. It gives itself according to the measure of the love it finds, so that however great is the charity that reaches out, by so much the eternal Worth grows upon it. And the more people bend towards each other up there, the more there is to love well and the more love there is, and, like a mirror, each reflects it to the other.][104]

The divine light, Virgil explains, races out to the souls of the blessed as rays to a luminous object. Their souls, acting as mirrors, then reflect that "infinito e ineffabile bene" to their neighbours, and this, Virgil says, is charity – what Aquinas calls *amicitia caritatis,* which is love of the other "for the sake of God." The more open the soul is to receive *carità,* the more of it the soul receives; the more there are who can participate in this reflection, the more love is there reflected to one's neighbours, as between one mirror and another. As in Aquinas's description of *amicitia caritatis*, Virgil emphasizes the directionality of *carità*, which proceeds first to God (the "principal in our loving," Aquinas says), and then, diffused as in a mirror ("come specchio"), reflects from one to the other. "Carità si stende," Virgil stresses, echoing Aquinas's claim that charity "se extendit" even to enemies. In its essence, though, this love is always an extension of the divine, which is its origin. It is distinct from and elevated above the contingent and vulnerable love of humankind. Virgil's "la sù," repeated twice in three tercets, marks the distance and differentiation of this higher kind of love from what we see below, even in Purgatory.

Virgil's account is confirmed in the heaven of Mercury. As soon as the pilgrim and Beatrice ascend, shot like an arrow to the second sphere, the "mille splendori" of the souls of the ambitious cry out "Ecco chi crescerà li nostri amori" [Behold one who will increase our loves].[105] Webb reads this verse in light of the transmutability characteristic of the relational identity of the souls in Paradise, and particularly of the pilgrim. She sees Virgil's reliance on the mirror imagery at the conclusion of his remarks in *Purgatorio* 15 as a rational misunderstanding of *carità*'s ever-increasing potency, the mirror image reducing this potency to mere "reciprocity or equivalency." I would stress, instead, the image's continuity with Virgil's explanation of *carità*, ever increasing ("più … più … più …") as more souls ascend to join the "triunfo etternal" of the blessed. A closer reading of the mirror image at the end of his account clarifies just how precisely he has presented the ontological unity of *carità*, even as it is experienced dynamically and to differing degrees. Rather than read Virgil's mirror imagery as mistakenly resolving the intensification of paradisiacal ardor in "reciprocity or equivalency," as Webb does, I would suggest that the mirror of Virgil's final verse highlights the unified genesis of *carità* as originating in God and reflecting more luminously as more mirrors arrive to diffuse its light. While the light and heat of *carità* may increase the more participants it finds, and while some souls may have an increased capacity for receiving and reflecting God's *carità*, divine love nevertheless burns as brightly in the soul of any one individual that receives it as it does in another.[106]

Returning to Piccarda's first words in the sphere of the moon, we see that it is heavenly *carità* that compels her to reply to the pilgrim's question, not the human *amistade* shared between her and the pilgrim in the world below. Where *amistà* is experienced differentially, the blessed perceive *carità* equally, to the fullest capacity of each soul. In the conversation that follows, Piccarda will untie the knot of hierarchy that had prevented the pilgrim from appreciating the fullness of her delight in divine love. Perhaps because of Piccarda's reference to the "corte" of heaven in verse 45, the pilgrim has misunderstood the paradisiacal hierarchy: he has confused *carità* and *amistà*. He innocently asks his friend, whom he has finally recognized despite her great resplendence:

Ma dimmi: voi che siete qui felici,
desiderate voi più alto loco
per più vedere e per più farvi amici?

[But tell me: you souls who are happy here, do you desire a higher place so as to see more and to make yourselves dearer friends to Him?][107]

The logic of the pilgrim's question (which John Took, in passing, calls "demonic") misinterprets the love the blessed hold for God as a particular *amistade*, which begs to be preferred above all others, to be more *amico* of God than the others are.[108] Following from Piccarda's reference to heaven's "corte," his question borrows the courtly language of sponsorship ("amici," as we saw in chapter 3), and he mistakenly frames the court of Heaven as a signorial court, where courtiers and clients vie for position as the nearest "amico" to the lord. Piccarda corrects him, beginning her discourse with that same purgatorial appellation that derives from *carità*, and not from a preferential *amistade*. "Frate," she begins, acknowledging Dante as a member of the paradisiacal *fratellanza collettiva* and not as her particular *amico*:

la nostra volontà quïeta
virtù di carità, che fa volerne
sol quel ch'avemo, e d'altro non ci asseta.
Se disïassimo esser più superne,
foran discordi li nostri disiri
dal voler di colui che qui ne cerne;
che vedrai non capere in questi giri,
s'essere in carità è qui necesse,
e se la sua natura ben rimiri.

[our will is quieted by the power of charity, which causes us to desire only what we have and does not make us thirst for anything else. If we desired to be higher up, our desires would be discordant with the will of him who assigns us here, which you will see is contradictory to these spheres, if to be in charity is here *necesse*, and if you consider well its nature.][109]

Asking the pilgrim to consider well the essence of paradisiacal *carità*, its "natura," Piccarda clarifies not only the necessity of *carità* over *amistà* in Paradise, but also the definition of *carità* in its relationship to individual desire or will. In her reasoning,

Piccarda follows Aquinas, who locates charity not in free will but in volition.[110] Her argument proceeds thus: one admitted to Paradise must have surpassed preferential *amistadi* and moved into divine *carità*. Charity, by its very nature and power, quiets each soul's *volontà*. To desire something (or someone) differently than what is desired by the supreme will would draw the soul out of accord with the fixed standards set by charity, a logical impossibility for those who have succeeded in correctly orienting volition. Such discordant desires would ultimately relegate that soul outside of the realm of blessedness.[111]

The quietude of *volontà* that Piccarda and the blessed have discovered upon setting preferential and possessive desires aside is precisely the peace that had been denied to a figure like Francesca in *Inferno* 5. Francesca's willfulness has prevented her from relinquishing attachment to her own desires and submitting to the "virtù di carità" – the power or force of divine charity, which grants quietude to the will in its act of acceptance ("la nostra volontà quïeta"). As Inga Pierson has demonstrated, such an act of submission represents not the lack of resolve that has historically been imposed on Piccarda, but a great moral conviction that triumphs over willfulness and discovers "the serenity that can only come from accepting the inscrutability of divine justice."[112] Had Francesca submitted like Piccarda did, aligning herself with divine force in her battle with desire, she would have found the peace that she so craves and that Piccarda enjoys: "'n la sua volontade è nostra pace," Piccarda concludes, for the desires of the "re" and "tutto il regno" cohere. It is not that the "re de l'universo" is not a friend to Francesca; it is that she, in her willfulness, refuses the "virtù di carità" that has always been extended to her. Francesca insists on her individualism and estrangement from others, rather than making herself mirror through which to reflect divine charity, as Piccarda, in her resolute submission, does.

From Piccarda's perspective, preferential human *amistà* indicates a deficiency of will. These preferential bonds, which would privilege one individual over another, represent lingering human desires, a will that has not yet ceased becoming, so that it may eventually reach its perfect conformity to the divine.[113] It is this deficiency that Piccarda explains to the confused pilgrim, recalling the lessons of his encounters with friends like Casella and Forese in *Purgatorio*: friendship may itself be a good – each friend aiding the other's mastery of the sense of virtue – but not when it is coupled with preference or possessiveness as *amistà*, which is redolent of ego. Possessiveness is the trap to which Francesca had succumbed, desiring that Love seize Paolo for her and her for Paolo ("prese costui … mi prese").[114] Friendship is to be sought, but only when it seeks the friend for the friend's sake, not for the self. Friendship must seek for the friend union with God, not the union that ties Paolo to Francesca and her to him, such that the bond "ancor non m'abbandona" [still does not abandon me]. Friendship, in other words, must look nothing like the *amistà* that Dante has discussed, even celebrated, elsewhere in his works. Any friendship that is not a direct specular reflection of the *amicitia caritatis* described by Aquinas, loving the other for the sake of God, marks a desire discordant with divine *carità*, which, as Piccarda makes plain, "è qui necesse."

Piccarda emphasizes the conformity of each individual's will to the divine will, repeating the details for the pilgrim, who is slow to relinquish his understanding of *amistà* and preference:

> Anzi è formale ad esto beato esse
> tenersi dentro a la divina voglia,
> per ch'una fansi nostre voglie stesse.

[Indeed, it is constitutive of this blessed *esse* to stay within God's will, and thus our very wills become one.][115]

It is, she reiterates, the very form of paradisiacal being ("è *formale* ad esto beato esse") that one constrain one's will, habituated by purgatorial practice, to accord with the divine will and hence with one another, becoming one will, united "dentro a la divina voglia." In other words, it is in the very metaphysical structure of Paradise that individual wills, in their multiplicity, conform to one will, not subordinate to the divine will but imitating it, conforming to its likeness.[116] The souls thus participate in God's will, in harmony with that will and with one another, under the unifying bonds of charity that Virgil's discourse of specularity and diffusion in *Purgatorio* 15 heralded.[117]

The pilgrim's question to Piccarda has not, however, been thoroughly resolved. Essentially, the pilgrim seeks to reconcile the hierarchy and differentiation of the heavenly court with the equality and unity of *carità*, mistaking the love between God and the blessed for preferential *amistà*. The pilgrim assumes that the love felt by the blessed is dispersed according to the same "gradi" that Dante had alluded to in the *Vita nova*.[118] In a sense, it turns out, he is correct: the "gradi dell'amistade" from his early depictions of exclusive friendships with individual interlocutors are here transmuted into a kind of "gradi di carità," hierarchical degrees of charity, a notion Dante might have gleaned from Richard of Saint Victor or other theological sources.[119] Piccarda explains that, despite its universal reach, charity is dispersed to varying degrees, according to the different capacities with which each blessed soul can receive it. Teodolinda Barolini elucidates Piccarda's paradoxical statement: "The single *più* of Piccarda's first speech has been tripled by the pilgrim, who suggests, reasonably enough, that the souls must want a '*più* alto loco / per *più* vedere e per *più* farvi amici.' He only sees the stigma of difference, and so Piccarda must explain further; rather than eliminate difference ontologically, she eliminates it psychologically."[120] Piccarda clarifies that although the blessed souls delight fully in the love of God, rendering equal what Barolini calls their "psychological" experience of blessedness, their capacity for receiving that delight ("ontologically") varies in degree:

come noi sem di soglia in soglia
per questo regno, a tutto il regno piace
com' a lo re che 'n suo voler ne 'nvoglia.
E 'n la sua volontade è nostra pace.

[how we are arranged from level to level through this kingdom, delights the entire kingdom, as well as the King who enamors us of his will. And in his will is our peace.][121]

The blessed souls are arranged hierarchically – according to *gradi* or, as here, *soglie* – but such a hierarchy is not indicative of preference, as it was construed in the *Vita nova* and in the Epistle to Cangrande. Just as in the *Vita nova* and the Epistle *amistà* was dispersed according to hierarchical structures that allot intimacy in degrees, so here, counterintuitively, *carità* – what Aquinas calls *amicitia caritatis* or, elsewhere, *amicitia Dei* – remains hierarchical in its structure.[122] Much as they were in the Epistle's careful rhetorical negotiation, hierarchies, and inequalities – particularly in the social order – are maintained in the heavenly spheres. But unlike the hierarchical configuration of *amistadi*, the distribution of *carità* varies in degree but not in quality: each of the blessed souls receives fully according to her capacity. Divine *carità* is thus dispersed differentially but not preferentially: God desires all the blessed souls equally, even as some are more endowed with the "virtù di carità" than others may be. For this reason, Piccarda concludes, "'n sua volontade è nostra pace": each finds serenity in conforming one's own desires with the will of God, discovering in that conformity the likeness that renders the court of heaven the *alter idem* of its Lord.

Conformity to the divine will does not entail uniformity.[123] Becoming the *alter idem* of God does not imply abandoning difference for the sake of likeness. The divine likeness that these souls mirror is both one and many: it is unified in the force of its love and in the ground of its being, but its expression – at least as it is performed for the wayfaring pilgrim – is multiform. Even as the blessed freely submit themselves to the will of God, they do not surrender their individual identities, histories, capacities, or – as will unfold over a series of encounters in *Paradiso* – their attachments.[124] They remain arranged hierarchically, *di soglia in soglia*, distinguished not by the fullness of their experience of blessedness but by the degree to which they are able to receive it. The *Commedia*, and in particular the *Paradiso*, refuses to yield multiplicity for the sake of homogeneity.

That the heavenly city's diversity mirrors that of the earthly city is made plain in the great celebration of human difference that unfolds in Dante's encounter with yet another friend, Carlo Martello, in the third heaven, Venus.[125] Much as Piccarda's explanation of blessedness bridges the paradox of complete fulfilment and differential distribution, so do Carlo Martello and his companions in the third sphere straddle the seeming contradiction between diversity and identity in the heavenly court. Insisting on difference as the essential and natural root of sociability ("esser diverse / convien di vostri effetti le radici"), Carlo Martello clarifies that the natural splendors of the forest of human society are the result of richly varied and differently cultivated seedlings, scattered "diversamente" [differently] and thus producing different fruits, some sweet, some bitter. The best outcome of this natural diversity in the world is the forest's abundant fruit, which Carlo alludes to when he recalls his budding affection for the pilgrim: "s'io fossi giù stato, io ti mostrava/ di mio amor più che le fronde" [if I had stayed down there I would have shown you more than the foliage of my love].[126] Particular affection is figured here as the abundant fruitfulness of human society, which enriches the earth, and provides differently to each according to divine providence.[127]

The individuated souls of the blessed are the hypostases of the bounteous diversity of being Carlo alludes to.[128] The ranks of the blessed, to whom beatitude has been dispersed "diversamente," differentiate themselves "di soglia in soglia," one from the other, as unique participants in the bonds of divine *carità*. But in their collective participation in it, they also enable its diffuse reflection, the unitive bond generated by this friendship of "the at-least-two." As the example of Orestes and Pylades showed to the envious penitents seeking to cultivate *amore*, the souls in Paradise – and especially in the heaven of Venus – practice love in two directions: an assimilative love that makes all souls the mirrors of divine *carità* and a reflective love that unites them, each to each, as distinct individuals. As John Took has shown, this twinned love is exemplified in these cantos of *Paradiso*, particularly in the notion that the soul would "inluiarsi" in God or "intuarsi" in its neighbour.[129] Without sacrificing one's identity as a singular participant in that reflection, one also realizes the truth of one's reality as grounded in the source of being itself, thus effacing – without annulling – the boundary that separates self from other.

As much as the figure of Carlo Martello celebrates human diversity and the particular affections which it bears as its fruit, his example also transcends that celebration as it shifts its focus from the beauties of the fruits of the diverse human forest to the ground of those beauties. Despite the resplendent and reciprocal joy of the beginning of the encounter, the meeting between Dante and his one-time friend ends unsentimentally, as Carlo suddenly returns his focus to the sun:

> E già la vita di quel lume santo
> rivolta s'era al Sol che la rïempie
> come quel ben ch'a ogne cosa è tanto.

[And already the life of that holy light had turned back to the Sun that fills it, as to the Good that is sufficient to everything.][130]

As swiftly and ardently as he had descended to speak with the pilgrim, so abruptly ("E già") does Carlo return his full attention from the bounteous fruits of *carità*'s abundant diffusion to the ground of beatitude itself. His redirected focus anticipates the contemplations of the blessed in their truth, which is sated only by the attention to the source of that truth. In other words, Carlo redirects his attention away from particular affection to affection itself.

Piccarda's first words to the pilgrim suggest that the heavenly court would reflect God's likeness ("che vuol simile a sé tutta sua corte").[131] But as each soul makes herself into a mirror of divine likeness, she does not abandon her individuality and alterity. To become "amico di Dio" means to become God's *alter idem*, united in will and reflective of charity, mirroring the source of love so as to enhance and intensify it, and in so doing realizing the fullness of both self and other as simultaneously single hypostasis and as substance.

The Eclipse of Friendship

We have seen, then, that friendship in the realms of salvation must be transmuted from its previous instantiations. It must uncover concord where there had been willful self-interest; it must move beyond preference without abandoning hierarchy; it must recognize the difference of each one while maintaining focus on the collective identity of all beings as divine Being. What then, in light of this discussion, are we to make of Beatrice's appellation "l'amico mio, e non de la ventura," with which I began this book? I have argued above that certain forms of friendship, in *Purgatorio* relabeled as brotherhood, act as a training ground for participation in *carità*. When friendships are goal-directed, oriented towards virtue, mutually beneficial, non-competitive, and non-possessive, they aid in the mastery of the "sense of virtue" towards which the practices of purgation mean to dispose the penitents. The pilgrim, too, must reorient his friendships – including his attachment to Beatrice – around these new practices. It is nothing new to say that Beatrice is the pilgrim's unique conduit to God's love.[132] But, we must ask ourselves, what will happen to his particular attachment to her once the pilgrim's soul has formally attained Paradise? Will he still consider her his beloved Beatrice, his mediator of divine love? And will she still call him "l'amico mio"?

Much as Anna Harrison has identified across Saint Bernard's Sermons, *Paradiso* offers conflicting answers to the question of special attachments between the saints.[133] The blessed retain their identifying characteristics, names, faces, and memories (cleansed of sin); and yet they simultaneously abandon anything that does not cohere with divine will. Vulnerability, special intimacy, preference – these conditions of human love cannot remain in the glory of eternity, particularly once that glory is enjoyed in its fullest expression following the resurrection of the body.

The theoretical abandonment of particular affections upon realizing one's beatitude, however, stands in tension with the much-discussed passage in *Paradiso* 14, as the souls react with visible delight at Solomon's account of the resurrection of the flesh:

> Tanto mi parver súbiti e accorti
> e l'uno e l'altro coro a dicer "Amme!"
> che ben mostrar disio d'i corpi morti,
> forse non pur per lor, ma per le mamme,
> per li padri, e per li altri che fuor cari
> anzi che fosser sempiterne fiamme.

> [So swift and eager were both choruses to say "Amen!" that they well showed their desire for their dead bodies, perhaps not for themselves alone, but for their mamas, for their fathers, and for the others who were dear to them before they became sempiternal flames.][134]

While the passage often elicits commentary on the souls' desire for the glorified body – a desire that paradoxically suggests that the bliss of Paradise is somehow incomplete – what is more puzzling here is the poet's justification of that desire: that the souls yearn not only for their own bodies but also for those that belong to "li altri che fuor cari."[135] In other words, each soul desires that his or her dearest companions will be reunited with their own bodies, so that these beloved souls may once again become visible and embraceable. Gabriele Muresu cautions readers not to indulge their own nostalgia or oversentimentality in considering these verses, claiming that "la dimensione del quotidiano e del familiare è del tutto estranea alla rappresentazione del Paradiso" [the dimension of the quotidian and the familiar is completely foreign to the representation of Paradise].[136] While Muresu may rightly recognize the risk of oversentimentality here, his caution to the reader seems misplaced: the text encourages the reader to indulge human affections here, as the poet himself has used a domestic explanation to justify paradisiacal bliss.

Manuele Gragnolati, by contrast, shows no such caution, reading the passage in *Paradiso* 14 as a demonstration of Dante's originality on questions of the sociability of the saints.[137] Gragnolati explains Dante's innovation thus:

> Bonaventure, for instance, writes that every saint is equally close to all the other saints: with the resurrection of the body, one will rejoice in other people's happiness as much as in one's own; in fact, Peter will rejoice in Linus's happiness even more than Linus does. What Dante's Solomon expresses is much more intimate than Bonaventure because it is not Peter rejoicing in Linus's and anyone else's glory, but each individual rejoicing at the idea of reunification with his or her dearest loved ones.[138]

Building on this interpretation in a later essay, Gragnolati reaffirms his earlier reading: "Dante's poem reveals that once one has relinquished earthly attachments and attained the beatific vision, one may again desire what is important for one's individuality. In the world of the *Commedia*, even in Heaven one is allowed, or even encouraged, to retain one's desires for oneself, for one's body and for the persons who mattered and continue to matter to one."[139]

The passage certainly seems to bear this out: each soul burns brightly and resounds its "Amme" to celebrate the recovery of the visible, tangible, embraceable body. The blessed respond with increased ardor as they anticipate the bliss of their paradisiacal companions, in which each one may mirror one's own bliss in the bodies and faces of all one's brothers and sisters in the heavenly family. But the passage here is clear: it is not each for all, but each for his or her own "cari," those who had been dear to them during their lives, the *passato remoto* of the verb making clear that this refers to an earthly and lived nostalgia for past loves. That they would again rejoice at the sight of the bodies of these dear ones implies their continued attachment to them.

It is not Solomon who expresses such intimacy, though, as Gragnolati claims. Instead it is the poet, who seeks to comprehend and justify the intensified ardor the pilgrim witnesses in the blessed souls. "Forse," perhaps, the poet says, the flash of enthusiasm displays their eagerness for their loved ones to be reunited with their bodies, as if an expression of their continued affection for them. Rachel Jacoff, perhaps attentive to the "forse" of the passage, is more cautious than Gragnolati without dismissing the possibility outright, as does Muresu. She notes, "*If* the desire for the bodies of those who were dear before they became sempiternal flames is legitimate, there is indeed room in heaven for our specific affective histories."[140] An equally plausible explanation here, which Jacoff's "if" and Dante's "forse" leaves open, is that the all-too-human poet has misinterpreted the particular affection of the saints for "li altri che fuor cari." Perhaps his still-human sensibility seeks to domesticate the intimacy of the saints – that it is not merely Peter rejoicing in Linus's happiness but Peter specifically rejoicing in the happiness of *his* friend. Exulting in the particular love his Beatrice has shown and continues to show him, relishing the beauty of her glorified eyes and smile, the poet perhaps misreads these cues as coherent with his own limited perception of paradisiacal community. Perhaps the poet's domestic, familiar, human explanation of the saints' celebratory "Amme!" misses the mark.

That the still-human poet may cling to the particular attachments of earthly existence is suggested by the pilgrim's momentary glimpse of full, ecstatic attention in *Paradiso* 10, just as he and Beatrice ascend to the Sun, where the conversation with Solomon will unfold. It is an easily overlooked, fleeting exchange, but one that remains suggestive of the ways in which particular friendships will not be displaced but eclipsed by the fires of heavenly ardor. To prepare for the ascent, the pilgrim centres all his attention on the intense light of the "quarta famiglia/

de l'alto Padre, che sempre la sazia" [fourth family of the high Father, who always satisfies them].[141] Beatrice, encouraging his concentration by stoking his gratitude, exclaims:

> Ringrazia,
> ringrazia il Sol de li angeli, ch' a questo
> sensibil t'ha levato per sua grazia!

> [Give thanks, give thanks to the Sun of the angels, who to this visible one has lifted you with his grace!][142]

Much as he had seen Carlo Martello do at the end of their encounter in the previous canto, the pilgrim directs his focus towards the Sun and its abundant light. Heartened by Beatrice's words, and bypassing her eyes, her smile, and her splendor, the pilgrim concentrates his awareness and his love exclusively on the source, unmediated by any other intercessor:

> Cor di mortal non fu mai sì digesto
> a divozione e a rendersi a Dio
> con tutto 'l suo gradir cotanto presto,
> come a quelle parole mi fec' io,
> e sì tutto 'l mio amore in lui si mise
> che Beatrice eclissò ne l'oblio.

> [Mortal heart has never been so concentrated to devotion and so swift to surrender itself to God with all consent, as at those words I became, and I so placed all my love in him that it eclipsed Beatrice with forgetfulness.][143]

The eclipse of Beatrice ("Beatrice eclissò") – as well as the pilgrim's capacity to forget her momentarily ("l'oblio") in his fleeting rapturous attention to divine Being – foreshadows the pilgrim's direct encounter with God, appropriately guided by Bernard of Clairvaux after Beatrice has ascended to rejoin the heavenly ranks.[144] But they also foreshadow the eventual subsumption of the pilgrim's particular attachment to his beloved Beatrice in his refocused attentions.[145] Directed by Beatrice's call to gratitude, the pilgrim does not supplant her as object of his affection, but instead passes through her love to "rendersi a Dio/ con tutto 'l suo gradir." The eclipse of Beatrice's love is not a displacement but a dilation, as his ardor enlarges to accommodate his increased affections.

Beatrice's response to her own eclipse in the pilgrim's mind confirms that he has directed his attentions correctly. The pilgrim forgets Beatrice only for a passing moment – immediately afterwards, he will again see her laughing eyes and dazzling smile, which will bring him back from the marvel of the unified Creator to the plurality of created phenomena. That smile is triggered by her approval of his forgetfulness:

> Non le dispiacque, ma sì se ne rise
> che lo splendor de li occhi suoi ridenti
> mia mente unita in più cose divise.

[She was not displeased but so smiled that the splendor of her laughing eyes divided my united mind into a plurality of things.][146]

She assents to his forgetting her, but the smile that accompanies her assent brings him back from his absorption into the highest order to the lower (though still splendid) beauty of creation. In the flash of *dilectio Dei* enjoyed in this moment, all lower forms of love have been subsumed into the one love of *carità*, which directs its devotion and concentration entirely on the source, conforming its agency to the divine will, and rendering all other loves the specular reflections of this central focus.[147] In this glimpse of ecstatic vision, the pilgrim finds his mind "unita," united with the divine mind as its *alter idem*: other, but so conjoined with it in likeness as to behold the "forma universal" [universal knot] that is the ground of being.[148] The plurality of creation is not resolved in the unity Dante glimpses, but is coextensive with it.

We may have expected the *Commedia*, in its encyclopedism or its sacrality, to resolve the dilemmas of friendship that have been discussed in this book. But the *Commedia* offers little resolution, instead answering the wisdom of a Solomon with the poet's persistent "forse." As all the texts under discussion in this book have shown, Dante is a poet who delights in unresolved paradoxes, tensions, dilemmas, and doubts. It is no accident that *Paradiso* in particular fluctuates between fixed doctrinal knowledge and spontaneous human practice, between ardent conviction and implacable doubt. The battle between doubt and certainty – a battle that drives the will to cohere with the intellect, so that it can sustain its clashes with the heavens, which would incline it towards incoherence – is at the very root of what it means to be human.[149] Confronting the irresolvable ambiguities of being in the world, both alone and with others, is for Dante our most pressing ethical responsibility.

The ethical dilemmas friendship raises for the medieval Christian poet – inclusivity and exclusivity, disinterestedness and advantage, hierarchy and equality, difference and identity – remain unsettled in the *Commedia.* These dilemmas are not resolved in the figure of Beatrice and her personal affection for the pilgrim. Hers is not a new and special friendship that reduces the ethical ambiguities of this relationship to a singular, inimitable reconciliation of *eros*, *philia*, and *caritas* in one unique instantiation. Beatrice's friendship is, rather, an intensification of those ambiguities, her particular affection for the pilgrim becoming the mirror through which the complexities and contradictions friendship introduces in Christian ethics are reflected and amplified.

In their particularity and alterity, each of our friends sustains us in the project of becoming ourselves, unfolding the coherence in our identities, and, in their distinction from us, mirroring back to us our uniqueness. At the same time, the boundaries of those plural and differentiated identities become, in the light of divine love, as distinct as a pearl on a white forehead. Within an "anthropology of the at-least-two," particular loves dilate, accommodating first a third, then a fourth, and so forth, until they embrace all within their diffuse grasp. It is thus that these individual attachments participate in the love that is God. The intersubjective love of the one for the other – an *alter idem* which, in its distinctiveness, reveals its likeness both with the one and with the divine – unfolds through the various paradoxes of relational identity and social life. In the final analysis, the dilemmas of friendship stand, sustained by the poet's unrelenting "forse." From this eschatological perspective, then, friendship is not an end but a beginning.

Epilogue: Friendship's Afterlife in Early Humanism

Within the genealogy of Western conceptions of friendship, the *Commedia*'s eschatological view would leave neither an immediate nor a lasting mark. The poem's attempt to sit with the tensions that friendship had created within late medieval ethical discourses – especially in their theological and soteriological expressions – would not profoundly shape the theories and practices of sociability promoted by the generation of early humanist writers that would follow. The early Italian humanists, Boccaccio and Petrarch chief among them, would emphasize the versatility and range of human friendship, its indisputable usefulness not only for moral growth and intellectual refinement, but also for self-interested promotion and personal advantage.[1] They favoured an expansive, adaptive attitude towards friendship that would eventually turn *amistà*, *amicizia*, and *amicitia* into such capacious terms that Renaissance Florentines could apply them to describe any number of their strategic social relationships.[2] In this way, they lean more on Dante's *opere minori* and the contemporary works with which they are engaged, and not his poetic and theological masterpiece, the *Commedia.* The *Commedia*'s eschatological picture of human sociability – and the specific tensions it sought to embrace – was inadequate to describe the word *amico*'s flexibility in the complex and multifaceted urban social spheres of late-Trecento and Quattrocento Italy.

Unlike what we see in the *Commedia*, however, the innovative, strategic, adaptable uses of the language of friendship evidenced elsewhere in Dante's works (and in those of his interlocutors) would resonate with the early humanist writers. Dante's *opere minori* and those with which they are in dialogue would anticipate the complex negotiations appropriate to the kind of worldly relationships that would become central to the humanists' conception of social life. The early humanists inherited their forebears' calculated language of *amistà* and *amicitia* and deployed it to great advantage across social and ethical discourses. The flexibility of friendship terms among the early humanists is frequently attributed to the revitalization of classical (especially Stoic) ideals found in the works of Cicero and Seneca, or to the social reorganization precipitated by the devastating plague of 1348.[3] The intellectual and social upheaval wrought by these changes cannot be underestimated. But, as this book has demonstrated, Italian vernacular authors had already for decades been expanding and reimagining the possibilities of friendship, beyond so-called *vera amicitia*, to accommodate an expansive and diverse array of social relations, encompassing not only conventional kinds of friendships but also those driven by rivalry, fealty, self-interest, sponsorship, collaboration, patronage, clientage. As we have seen, late-Duecento and early-Trecento writers did not root *amistà* in an abstract conception of sociability. Instead, they would deploy the term strategically, leaning into friendship's various roles across the range of human relationships in urban life. Their writings would refashion the role of private friendship within dynamic systems of exchange, in which one's *amici* could do much more than make one a better person. Dante and his interlocutors had sought to negotiate around the tensions friendship raised for the late medieval Christian writer: inclusivity or exclusivity, disinterestedness or self-interest, equality or hierarchy, likeness or difference. In their use of the language of *amistà*, they show they are committed to the possibility that friendship would accommodate paradoxical ethical standpoints and straddle multiple (even conflicting) social positions. They viewed their friendships as embedded within overlapping networks of honour, authority, power, reputation, and fame. Attending to the ways that the language of friendship is determined by strategic practice, and how friendships themselves are embedded in multiple networks, we can more clearly see how the practical interventions of Dante and his interlocutors anticipate those of the succeeding generation of writers. Their articulations of both friendship's problems and its possibilities lay the groundwork for how their immediate successors – the early humanists – would validate the various, complex, flexible, and sometimes morally ambivalent forms that friendship could take across the social spectrum.

The humanist conception of friendship was far from monolithic. Authors used the term "amico" to denote a wide range of relationships, from spouses to business partners, patrons to disciples. In his sociological study of Quattrocento letters, Paul D. McLean observes, "in Florence, the word *amici* (friends) has several meanings, from very general ones to very particular ones.... Readers of letters had to figure out which level of generality of *amicizia* was meant by letter writers who invoked it, but the wording also left the meaning ambiguous, to allow petitioners to reframe their intentions after the fact."[4] Instrumental relationships, like those McLean has examined, frequently used the capacious language of *amicizia*, particularly in relationships of mutual benefit like patronage. Far from representing a cynicism or scepticism about friendship – as the great historian of medieval monastic friendship Brian Patrick McGuire would have it – the humanists instead wholeheartedly celebrated complex and multifaceted human relationships, particularly as they are expressed through *amistà* or *amicitia*.[5] Where McGuire's monks may have viewed friendship through the narrow lens of a *vera amicitia* – directed solely towards the production of Christian virtue – Petrarch, Boccaccio, and their immediate successors adopted the wide-ranging definitions and practices of friendship that their predecessors had promoted and disputed.[6]

Whatever their disputes around the specific constructions, duties, objectives, and advantages of private friendship, the worth as such of cultivating personal attachments was, for the humanists, never a matter of dispute. As historians Carolyn James and Bill Kent have suggested, "new and old ideas about friendship, as well as friendships themselves of almost every variety imaginable, flourished" across Europe in the two centuries following Dante's death.[7] Across literary genres – letters, diaries, commonplace books, translations, and so forth – evidence makes plain that, as James and Kent claim, "words denoting friendship were on almost everyone's lips."[8] Indeed, humanist writers took as a given both the moral and the instrumental value of private friendship. In several noteworthy instances, they used the theme of friendship as the backdrop for ostentatious displays of literary prowess: Boccaccio, for one, used friendship in an early letter as a "proving ground" through which he could display his literary talents to a friend.[9] Likewise, it is not for nothing that friendship would be the subject of the *Certame coronario* Leon Battista Alberti would organize in 1441, through the patronage of Piero de' Medici.[10] In each of these cases, the value of friendship is asserted as an established fact, so that the participants can use it as a template through which to exhibit their literary and philosophical prowess. While they debated the possibility of achieving Ciceronian *vera amicitia* (virtue friendship in the strictest sense) in the real world of political and instrumental advantage, or while they disputed whether communities of friends should come together in Stoic manliness or in compassionate vulnerability, they did not hesitate to praise friendship as the vehicle through which their ends could be achieved.[11] They did not question, as their predecessors had, whether friendship itself was good for the makeup of human society. Private friendship, even in its instrumental forms, would not be treated as suspect but as precious, even invaluable.

The contrast between theory (where friendship was construed along the lines of Ciceronian *vera amicitia*) and practice (where one would speak equally of prospective patrons, political allies, and distant acquaintances as *amici*) is manifest across the corpora of the leading luminaries of early humanism. Boccaccio, for one, celebrates in theoretical terms the likeness generated by *vera amicitia* in his fictions, while simultaneously in his correspondence he utilizes the language of friendship to secure very strategic practical objectives.[12] In his discussion of Boccaccio's take on friendship in his epistles to two friends of his youth, for example, Jason Houston describes a letter from Boccaccio to his friend Niccolò Acciaiuoli, in which "Boccaccio undertakes the rather delicate task of converting Acciaiuoli from a friend to a patron."[13] Employing a steady stream of classical tropes and exemplary friendships, Boccaccio attempts to flatter his Neapolitan friend with the laudatory language of classical *amicitia* to secure his sponsorship. His attempt apparently fails. But the readiness with which Boccaccio relies on the language of friendship to bring about personal advantage – and, especially, the seeming lack of ethical unease the author feels in eliding the rhetoric of *vera amicitia* with that of self-interest or across status divides – suggests that the previous generation of writers have succeeded in resolving the tensions that had plagued their broader application of the terms *amico*, *amistà*, and *amicitia* in their own works. Even a figure of stalwart ideals and resolute moral commitments such as Petrarch employed the term to strategic ends and with internal contradictions, applying it to both distant patrons and intimate allies.[14] As Hannah Wojciehowski has observed, in his correspondence Petrarch would speak even of patrons with deep and abiding affection.[15] Boccaccio and Petrarch alike use the term "amicus" to refer equally to patrons as to intimates without any of the apparent discomfiture we saw in chapter 3, for example, where I discussed Dante's apologia for using the term in his address to his patron Cangrande della Scala.

In their celebration of friendship's complexities and ambiguities, the early humanists show themselves the heirs of Dante and his interlocutors. I do not mean to suggest that Petrarch, Boccaccio, and their contemporaries pored over, for example, Dante's *De vulgari eloquentia* or Epistle to Cangrande and so deeply assimilated Dante's approach to *amicitia* with a collaborator or a sponsor that they were then enabled to straddle the same conflicting social and ethical positions in their own correspondence. I would contend, however, that it is crucial to read the *amicitia* theorized and practiced by the early humanists as part of a continuum with the generation of writers immediately preceding theirs, and not, as it often has been, as the result of a cultural and ideological rupture. In considering the writings of the later generation as part of a continuum, we can see more precisely how the negotiations of the earlier generation impacted the social, political, and literary friendships sought and cultivated by the early humanists, for whom friendship became the most critical and most flexible category of social engagement.

Notes

Introduction: The Dilemmas of Friendship in Dante's Italy

1 *Inferno* 2.61. This and all citations and translations of Dante's *Divine Comedy* follow *The Divine Comedy of Dante Alighieri*, ed., and trans. Robert M. Durling, introduction and notes by Ronald L. Martinez and Robert M. Durling, 3 vols.

2 See, most prominently, Modesto, *Dante's Idea of Friendship*. See also Ciabattoni, "Dante's Rhetoric of Friendship"; Maldina, "A Classicising Friar"; Masciandaro, *The Stranger as Friend*, 27–8; Mazzaro, "From *Fin Amour* to Friendship."

3 *De amicitia* 26. All citations and translations of Cicero's dialogue follow Cicero, *How to be a Friend.* I have also consulted Falconer's translation of *De amicitia* for the Loeb Classical Library.

4 Mews, "Cicero and the Boundaries of Friendship," 376.

5 The relationship is implicit in *Convivio* 2.12.3, when he professes that he turned to *De amicitia* for consolation after Beatrice's death. But he reserves the terms of friendship in that text for abstractions, chiefly the Italian vernacular and Lady Philosophy.

6 On the three terms, which are used relatively interchangeably across Dante's works (with *amistà* appearing most frequently, by a slim margin), see the contributions on the terms "amica," "amicizia," "amico," "amistà," and "amistanza," by Pasquini in *Enciclopedia dantesca.* See also Pasquini, "Concezione e lessico."

7 I borrow the term "poetic agora" from Barolini, "Semantics of Friendship," 49. See also Barolini, "A Young Man."

8 Wojciehowski, "Petrarch: First Modern Friend."

9 On the disruption in friendship theory caused by the introduction of Aristotle's *Ethica Nicomachea* to medieval Christian ethics, see Sère, *Penser l'amitié*, 17.

10 On the changes in the discourse of friendship in the early years of secular humanism, see James and Kent, "Renaissance Friendships," 116. See also Sère, *Penser l'amitié.*

11 In addition to the two essays cited above ("A Young Man" and "Semantics of Friendship"), see also the relevant introductory essays in Barolini, *Dante's Lyric Poetry*, and her discussion in "Sociology of the *Brigata.*"

12 McLean, *The Art of the Network*, 15.

13 James and Kent, "Renaissance Friendships," 117.

14 On pre-Christian and early Christian responses to the incompatibility between universal love and particular friendship, see Cassidy, "He Who Has Friends"; White, *Christian Friendship*. On friendship in monastic rule and thought across the Middle Ages, see McGuire, *Friendship and Community*.

15 The phrase is McGuire's (*Friendship and Community*, 231).

16 For an overview of the language of *amicitia* in these letters, see Haseldine, "Friendship Networks in Medieval Europe," 6988; Haseldine, "Friends or *amici*?" See also McGuire, *Friendship and Community*. For specific studies on individual letter-writers, see Haseldine, "The Politics of Friendship"; Haseldine, "Friends, Friendship and Networks"; Haseldine, "The Friendship Circle of Peter of Celle"; McLoughlin, "*Amicitia* in Practice"; Nederman, "Theory and Practice."

17 See Haseldine, "Friends or *amici*?," on the contrasting languages of personal affection and of impersonal *amicitia* in the letter collections of the twelfth-century monastic luminaries.

18 McEvoy, "Aelred of Rievaulx's 'De spirituali amicitia,'" 402. On Aelred's treatise, in addition to McEvoy, see Classen, "Introduction," in *Friendship in the Middle Ages*; McGuire, *Friendship and Community*; Mews, "Cicero and the Boundaries of Friendship."

19 On the resistance to Aelred's views from within his own community and in the immediate wake of his abbacy, see McGuire, *Friendship and Community*.

20 Critical assessments of Cicero's legacy among twelfth-century writers are available in McEvoy, "The Theory of Friendship"; Mews, "Cicero and the Boundaries of Friendship"; Ziolkowski, "Twelfth-Century Understandings." As a testament both to the staying power of Cicero's *De amicitia* across the Middle Ages, and to its resurgence of popularity in the twelfth century, Mews cites an astonishing statistic: of extant medieval manuscript copies of the *De amicitia*, scholars have discovered three dating from the ninth century, three from the tenth, twelve from the eleventh, and some forty from the twelfth.

21 *De amicitia* 20. On the uses of the citation, see Mews, "Cicero and the Boundaries of Friendship," 373 and 380.

22 Mews, "Cicero and the Boundaries of Friendship."

23 *De amicitia* 15.

24 *De amicitia* 32.

25 *De amicitia* 15.

26 For a compelling challenge to the notion that the good of friendship is necessarily a moral good, see Nehamas, "The Good of Friendship"; and Nehamas, *On Friendship*.

27 In fact, Pangle has suggested that even Cicero did not share Laelius's idealized view, as the exacting demands of friendship in Laelius's account are irreconcilable with the particularities of competitive urban life in the Republic. See Pangle, *Aristotle and the Philosophy of Friendship*.

28 Nathan, *Amicitia di Maestro Boncompagno da Signa*, 10. All following citations of the Latin text come from Nathan's edition, with English translations from *Boncompagno da Signa*, trans. Dunne.

29 See, for example, Peraldus's chapter "De vera amicitia" (1.4.15), which leans on Ciceronian idealizations throughout: Guilelmus Peraldi, *Summa virtutum ac vitiorum*. See also the sermon of Servasanto da Faenza, who unites friendship with Christ to the Apostolic mission, and who leans on Seneca, Aristotle, and other classical authorities to differentiate true from false friendship. Both examples are discussed in Maldina, "A Classicising Friar."

30 The voice of Reason, the arbiter of the dialogue, concludes the discussion by drawing the distinction (following Augustine's *City of God*) between earthly and heavenly friendship, and claims that Soul has only elected to discuss heavenly friendship in her response to Body's questions. This is a puzzling claim for Reason to make, given that the bulk of Soul's response consists of listing the twenty-three types of false friendship. See the discussions of Boncompagno da Signa's *Amicitia* in McGuire, *Friendship and Community*, 379–82; Mews and Chiavaroli, "The Latin West," 91–3.

31 Boncompagno, *Amicitia* 12.

32 Boncompagno, *Amicitia* 19 and 30. See also McGuire, *Friendship and Community*, 381.

33 Boncompagno, *Amicitia* 39.

34 I have amended Dunne's translation here. See the discussion in Cicero, *De amicitia* 69–73. On Boncompagno's desire to distance his theory from Cicero's, while maintaining that Cicero is his principal adversary, see Nathan's preface to her edition of the *Amicitia*, 24–5.

35 Boncompagno, *Amicitia* 39.

36 Boncompagno's treatise was not without its own imitators, most prominently Brunetto Latini, who relies on Soul's enumeration of false friends to draw distinctions with *vera amistà* in his *Favolello*.

37 See *Convivio* 2.12.3: "E udendo ancora che Tulio scritto avea un altro libro, nel quale, trattando dell'Amistade, avea toccate parole della consolazione di Lelio, uomo eccellentissimo, nella morte di Scipione amico suo, misimi a leggere quello" [And hearing further that Tully had written another book in which, while discussing Friendship, he had addressed words of consolation to Laelius, a man of the highest merit, upon the death of his friend Scipio, I set about reading it]. All citations of *Convivio* follow Fioravanti's edition, included in Dante Alighieri, *Opere. Volume secondo: Convivio, Monarchia, Epistole, Egloge*, eds. Fioravanti et al. Translations are cited from *Il Convivio (The Banquet)*, trans. Lansing.

38 See De Robertis, *Il libro della* Vita Nuova. See also Modesto's reading of *eros*-as-*amicitia* in the pilgrim's relationship to Beatrice in the *Commedia*, which is one of the central premises of her 2015 book *Dante's Idea of Friendship*.

39 McGuire, *Friendship and Community*, 404.

40 *Ethica Nicomachea* 8.3 (1156a6–b32).

41 I will refer throughout to the Latin translations of Aristotelian terms, relying on the Grosseteste translation: Aristoteles Latinus, *Ethica Nicomachea, traslatio Roberti Grosseteste Lincolniensis sive 'Liber Ethicorum,'* ed. Gauthier. Translations of Grosseteste's Latin are my own.

42 *Ethica Nicomachea* 9.5 (1167a12).

43 On the dispute in the commentaries over whether or not friendship is a virtue, given the puzzling assertion that opens Aristotle's account of friendship, "Est enim virtus quaedam vel cum virtute" [for it is a virtue or it involves virtue], see Sère, *Penser l'amitié*, 68–76. On Aristotelian friendship as activity, see Pangle, *Philosophy of Friendship*, 55.

44 *Ethica Nicomachea* 8.1 (1155a20–22). On the exclusive and preferential nature of Ciceronian friendship, see *De amicitia* 20: "ita contracta res est et adducta in augustum, ut omnis caritas aut inter duos aut inter paucos iungeretur" [friendship is selective so that its affection joins together only two or at most a few people].

45 *Ethica Nicomachea* 8.8 (1159b1–2).

46 On the many and varied responses to the question of equality in friendships, see Sère, *Penser l'amitié*, especially chapter 3, "Amitié et ordre social: Réduction d'une aporie," 101–51.

47 *Sententia libri Ethicorum* L. VIII, lectio 8 (1649): "Sic enim, dum se invicem amant secundum suam dignitatem, etiam illi qui sunt inaequalis condicionis poterunt esse amici, quia per hoc aequabuntur; dum unus eorum quo magis deficit in bonitate, aut in quacumque excellentia, eo plus amat" [Thus, when people love one another according to their worth, even those who are of unequal condition can be friends because they are made equal in this way – provided that the one who is more lacking in goodness or some other excellence loves that much more]. Latin citations of the *Sententia* here and throughout are from the Library of Latin Texts edition of *Sententia libri Ethicorum*, ed. Leonina. The English translation is that of Litzinger.

48 *Sententia libri Ethicorum* L. VIII, lectio 7 (1632). See also Sére, *Penser l'amitié*, 104.

49 Later traditions would upend Thomas's prohibitions on friendships with God and the king. In fact, in the fourteenth and fifteenth centuries, commentators reversed Thomas's position entirely, claiming that the only virtuous friendships in political life are those between kings and their subjects, and disavowing as false the friendships of equals in organizations like confraternities. See Sère, *Penser l'amitié*.

50 In *Penser l'amitié*, Sère conducts a careful historical analysis of what she calls the "acculturation" of the *Nicomachean Ethics* from the thirteenth to the fifteenth centuries. Although much of her work treats commentaries that postdate the period under consideration here, her analysis of the Albert-Thomas line of thought is relevant to the present discussion.

51 Liuzzo Scorpo, *Friendship in Medieval Iberia*, 18; McEvoy, "The Theory of Friendship," 30–2.

52 Classen, "Introduction," in *Friendship in the Middle Ages*, eds. Classen and Sandidge,37–9; Liuzzo Scorpo, *Friendship in Medieval Iberia*, 19–20; Sère, *Penser l'amitié*, 67–100 and

270–84. On Christian *caritas* and classical *amicitia*, see McEvoy, "The Theory of Friendship," 30–2.

53 Sère, *Penser l'amitié*, 67. For a discussion of how this plays out in the commentaries, see her chapter "Amitié et vertu: Réemploi d'un *topos*," 67–100.

54 See, for example, Thomas, who clarifies that such friends do not love "quod ipse in se" [what he is in himself], but only what is incidental to him. *Sententia libri Ethicorum* L. VIII, lectio 3 (1566).

55 As Sère comments, "Pour les médiévaux, le langage est clair: l'ami, c'est l'allié" [For medieval people, the language is clear: a friend is an ally] (*Penser l'amitié*, 15).

56 See Liuzzo Scorpo, *Friendship in Medieval Iberia*, 16 and 19–20.

57 See again Sère's claim that the introduction of Aristotle's works into late medieval Latin Christendom produced "un choc sensible" [a perceptible shock] on mid-thirteenth-century intellectual culture across Europe (*Penser l'amitié*, 17). See also McEvoy, "The Theory of Friendship," 13–15 and 25–9.

58 Ciabattoni alludes briefly to the distinction in his essay "Dante's Rhetoric of Friendship," 100. Modesto explores each of the ancient thinkers in turn, in relation to *Convivio*, although she sees the two ancient authors as fundamentally in line with one another on friendship: see "Classical Friendship: Aristotle and Dante's *Convivio*," 20–42, and "Cicero's *De Amicitia* and Dante's *Convivio*," 43–57, in *Dante's Idea of Friendship*.

59 Brunetto Latini alludes across his works to friendship's pivotal role in fostering civic peace, particularly in the *Tresor*, but also in the *Rettorica*, as will be discussed below in chapter 1. In the *Favolello*, which closely follows Boncompagno's *Amicitia*, Brunetto is more cynical about the practice of friendship within intellectual society, but he nevertheless insists that "verace amicizia" has the power to bind individuals and spur them towards developing virtue, even within corrupt environments. Citations from *Li Livres dou Tresor* are from Brunetto Latini, *Li Livres dou Tresor*, eds. Baldwin and Barrette. English translation cited from Brunetto Latini, *The Book of the Treasure (Li Livres dou Tresor)*, trans. Barrette and Baldwin.

60 *Li Livres dou Tresor* 2.43.6.

61 *Li Livres dou Tresor* 2.105.

62 *Li Livres dou Tresor* 2.106.

63 *Li Livres dou Tresor* 2.43.3.

64 *Li Livres dou Tresor* 2.104.1.

65 See, most notably, De Robertis, *Il libro della* Vita nuova; Mazzaro, "From *Fin Amour* to Friendship," 121–37; Modesto, *Dante's Idea of Friendship*. On Dante's reliance on classical friendship theory more broadly, see Falzone, "Il *Convivio* e l'amicizia," 55–101; Sebastio, "Un tema dantesco: l'amicizia," 347–63.

66 On "transformation," see the titles of two recent studies of the friendship theme in Dante's works: Mazzaro, "From *Fin Amour* to Friendship: Dante's Transformation," and Modesto, *Dante's Idea of Friendship: The Transformation of a Classical Concept*. "New" and "special" are Ciabattoni's words ("Dante's Rhetoric," 97), and "spiritual friendship" is from Modesto, *Dante's Idea of Friendship*, 19.

67 See, for example Armour, "Friends and Patrons," 102–30; Barolini, "A Young Man"; Ciabattoni, "Dante's Rhetoric of Friendship"; Modesto, *Dante's Idea of Friendship*, 75–92. There is of course also a vast bibliography on Dante's relationships with individual friends, such as Cino da Pistoia, Forese Donati, and, chiefly, Guido Cavalcanti.

68 *De amicitia* 20.

69 On Beatrice as friend, see most notably Mazzaro, "From *Fin Amour* to Friendship," 121–37; Modesto, *Dante's Idea of Friendship*, especially 93–133. On Virgil, see especially Masciandaro, *The Stranger as Friend*, 24–8; Modesto, *Dante's Idea of Friendship*, 93–114; Raffa, "A Beautiful Friendship," S72–S80.

70 Bourdieu, *Outline of a Theory of Practice*, especially 1–30 and 72–95; Bourdieu, *The Logic of Practice*, trans. Nice, especially 52–134. See also Swartz's chapters "Habitus: A Cultural Theory of Action" (95–116) and "Fields of Struggle for Power" (117–42) in *Culture and Power: The Sociology of Pierre Bourdieu.*

71 Bourdieu, *Outline of a Theory of Practice*, 12; Bourdieu, *The Logic of Practice*, 100.

72 Bourdieu, *The Logic of Practice*, 100.

73 Mullett, "Power, Relations, and Networks," 257.

74 On friendship in monastic life, see Haseldine, "Monastic Friendship in Theory and Action," eds. Classen and Sandidge, 349–93; Haseldine, "Friends or *amici*?," 43–58; Haseldine, "The Politics of Friendship in the Letters of Peter the Venerable," 251–80; Haseldine, "Friends, Friendship and Networks in the Letters of Bernard of Clairvaux," 243–80; Haseldine, "The Friendship Circle of Peter of Celle," 237–60; McGuire, *Friendship and Community*; McLoughlin, "*Amicitia* in Practice: John of Salisbury," 165–81. On aristocratic and courtly literature and culture, see Hyatte, *The Arts of Friendship*; Jaeger, *Ennobling Love.* For the specific case study of the shifting rhetoric of friendship at the court of Alfonso X of Castile, see Liuzzo Scorpo, *Friendship in Medieval Iberia.* On friendship in academic and intellectual circles, and especially but not exclusively Scholasticism, see Lefler, *Theologizing Friendship*; McLoughlin, "*Amicitia* in Practice: John of Salisbury," 165–81; Nederman, "Friendship in Public Life," 385–97; Schwartz, *Aquinas on Friendship*; Sère, *Penser l'amitié.*

75 On epistolary friendship in the medieval period, see the works of Haseldine, cited throughout, as well as Delle Donne, "*Amicus amico*: l'amicizia nella pratica epistolare del XIII secolo," 107–26; Hartmann, "L'*amicitia* nei primi comuni italiani," 31–55; Hartmann, "Eloquence and Friendship," eds. Steckel, Gaul, and Grünbart, 67–86; McLoughlin, "*Amicitia* in Practice: John of Salisbury," 165–81. On letters and networks in the Renaissance, see, among others, Kent, *Friendship, Love, and Trust*; McLean, *The Art of the Network*; Najemy, *Between Friends.*

76 The phrase comes from Sère (*Penser l'amitié*, 385), who credits Jean Buridan's original commentary on the *Ethics* with articulating a new theory of humanist friendship which would emerge differently across the regions of Europe, following the decade 1340–50. On the civic humanists, see Sère, *Penser l'amitié*, 370–85. Although Sère

sees this theory of friendship first articulated in Buridan, I contend that similar discussions already animate, albeit less explicitly, the ways in which the Italian vernacular writers of the preceding generation employed the language of *amicizia* and *amistà*.

77 The literature on humanist conceptions of friendship is vast. See, for example, Classen, "Introduction," in *Friendship in the Middle Ages*, 60–7; Fenzi, "Petrarca e la scrittura dell'amicizia," ed. Berra, 549–89; Hyatte, *The Arts of Friendship*; James and Kent, "Renaissance Friendships"; Kent, *Friendship, Love and Trust*; Kircher, *Living Well*, especially 187–94; Langer, *Perfect Friendship*; Sère, *Penser l'amitié*, 370–85; Sherberg, *The Governance of Friendship*; Wojciehowski, "Petrarch and His Friends," eds. Ascoli and Falkeid, 26–35; Wojciehowski, "Petrarch: First Modern Friend," 269–98. See also the collection of essays in *Friendship and Sociability in Premodern Europe: Contexts, Concepts, and Expressions*eds. Gill and Prodan.

78 On the various ways *amicitia* is used to describe diverse social relations in the Renaissance, see, for example, Hyatte, "Complementary Humanistic Models," 251–61; Leushuis, *Le mariage et l'"amitié courtoise"*; McCue Gill, "Vera Amicizia"; Wojciehowski, "Petrarch and His Friends," 26–35; Wojciehowski, "Petrarch: First Modern Friend," 269–98. See also the essays collected in the volume edited by McCue Gill and Prodan (*Friendship and Sociability*), particularly Baker, "Italian *Familiaritas* and Petrarch's Community of Friends," 125–52; and Sacks, "Commercial Exchange as a Form of Friendship in Renaissance Thought," 273–312.

79 Although I will reference other works of Dante's (most notably *Convivio*) throughout, I do not give those works extensive treatment, because of the great distinction between the figurative approach to friendship in those works and its tactical use for strategic social intervention in the four principal texts treated here.

80 On Bourdieu's theory of *champs*, see especially, "Séminaires sur le concept du champ, 1972–1975," reprinted with introduction by Champagne, 4–37. An overview of Bourdieu's theory can be found in Swartz, *Culture and Power*, 117–42.

81 In his collected "Séminaires," Bourdieu notes, "Dans un champ, on joue à un jeu déterminé qu'il faut définir à chaque fois dans sa spécificité" [In a field, one plays a precise game that must be defined each time in its specificity] (13).

1 Exclusivity: The Piazza

1 Lewis, *The Four Loves*, 75.

2 *Vita nova* 16.10 [25.10] and 21.1 [32.1]. Citations from the *Vita nova* follow Gorni's edition, with his numbering. This and all citations of *Vita nova* are from Dante Alighieri, *Opere. Volume primo: Rime, Vita nova, De vulgari eloquentia*, eds. Giunta, Gorni, and Tavoni. I have included Barbi's chapter divisions in brackets following each citation. Unless otherwise noted, translations of the *Vita nova* are cited from Dante Alighieri, *Vita Nova*, trans. Frisardi. Here I have slightly amended Frisardi's translation.

3 *Vita nova* 2.1 [3.14].
4 *Vita nova* 2.1 [3.14], 15.3 [24.3], 15.6 [24.6], 16.10 [25.10], 19.10 [30.3], and 21.1 [32.1].
5 *Convivio* 2.12.3–5.
6 The most prominent recent intervention to favour the biographical reading is Modesto's chapter on Cavalcanti in *Dante's Idea of Friendship*, 79–84.
7 The ideological reading tends to be more common, and often these interpretations will weave biographical concerns (especially over the poets' supposed "falling out") into the discussion of ideological conflict. On ideological distinctions between Dante and Guido, see, for example, several of the essays in Ardizzone, *Guido Cavalcanti tra i suoi lettori*. See also Ardizzone, *Guido Cavalcanti: The Other Middle Ages*; Ciabattoni, "Dante's Rhetoric of Friendship," eds. Gill and Prodan, 97–123; Ghetti, *L'ombra di Cavalcanti e Dante*; Hainsworth, "Cavalcanti in the *Vita Nuova*," 586–90; Harrison, *The Body of Beatrice* 69–90; Malato, *Dante e Guido Cavalcanti*; Tanturli, "Guido Cavalcanti contro Dante," eds. Gavazzeni and Gorni, 3–13.
8 See *Purgatorio* 11.97–9. On the "Oedipal drama" and "Oedipal structure" of this relationship, see Harrison, *Body of Beatrice*, 82–3. On the two Guidos referred to in the tercet, see Barolini, *Dante's Poets*, 123–53; Bowe, *Poetry in Dialogue*, 123–37.
9 Barolini, "A Young Man," 39–61, particularly 58–9.
10 In addition to Barolini, "A Young Man," see also the relevant introductory essays in her *Dante's Lyric Poetry*; and Barolini, "Dante and the Semantics of Friendship," 46–69.
11 Barolini, "Semantics of Friendship," 49.
12 I borrow the metaphor of the piazza from Ahern, "The Reader on the Piazza," 18–39.
13 On the *tenzone* and *rime di corrispondenza* see Giunta, *Due saggi sulla tenzone*; Giunta, *Versi a un destinatario*; Kleinhenz, "Adventures in Textuality"ed. Robins; Santangelo, *Le tenzoni poetiche*.
14 Lewis, *The Four Loves*, 75.
15 See, for example, the late-thirteenth-century sermons of Servasanto da Faenza, whose engagement with Cicero, Seneca, Boethius, Valerius Maximus, and Aristotle is demonstrated by Maldina, "A Classicising Friar," eds. Gaimari and Keen, 30–45.
16 *Amistade d'envidia è medicina*, vv. 3–4: "preziosa è sua vertude fina / e bono è 'l maggio di natura umana" [its refined power is precious, and it is the highest good of human nature]. The text of the sonnet follows Guittone d'Arezzo, *Rime*, ed. Egidi, 243. Translations are mine.
17 *Amistade d'envidia è medicina*, vv. 5–8: "Luce del mondo e spezial larga vina, / che 'n terra fai di bene onni fontana, / pane de vita e de dolzor cocina, / devina grazia en lei giunge mondana" [Light of the world and particularly generous vein, that produce every fountain of good on earth, bread of life and sweet sustenance, in it divine grace is joined to the worldly].
18 *Amistade d'envidia è medicina*, vv. 12–14: "Vivendo senza lei mort'è ciascono, / e pover tutto'l piú ricco signore, / e miser fort' e vil tutto 'l piú caro" [Living without her is death for anyone, and the richest lord becomes completely poor, and the strong wretched and what is dearest all worthless].

19 On the tradition of female *invidia* from Ovid and Andreas Capellanus to Italian Renaissance humanists and poets, see Feng, "Desiring Subjects," ed. Falkeid and Feng, 75–91.

20 For Guittone's theory of envy, see the corresponding sonnet in the cycle of the vices, *Invidia, tu nemica a catun see.*

21 *Inferno* 1.109–11.

22 Indeed, Guittone may have believed that there is no inherent philosophical conflict between the Aristotelian model of individual friendship and the Christian model of a universal brotherhood. See Margueron, "La notion d'amitié," 415.

23 On the civic benefits of literary friendship, see Margueron's remark ("La notion d'amitié," 422): "Guittone groupe autour de sa personne une société d'esprits qui goûtent l'étude ou la controverse portant sur la poésie, la morale, la théologie, une république littéraire qui coiffe les multiples communes de l'Italie centrale du *Duecento*" [Guittone gathers around himself a society of minds who enjoy the study or debate over poetry, morality, theology, a republic of letters that covers the numerous *comuni* of central Italy in the Duecento].

24 On the correlation between vernacular correspondence poems and oratorical disputation ("tencione o tacita o espressa," *Rettorica* 76.16), see Ahern, "The New Life of the Book," 2–3; Giunta, *Versi a un destinatario*, 176–81; Milner, "The Limits of Civic Republican Discourse," 172; Steinberg, *Accounting for Dante*, 71. Citations from Brunetto's *Rettorica* follow *La Rettorica di Brunetto Latini*, ed. Maggini. Translations are my own.

25 Copeland and Sluiter, *Medieval Grammar and Rhetoric*, 754. See also Cox, "Ciceronian Rhetoric in Italy," 239–88; Cox, "Ciceronian Rhetoric in Late Medieval Italy"; Milner, "The Limits of Civic Republican Discourse"; Milner, "Communication, Consensus and Conflict," 365–401; Steinberg, *Accounting for Dante*, 70–3.

26 *Rettorica* 2.5.

27 On the use of the terminology of *amicitia* within twelfth-century *artes dictandi*, see Hartmann, "L'*amicitia* nei primi comuni italiani," 44–5. On Boncompagno's *Amicitia* and Brunetto's *Favolello*, see Introduction, above.

28 *Rettorica* 2.6.

29 On the exclusionary nature of the cultivation of these bonds, crucial to the present study, see Milner, "The Limits of Civic Republican Discourse."

30 *Rettorica* 1.4.

31 *Rettorica* 1.10.

32 I will return to the instrumental relationship between Brunetto and "suo porto" [his port] below, in chapter 2.

33 Cox and Milner have both emphasized the "adversarial nature of Ciceronian rhetorical instruction … and its moral ambivalence relative to prevailing Christian speech ethics, attributes which perfectly suited the conflictual arena on communal politics in this period" (Milner, "Communication, Consensus, and Conflict," 369).

34 Milner, "The Limits of Civic Republican Discourse," 173.

35 *Rettorica* 2.2.

36 On the *tenzone* as a social tool to negotiate one's literary standing, see Ahern, "The Reader on the Piazza"; Alfie, *Dante's Tenzone*; Barolini, "A Young Man"; Bowe, *Poetry in Dialogue*, especially 3–9; Giunta, *Due saggi sulla tenzone*; Giunta, *Versi a un destinatario*; Steinberg, *Accounting for Dante*, especially 61–94. Much of the following discussion of friendship practices in *tenzone* exchanges was also elaborated in Coggeshall, "Jousting with Verse."

37 Bowe convincingly argues that the *tenzone* is more properly considered a "mode" than a "genre"; see *Poetry in Dialogue*, 7: "there is a procedural aspect to the *tenzone* that justifies a categorical blurring for which 'genre' may not sufficiently allow. *Tenzoni* play out through the interaction between texts." Giunta draws distinctions between a formal *tenzone* and other *rime di corrispondenza*; see especially *Versi a un destinatario*, 168–9. I consider the *tenzone* a more public enterprise than Giunta does: I disagree with Giunta's classification of certain themes as "private" and instead treat all the poetry under analysis here as being performed for an audience greater than the two explicit interlocutors.

38 For discussion of the impact of conflictual communal politics on rhetorical conventions in the late medieval period, see especially Milner, "Communication, Consensus, and Conflict."

39 I borrow the metaphor of the *agora*, entirely appropriate to descriptions of public and competitive lyric exchange among late-Duecento poets, from Barolini. "A Young Man," 40.

40 See Steinberg, *Accounting for Dante*, 145: "Whether it was experienced primarily as a private or public document, Vaticano 3793 illustrates how early vernacular texts were experienced in specific social 'places.' The manuscript was produced by merchant elite writers for merchant elite readers, and later possessors of the manuscript were also drawn from the mercantile and bourgeois classes. Many of the poets collected in the anthology were representative of the political elite in thirteenth-century Florence, and their participation in the culture of the *tenzone*, attested to in the various *tenzoni* in the sonnet section, underlines the importance of Italian poetry for maintaining political and social cohesiveness. Ultimately, the Vatican anthology demonstrates the municipality of contemporary poetry, how it portrayed, served, and reinforced specific social groups."

41 Antonio da Tempo, *Summa artis rithmici vulgaris dictaminis*, par. 62, cited in Giunta, *Due saggi*, 11.

42 Gidino da Sommacompagna, *Trattato e arte de li Rithimi volgari* 8.5, cited in Giunta, *Due saggi*, 15. My emphasis.

43 Bourdieu, *The Logic of Practice*, 100.

44 Bourdieu, *The Logic of Practice*, 100.

45 Bourdieu, *The Logic of Practice*, 81.

46 Bourdieu, *The Logic of Practice*, 100.

47 Kumar, "Reading *Tenzoni* in a Ludic Key." For readings of communal lyric exchanges in a key of irony or aggression, see Barolini, "A Young Man"; Barolini,

"Semantics of Friendship"; Martinez, "Specter of Idolatry," 297–324. On the role of vituperation and insult within *tenzoni* see Alfie, *Dante's Tenzone*. On the aggressive use of the term "amico" in the exchange between Dante Alighieri and Dante da Maiano, see especially Barolini, whose essay "A Young Man" reads the exchange as polluting with rivalry the practice of authentic *amicizia* between poets.

48 On the exchange, specifically the abbot's tactful rebuke, see Kleinhenz, *The Early Italian Sonnet*, 64–8.

49 *De amicitia* 88–9: "Una illa sublevanda offensio est, ut et utilitas in amicitia et fides retineatur; nam et monendi amici saepe sunt et obiurgandi, et haec accipienda amice *cum benevole fiunt* … Molesta veritas, siquidem ex ea nascitur odium, quod est venenum amicitiae; sed obsequium multo molestius, quod peccatis indulgens praecipitem amicum ferri sinit" [And one occasion for offense we must learn to accept if we want a friendship that is useful and trustworthy is listening to the advice and criticism of a friend *when given in the spirit of goodwill* … Truth can indeed be troublesome if it brings about hatred, which is poison to friendship; but much worse is the kind of indulgence and acquiescence that allows a friend to rush headlong into destructive behaviour]. Emphasis added. I am grateful to Akash Kumar for this insight.

50 On friendship across Guittone's works, primarily in the letters, see Margueron, "La notion d'amitié." On dialogism in his pre- and post-conversion poetry, see Bowe, *Poetry in Dialogue*, 21–58.

51 Kleinhenz, *The Early Italian Sonnet*, 94–7; Barolini, "Semantics of Friendship," 48–9. Bowe offers an astute analysis of the changing shape of Guittonian dialogue over the course of the poet's career through close readings of Guittone's exchanges with "Mastro Bandino, amico." See *Poetry in Dialogue*, 50–7.

52 On the coherence of group identity among Guittonian poets, see Hainsworth, "Dante and Monte Andrea," eds. Barnes and Petrie, 153–77.

53 Peter Hainsworth points out that the Guittonian poets, Monte Andrea included, tend to exhibit a distinctive "internal coherence as a group" ("Dante and Monte Andrea," 153) that sets them apart from their peers and interlocutors within communal literary networks. Their repeated calls for friendship with their interlocutors are symptomatic of their striking group identity.

54 On the formal elements of the exchange, see the discussion in Hainsworth, "Dante and Monte Andrea," 161–2.

55 For the scant biographical information on Schiatta di Albizzo Pallavillani, see the entry "Schiatta Pallavillani" in Asor Rosa, *Letteratura italiana. Gli autori*, vol. 8.2, 1607.

56 Hainsworth, "Dante and Monte Andrea," 155.

57 Monte Andrea's lyrics are cited from Monte Andrea, *Rime*, ed. Minetti. On this exchange, Minetti glosses: "La tenzone è promossa da Schiatta, cui lo zelo amicable … vieta di rimanere indifferente di fronte alle chiacchiere che rampollano, sempre meno benevoli, intorno agli eccessi dell'appassionatissimo ed … imprudente compagno" [The *tenzone* is initiated by Schiatta, whose friendly zeal … prevents him

from remaining indifferent in the face of the increasingly less kindly chatter that is arising about the excesses of their very impassioned and … reckless companion]. See Monte Andrea, *Rime*, 168.

58 In their political exchange, a *sonetto raddoppiato* written "a quattro mani," which begins *Non isperate, ghibellin', socorso,* it is Schiatta who uses the epithet for Monte (3, 20). Monte does not replicate Schiatta's choice of epithet, identifying Schiatta instead by his (opposing) political affiliation, "ghibellin'" (1, 25).

59 Monte Andrea, *Rime*, 178.

60 For a subtle reading of the politics that inform their exchanges (in particular Cavalcanti's *Una figura della donna mia* and Orlandi's response *S'avessi detto, amico, di Maria*), see Alfie, "Politics and Not Poetics," 209–24. On the ideological differences evidenced in the same exchange, see Martinez, "Specter of Idolatry," 297–324.

61 Martinez, "Specter of Idolotry," 311.

62 The word "amico" in fact only appears once in Cavalcanti's corpus, addressed to Bernardo da Bologna, whom he calls "Bernardo amico mio."

63 See Barolini, "A Young Man," 58–9.

64 Steinberg discusses the "specter of insincerity" that troubles the culture of the *tenzone*, which emphasizes the ritual elements of exchange over the moral power of the message (*Accounting for Dante*, 79).

65 The precise date of the sonnet exchange is impossible to determine. Of Giannini, the only surviving record of his activities in Pisa is dated to 1283. Because Si. Gui. cannot be identified with confidence, scholars cannot be certain of the dates of the exchange; but it can reliably be placed in the second half of the thirteenth century, probably in the last two decades. See Contini, *Poeti del Duecento*, vol. I, 331–3.

66 The Italian text follows Contini, *Poeti del Duecento*, 332. My translation.

67 Contini, following Zambrini, identifies the poet as Siribuono iudice, whose name was corrupted in the manuscript and so appears Si. Gui. instead of Si. Giu.; Zaccagnini, by contrast, claims that Si. Gui. should be identified either as "Similiante quondam Guidi" or a "Signorante di Giunta di porta Guidi," which identification Contini refutes. See *Poeti del Duecento*, 331.

68 In addition to his reply to Giannini, only one sonnet remains; like the reply to Giannini, this sonnet appears only in the Laurentian manuscript Redi 9 and appears as part of a *tenzone*).

69 "Il rimatore pisano aveva ricercato d'amicizia il Pistoiese, la cui fama, dic'egli, era arrivata ai suoi orecchi, e questi si mostra ben lieto d'essergli amico. Le altre parole di lode, colle quali il Giannini esalta il merito del Pistoiese, a cui tanto desidera di farsi conoscere … ci farebbero credere che nel misterioso Si. Gui. si nascondesse un poeta di vaglia; ma d'altra parte si pensi che *anche poeti mediocrissimi* allora si scambiavano con molta disinvoltura le piú sperticate lodi" [The Pisan poet had sought friendship with the Pistoian, whose fame, he says, had reached his ears, and the latter is happy to be his friend. The other words of praise, with which Giannini exalts the worth of the Pistoian, whose acquaintance he greatly desires to make …

would make us believe that a poet of great worth is hidden behind the mysterious Si. Gui.; but on the other hand, one might presume that at the time *even very mediocre poets* exchanged the most lavish praises with great ease] (my emphasis). Zaccagnini, *I rimatori pistoiesi*, ci–cii.

70 The exception is Giunta (*Versi a un destinatario*, 167–70), who discusses the exchange briefly, characterizing it as a private exchange between two biographical friends that has no explicit subject matter. I would counter that the subject matter of the exchange is the theory of friendship itself, and that it is more appropriate to read these texts as a theoretical intervention than an occasional exchange.

71 Cf. Giunta, *Versi a un destinatario*, 168–9.

72 See *Rettorica* 3: "Ma quelli il quale s'arma sie d'eloquenzia che non possa guerriare contro il bene del paese, ma possa per esso pugnare, questo mi pare uomo e cittadino utilissimo et amicissimo alle sue et alle publiche ragioni" [But he who arms himself with eloquence – not to wage war against the good of his country, but to fight for it – he seems to me a very useful man and citizen, deeply committed to his own interests and to those of the general public]. I will return to this citation below.

73 On the verb "pugnare" across Dante's corpus, see Bufano, *Enciclopedia dantesca*, s.v. "pugnare"; Kleinhenz, "Reading the *Divine Comedy*," 76–7.

74 Barolini, "Semantics of Friendship," 49. See also "A Young Man," 40 and 56.

75 On *tenzone*-participation as a mirror of "deliberative democracy" in the communal setting, see also Steinberg, *Accounting for Dante*, 71.

76 We might see the use of friendship terminology in these contentious poems as participating in the same "aestheticizing" of political division that Steinberg identifies in the compilation of Vaticano 3793. See *Accounting for Dante*, 72.

77 Barolini, "A Young Man," 59–60. See also Pasquini, "Concezione e lessico," 147–50.

78 See Pasquini, "Concezione e lessico," 147, following Marti, "Introduzione," in *Poeti del Dolce stil nuovo*, 22–3. See also Marti's entry on the "Stil nuovo" in the *Enciclopedia dantesca*, where he writes, "Questa spinta verso il nuovo fu vivamente sentita dal gruppo dei poeti stilnovisti, che amarono quasi rinchiudersi in un loro raffinato isolamento, differenziandosi e caratterizzandosi" [This push towards the new was deeply felt by the group of stilnovist poets, who loved to almost close themselves off in their cultivated isolation, differentiating themselves and setting themselves apart]. He goes on to claim that the group members are united in a friendship based on stylistic and ideological affinities.

79 See Barolini, "A Young Man," 59–60: "The fact that Dante writes one of the world's great poems of friendship without using the word 'amico' suggests that the word was still redolent to him of rivalry and competition, that – at least when used in poetry, where it had such a clear history – it still betokens a ritualized formula of address used between two men who are rivals, not friends." See also Pasquini, "Concezione e lessico," 148.

80 On the unique vision of friendship put forth in *Guido, i' vorrei*, see also Fontes Baratto, "L'amitié en questions," 9–28.

81 On the sonnet's relationship to the *plazer*, see Kleinhenz, *The Early Italian Sonnet*, 215.

82 The text of the poem follows Giunta's edition in Dante Alighieri, *Opere. Volume primo: Rime, Vita nova, De vulgari eloquentia*, eds. Giunta, Gorni, and Tavoni. The English text comes from Barolini's edition, with Lansing's translation: *Dante's Lyric Poetry: Poems of Youth and of the 'Vita Nuova' (1283–1292).*

83 Barolini, "Guido, i' vorrei che tu e Lapo ed io," in *Dante's Lyric Poetry*, 115.

84 Arendt, "Philosophy and Politics," 80.

85 Arendt, "Philosophy and Politics," 82.

86 *Rettorica* 3: "Ma quelli il quale s'arma sie d'eloquenzia che non possa guerriare contra il bene del paese, ma possa per esso pugnare, questo mi pare uomo e cittadino utilissimo et amicissimo alle sue et alle publiche ragioni" [But he who arms himself with eloquence – not to wage war against the good of his country, but to fight for it – he seems to me a very useful man and citizen, deeply committed to his own interests and to those of the general public]. We should, of course, note Brunetto's use of the adjective "amicissimo" to describe the commitments of the man who would fight for the common good.

87 Lewis, *The Four Loves*, 75.

88 Barolini notes a similar movement in Dante's sonnet *Sonar bracchetti*, in which the poet describes the ways that the experience of love excludes him from masculine company, feminizing him. *Sonar bracchetti*, in contrast to *Guido, i' vorrei*, does not celebrate this exclusionary impulse: it is marked by an "ambivalence" about the abandonment of masculine values to dedicate oneself wholeheartedly to the feminized sphere of Love's faithful. See Barolini's essay on *Sonar bracchetti e cacciatori aizzare* in her edition of *Dante's Lyric Poetry*, 107–8.

89 *De amicitia* 20. Laelius restricts the best forms of friendship even further, claiming that in all of history only two or three such pairs of friends have existed.

90 See the introductory essay on *Guido, i' vorrei che tu e Lapo ed io* in Barolini's edition of *Dante's Lyric Poetry*, 113–21. Barolini sees this insistence in the grammatical staccato of the first verse, which distinguishes each of the three names – laid out in polysyndeton – only to combine them in the second to a single "noi." She calls this a "distant preview" of *Paradiso*'s attempts to articulate in verse the mystery of the Trinity, which is itself a model of the solidarity of the souls in Paradise (*Dante's Lyric Poetry*, 116). At issue, I would argue, is that the antisocial impulse at the heart of the sonnet needs to be addressed, before this exclusionary vision of friendship can resonate with the radically inclusive model of paradisiacal friendship. I return to this argument in the final chapter, on the *Commedia.*

91 Barolini, *Dante's Lyric Poetry*, 115.

92 Barolini argues that, in much the same way that the Trinity is Three in One and One in Three, so these friends, carried along "al voler vostro e mio," "vivendo sempre in un talento," are simultaneously three individuals who are of one mind and one fancy. Barolini, *Dante's Lyric Poetry*, 116.

93 Barolini, *Dante's Lyric Poetry*, 107–8.

94 On Guido's *risposta* as indicative of particularly Cavalcantian themes, see West, "A Short-Lived Enchantment," 17–25.

95 Milner, "The Limits of Civic Republican Discourse," 163–4.

96 *Vita nova* 1.20 [3.9]. The "fedeli d'amore" return later in the narrative, called out by the sonnet *Venite a 'ntender li sospiri miei*, which addresses the "cor gentili." In the accompanying divisions, the speaker explains that in the first part he calls "li fedeli d'amore, che m'intendano." See *Vita nova* 21.4–5 [32.4–5].

97 *Vita nova* 1.20 [3.9].

98 *Vita nova* 2.1 [3.14].

99 *Vita nova* 2.1 [3.14].

100 See De Robertis, *Il libro della "Vita Nuova"*; Singleton, *An Essay on the* Vita Nuova. De Robertis's classic study of the *Vita nova*, which argues for Dante's dependence on Cicero's *De amicitia* for his articulation of the theory of disinterested love at the centre of the *Vita nova*'s discourse. The exclusionary vision of friendship that undergirds the *libello*'s picture of social relations is the flipside of the celebratory readings of friendship's blessings that frequently appear in *Vita nova* criticism; in addition to De Robertis, see Mazzotta, "Language of Poetry," 1–16; Modesto, *Dante's Idea of Friendship*, 79–84; among others.

101 *Vita nova* 2.3 [4.1]. Over Frisardi's "spitefully curious," which captures the spirit of Dante's term, I have opted for a more literal translation, in order to emphasize the contrast between the "amici" in the previous sentence with the "invidia" of these slanderers.

102 On the spatial metaphors of the piazza and the bedchamber in the *Vita nova*, see Ahern, "The Reader on the Piazza," and Ahern, "The Implied Reader."

103 *Vita nova* 21.1 [32.1].

104 Gorni, "*Vita nova*, libro delle 'amistadi' e della 'prima etade,'" in *Dante prima della* Commedia, 133–47, especially 138–9.

105 Aelred, for example, lists the "quatuor gradus" of perfect friendship as *electio*, *probatio*, *admissio*, and "rerum divinarum et humanarum cum quadam charitate et benevolentia summa consensio" (cited in Gorni, *Dante prima della* Commedia, 138).

106 *Conferences* 16.14.1–2. This and all citations from the *Collationes patrum* are taken from John Cassian, *Opera omnia*. The translation is cited from John Cassian: *The Conferences*, trans. by Ramsay.

107 *Conferences* 16.14.4.

108 Indeed, I find it unlikely that the young Dante derived his notion of the hierarchical ranking of friends from Cassian, given the divergence in the greater concerns of their respective works. Cassian's principal concern in *Conference* 16, "De amicitia," is with the preservation of a friendship against its dissolution, especially resulting from anger and blame. Within this broader discussion appears the short intervention on preferential love. The similarities in their use of the term to suggest a hierarchical ranking among friends are, nevertheless, worthy of note.

109 Even the *fedeli d'amore* are subject to the division of in-group from out-group, as they are differentiated according to their intellective capacities. As if it is not enough to restrict his audience to those who are true servants of love, the speaker categorizes even these "fedeli d'amore" according to a strict, hierarchical ranking: "questo dubbio è impossibile a solver a chi non fosse in simile grado fedele d'Amore" [this obscurity cannot be resolved by one who is not, to a similar degree, one of Love's faithful] (*Vita nova* 7.14 [14.14]).

110 For discussion of "insiders" and "outsiders" in the *Commedia*, particularly as regards citizenship, see Honess, *From Florence to the Heavenly City*, 14–36 and 71–106.

111 *Vita nova* 10.33 [19.22]. The same restrictive move happens later in the narrative, as the speaker divides the audience into "chi non guarda sottilmente" [who doesn't consider things subtly] and "chi sottilmente le mira" [whoever subtly looks at them] (*Vita nova* 22.2 [33.2]). See also Durling's brief gesture at Dante's "scornful elitism" towards his audience in *Vita nova*, as compared to his post-exilic works: Durling, "The Audience(s)," 28–9.

112 See, for example, Gorni's note that the addition is "dettata da modestia" [dictated by modesty], and Stefano Carrai's comment, which calls this a "professione di modestia" [declaration of modesty].

113 *Vita nova* 16.10 [25.10].

114 On the use of personal pronoun "noi" in *Guido, i' vorrei*, see Barolini, *Dante's Lyric Poetry*, 116, and above.

115 See Giunta, *Due saggi sulla tenzone*, 80–2.

116 Bowe has likewise discussed Dante's moves towards "erasure or absorption of the lyric past," particularly in terms of the *Commedia*. See especially the concluding remarks of his *Poetry in Dialogue*, 205–8 (citation 208).

117 On Dante's poem and Cecco's critical reply, *Dante Alighier, Cecco, tu' serv'e amico*, see Barolini, *Dante's Lyric Poetry*, 294–300.

118 *Vita nova* 27.6 [38.6].

119 *Vita nova* 5.24 [12.17].

120 *Vita nova* 1.1 [1.1].

121 See Gorni's note to *Vita nova* 16.1: "persona indefinita, che forse, dopo le speculazioni del precedente paragrafo, non è inopportuno identificare con Guido Cavalcanti, singolarmente degno di chiarimento su ogni punto" [undetermined person, who perhaps, after the speculations of the previous paragraph, it is not inappropriate to identify with Guido Cavalcanti, uniquely worthy of clarification on every point].

122 I draw the idea of Guido's "haunting" the *Vita nova* from Harrison, "The Ghost of Guido Cavalcanti," in *The Body of Beatrice*, 69–90, and his "The Ghost of Guido Cavalcanti, Revisited," in Ardizzone, *Guido Cavalcanti tra i suoi lettori*, 119–30.

123 Mazzotta pits the fullness of conversation with Cavalcanti against the silence of Beatrice: "Friendship comes forth as a metaphor for an intellectual conversation, for a certain benevolence of minds on account of which the two friends, in good will,

'turn together,' exchange and communicate ideas, share the secrets of their craft, decipher and penetrate each other's fablings" ("Language of Poetry," 5).

124 *Vita nova* 1.13 [3.2].

125 The suggestion is Marco Santagata's, in his biography of the poet: *Dante: The Story of His Life*, 7–8.

126 *Vita nova* 7.1 [14.1] and 27.4 [38.4], with some slight difference in the phrase.

127 Bowe has discussed these dialogic practices in the poetry of Guido Cavalcanti, which he calls a performance of "polyphonic identity." See *Poetry in Dialogue*, 104–14.

128 *Vita nova* 14.24 [23.24]: vv. 54–6 of the *canzone Donna pietosa e di novella etate.*

129 *Vita nova* 14.5 [23.5]. Emphasis added.

130 Arendt, "Philosophy and Politics," 86. Suzanne Stern-Gillet argues that this being-with-oneself is also the root of Aristotle's theory of friendship; see her *Aristotle's Philosophy of Friendship*.

131 *Vita nova* 14.3 [23.3]. See also *Vita nova* 10.10 [18.8], 24.3 [35.3], 27.2 [38.2], 29.2 [40.2], 29.3 [40.3], 29.4 [40.4], and 29.5 [40.5].

132 Ahern, "Implied Reader," 8.

133 *Vita nova* 31.1 [42.1]. On the shift in audience in the last chapters of the *Vita nova*, see Luzzi, "Literary History and Individuality," 170–1.

134 On the concluding chapter of *Vita nova* as a "threshold of silence" at which the poet is suspended, see Harrison, *Body of Beatrice*, 129–43: "The futurity that claims the work as a whole pervades these moments of silence" (141).

135 Giunta makes a similar claim in *Due saggi sulla tenzone*, 80–2. On the construction of *auctoritas* in the *Vita nova*, see Ascoli, *Dante and the Making*, especially 178–201.

136 See *Purgatorio* 24.52–60.

2 Self-Interest: The University

1 On the shifts in Dante's poetic practice during this "periodo di radicali ripensamenti," and especially the role of Cino da Pistoia as interlocutor and foil for these shifts, see Livraghi, "Dante (e Cino)," 65.

2 The precise dating of *De vulgari* – as well as the roughly contemporaneous *Convivio* – is debated. As will be discussed, Mirko Tavoni assigns composition of *De vulgari* to the period from mid-1304 to mid-1306, during which Tavoni conjectures a sojourn in the city of Bologna. Marco Santagata's biography largely follows Tavoni, assigning composition to the years 1304–6. In his recent biography, Giorgio Inglese gives a slightly earlier *terminus ante quem*: February 1305. Petrocchi, earlier, had argued for even earlier dates: between autumn 1303 and winter 1304, although he concedes that the second book might have been composed later than this. See the discussions in Inglese, *Vita di Dante*, 82–3; Petrocchi, *Vita di Dante*, 108; Santagata, *Dante*, 174–86; Tavoni, "Introduzione," in *De vulgari eloquentia*, ed. Tavoni, in Dante Alighieri, *Opere. Volume primo: Rime, Vita nova, De vulgari eloquentia.*

3 On Cino as imitator, see De Robertis, "Cino e le 'imitazioni'," 103–77; Marrani, "Ai margini della *Vita Nova*," 757–76. The reference to Cino as "stopgap" comes from Teodolinda Barolini, *Dante's Poets*, 135. On Cino's relationship to the city of Bologna and its literary circles, see De Robertis, "Cino e i poeti bolognesi," 273–312; Tavoni, "Introduzione," 1092–6, 1110–16. On Cino's distinct contributions to Dante's poetic development and to the landscape of Trecento literature and culture, see especially the collected essays in Arqués Corominas and Tranfaglia's volume *Cino da Pistoia nella storia della poesia italiana*. See also Brugnolo, "Cino (e Onesto) dentro e fuori la *Commedia*," 369–86; Hollander, "Dante and Cino da Pistoia," 201–31; Livraghi, "Dante (e Cino)," 55–98; Picone, "Dante e Cino: Una lunga amicizia," 39–54; Scott, "Cino da Pistoia and Dante," 26–37.

4 See Ascoli, *Dante and the Making*, 149–69; Barolini, "Semantics of Friendship," 56–60. Barolini notes the lack of scholarly interest in what she calls the "semantic and ultimately philosophical content of this remarkable phrase," which she describes as "strangely alive and dynamic" ("Semantics of Friendship," 57).

5 Barolini, "Semantics of Friendship," 56–60.

6 See, for example, *De vulgari eloquentia* 1.15.6, where Dante lists four Bolognese poets (Guido Guinizzelli, Guido Ghislieri, Fabruzzo and Onesto), explaining that "doctores fuerunt illustres et vulgarium discretione repleti" [these were distinguished men of learning who fully understood the nature of the vernacular]. Citations of the text follow *De vulgari eloquentia*, ed. Tavoni, in Dante Alighieri, *Opere. Volume primo: Rime, Vita nova, De vulgari eloquentia*, eds. Giunta, Gorni, and Tavoni. Translations (with slight modifications, as indicated) of *De vulgari eloquentia* are from Dante, *De vulgari eloquentia*, trans. Botterill. On Cino's correspondence with other poets on the Bolognese literary scene, see De Robertis, "Cino e i poeti bolognesi." See Christopher Kleinhenz's remarks on Cino's role as mediator between literary schools in *The Early Italian Sonnet*, 148.

7 *De vulgari eloquentia* 1.19.1: "Hoc enim usi sunt doctores illustres qui lingua vulgari poetati sunt in Ytalia, ut Siculi, Apuli, Tusci, Romandioli, Lombardi, et utriusque Marchie viri" [This is the language used by the illustrious authors who have written vernacular poetry in Italy, whether they came from Sicily, Apulia, Toscany, Romagna, Lombardy, or either of the Marches]. On the "*curia* in exile," see Ascoli, *Dante and the Making*, 138. On exile as central condition of the poet's claims – personal, political, and poetic – in *De vulgari*, see Keen, *Dante and the City*, 92–122; Shapiro, *Dante's Book of Exile*.

8 "L'*Universitas* medievale si configura, in un certo senso, come 'fenomeno di massa,' intendendo l'espressione non solo nel senso numerico del termine 'massa,' ma anche e soprattutto in quello di coscienza di un vasto ed omogeneo strato della popolazione all'interno delle singole "città universitarie." Si trattò, infatti, dell'organizzarsi spontaneo in associazione, a difesa di precise aspirazioni e di veri o supposti diritti, da parte di una vastissima pluralità di soggetti, i quali costituivano – o aspiravano ad essere – l'élite del pensiero" [The medieval *Universitas* configures

itself, in a certain sense, as a "mass phenomenon," intending the expression not only in the numerical sense of the term "mass," but also and especially in that of the awareness of a vast and homogeneous stratum of the population inside the individual "university cities." In fact, it was a matter of organizing spontaneously in fellowship, in defense of precise aspirations and of real or presupposed rights, on behalf of an extremely vast plurality of subjects, who constituted – or aspired to be – the intellectual elite]. The intellectual community surrounding the university is, in Luigi Pellegrini's definition, a collective association of individuals who aspire to the professionalization of knowledge. See Pellegrini, *L'incontro tra due "invenzioni" medievali*, 3–5 (citation pp. 3–4). On the professionalization of the "intellectual" and the legitimization of the academic class, see Le Goff, *Intellectuals in the Middle Ages*.

9 Terpstra, "Introduction," in *Bologna. Cultural Crossroads*, xvii–xxi (citations x. For a historical profile of the medieval city, see Milani, *Bologna*. On the intersections of academic and literary spheres in medieval Bologna, see Anselmi and Scioli, "Literary Culture in Bologna," 499–529.

10 Terpstra, "Introduction," xxi.

11 *De vulgari eloquentia* 1.15.6: "qui doctores fuerunt illustres et vulgarium discretione repleti" [Yet these were distinguished men of learning, who fully understood the nature of the vernacular].

12 See *De vulgari eloquentia* 1.15. On Bologna as an undoing of Babelic *confusio*, see Ascoli, *Dante and the Making*, 172–4.

13 Tavoni, "Introduzione," 1113–16. On Dante's relationship to Bologna, see also the studies of Pasquini, "Dante e Bologna," 277–96; and "Dante e lo Studio," 61–80.

14 See Tavoni, "Introduzione," especially 1067, 1113–16.

15 Tavoni, "Introduzione," 1115: "Dunque, ancor più che indizi del fatto che il trattato sia stato scritto *a* Bologna, io vedo in esso indizi che sia stato scritto *per* Bologna" (emphasis in original).

16 Tavoni, "Introduzione," 1092–6, 1113–16.

17 Tavoni, "Introduzione," 1095.

18 See, for example, Giorgio Inglese's biography, which rejects the notion that Dante was residing in Bologna during his authorship of *De vulgari eloquentia* – pointing instead to Gherardo da Camino's Treviso – but still conceding that Tavoni's "*per* Bologna" hypothesis is credible. Inglese, *Vita di Dante*, 83.

19 On the learned audience of *De vulgari eloquentia*, see Durling, "The Audience(s)," 29–32. On the *De vulgari*'s transhistorical notion of literary culture and its intersections with Dante's autobiography, see Luzzi, "Literary History and Individuality," 161–88.

20 On the dynamism of the university city and its related intellectual networks, see Pellegrini, *L'incontro tra due "invenzioni" medievali*, 3–5; Zaccagnini, *La vita dei maestri*.

21 Zaccagnini, *La vita dei maestri*, 33.

22 Zaccagnini, *La vita dei maestri*, 18–41.

23 Zaccagnini, *La vita dei maestri*, 31–3.

24 See Ruth Mazo Karras's discussions of disputational practices and bonding mechanisms as expressions of masculine development in "Separating the Men from the Beasts: Medieval Universities and Masculine Formation," in *From Boys to Men*, 67–108, especially 83–100. See also Zaccagnini, *La vita dei maestri*, 22–7. Zaccagnini describes the example of Ugolino di Zambono, "uno dei dottori di minor fama" [one of the *doctores* of lesser renown], who dared to challenge the great jurist Francesco d'Accorso. As a result of his challenge to Francesco's honor he was exiled by the Comune. Zaccagnini points out that the animosity between the professors did not extend to their disciples, with whom masters would often enter into close-knit friendships (27–8).

25 On Boncompagno's treatise, see the introduction above. See also Dunne, "Good Friends or Bad Friends?," 147–66.

26 On the "two Dantes" of *De vulgari eloquentia*, see Ascoli, *Dante and the Making*, 130–74.

27 Ascoli, *Dante and the Making*, 137.

28 Here I follow Inglese (*Vita di Dante*, 86–7), who argues that Dante worked on *De vulgari* from 1304 to 1306, and that he may have begun working on the first books of *Convivio* as early as 1304, even if the fourth book was certainly not begun until after the death of Gherardo da Camino in March 1306.

29 De Robertis, *Il libro della "Vita nova"*; Modesto, *Dante's Idea of Friendship*.

30 Barolini also notes the Ciceronian turn of the works in this period, but focuses her analysis on the relationship between friendship and the affirmation of individual identity as "alter idem" of the friend. See the discussion in Barolini, "Semantics of Friendship," 56–60.

31 Barolini, "Semantics of Friendship," 56. That the *De vulgari* engages in a performance of friendship is certainly the case, which is why in this project, at the intersections of sociology and literary criticism, I have chosen to focus on *De vulgari eloquentia*'s performance of friendship over *Convivio*'s philosophizing divorced from social life.

32 On the relationship between *De vulgari* and Aquinas's commentary on Aristotle's *Politics*, see Tavoni, "Introduzione," 1068: "È infatti nella pagina di apertura della *Politica* di Aristotele commentate da san Tommaso che Dante ha trovato la nozione di *locutio*, che egli pone come *subiectum* del suo trattato, definita come la facoltà distintiva dell'uomo che fa sì che l'uomo sia animale *politico*. Poiché il linguaggio è stato dato solo all'uomo; poiché il fine del linguaggio è che gli uomini possano comunicare fra loro circa il bene e il male, il giusto e l'inguisto, l'utile e il nocivo; e poiché la natura non fa nulla di inutile, ne consegue che l'uomo ha come proprio fine, per natura, la società civile" [It is in fact in the opening page of Aristotle's *Politics* commented by Saint Thomas that Dante found the notion of *locutio* (speech) that he poses as the *subiectum* (subject) of his treatise, defined as the distinctive faculty of man that makes man a *political*

animal. Since language was given only to man; since the purpose of language is that men can communicate with one another about good and evil, just and unjust, useful and harmful; and since nature does nothing useless, it follows that man has, by nature, civil society as his aim].

33 Ascoli, *Dante and the Making*, 167. See also Luzzi, "Literary History and Individuality," 162–6.

34 *De vulgari eloquentia* 1.2.5.

35 On *locutio* as revelation of self to other, see Rosier-Catach, "Dante, gli angeli e gli animali," 438–40.

36 On *amicabile commertium* and the social order, see Honess, *From Florence to the Heavenly City*, 152, with reference to Brunetto Latini.

37 Honess, *From Florence to the Heavenly City*, 152 n. 4. See also chapter 1, above.

38 See Guittone d'Arezzo's sonnet *Amistade d'envidia è medicina*, quoted and discussed above in chapter 1. See also Ascoli (*Dante and the Making*, 153), who uses the terminology of healing to describe the phenomenon of language, calling it a "necessary *remedy* for the limits of individual human reason" (my emphasis).

39 On Dante's polysemous conception of *civitas*, see Brilli, "*Civitas*/Community," 353–67. See also Honess, *From Florence to the Heavenly City*, especially 37–70; Keen, *Dante and the City*, especially 8–15; Lummus, *The City of Poetry*, especially chapter 2, "Dante Alighieri, Poet Without a City," 63–111.

40 *Rettorica* 2.5–6. See above, chapter 1.

41 See Ascoli, *Dante and the Making*, 151–4; Corti, "Dante e la Torre di Babele," 250–6; Luzzi, "Literary History and Individuality," 166.

42 *De vulgari eloquentia* 1.3.1.

43 See Ascoli, *Dante and the Making*, 152: "Throughout the text, in any case, Dante stresses that the tertiary Fall of Babel creates a historical situation where the *dispersio* and variety of dialects approach as a limit a condition of radical individuality and incommunicability. Every little town, each Petramala, thinks its 'proprium vulgare' is the best way of speaking (1.6.2)."

44 Luzzi ("Literary History and Individuality," 166) attributes to poetry the power to mediate between individual, everyday language, and the public voice of the community.

45 *Convivio* 1.1.8. Here I have amended Lansing's translation, which removes Dante's emphasis on the individuality of human relationships.

46 Ascoli, *Dante and the Making*, 141.

47 See *Convivio* 2.12.3. For the popularity of Cicero's dialogue in the medieval Christian West, see the introduction to this book. On the poet's public alignment of himself with Cino over Guido, see Barolini, "Semantics of Friendship," 56–60.

48 *De amicitia* 20.

49 *De amicitia* 20. For the implicit critique of Stoic views on friendship here and elsewhere in the dialogue, see Pangle, *Aristotle and the Philosophy of Friendship*, 114–17. See also Grayling, *Friendship*, 47.

50 On *Laelius* and its afterlife in the Middle Ages, see especially Mews, "Cicero and the Boundaries of Friendship," 369–84.

51 *De amicitia* 19.

52 See Grayling, *Friendship*, 46–8.

53 Cicero advises that, in order to protect against the dissolution of friendships, we must be certain "ut ne nimis cito diligere incipient, neve non dignos" [that you don't love too quickly and don't give your friendship to those unworthy of it] (*De amicitia* 78) and that "magis vituperanda est rei maxime necessariae tanta incuria" [our carelessness regarding something as important as friendship deserves the strongest condemnation] (*De amicitia* 86).

54 *De amicitia* 26–31. See also 50: "quidem, Fanni et Scaevola, constet, ut opinor: bonis inter bonos quasi necessariam benevolentiam, qui est amicitiae fons a natura constitutus" [my young friends, I think it's clear that good people have, so to speak, a necessary affection for good people, because nature has established this as the source of friendship].

55 *De amicitia* 31.

56 On the matter of reciprocity in Cicero's theory of friendship, see Leach, "Absence and Desire," 3–20, especially 11–12.

57 *De amicitia* 58. See also Leach, "Absence and Desire," 15.

58 *De amicitia* 58.

59 That reciprocity and the economy of friendly exchange are so central to Laelius's account is the greatest liability of his praise of perfect friendship; this focus will trouble the remainder of the dialogue. Laelius's vision is staked on equality between the two partners, and this principle of resemblance is easily thrown off balance in the strict system of Roman rank. According to Leach, "this struggle [to maintain such mirroring equality between friends] is among the most interesting aspects of the essay" ("Absence and Desire," 13–14).

60 Jaeger, "Friendship of Mutual Perfecting," 185–200.

61 *De amicitia* 32.

62 In relation to Laelius's emphasis of friendship's exacting demands, Pangle has concluded that Cicero systematically undermines his own character's account. See Pangle, *Aristotle and the Philosophy of Friendship*, 107–22.

63 See *De amicitia* 15. See also Mews, "Cicero and the Boundaries of Friendship," 370–2.

64 On the influence of Cicero's treatise on Christian readers, see especially Classen, "Introduction," in *Friendship in the Middle Ages*, 8–9; McEvoy, "The Theory of Friendship"; Mews, "Cicero and the Boundaries of Friendship"; Ziolkowski, "Twelfth-Century Understandings."

65 De Robertis, *Il libro della "Vita nova,"* 93–4. Filippa Modesto reads in similar terms the influence of *De amicitia* on Dante's thinking about friendship, addressing in particular *Convivio* and Beatrice's "friendship" as articulated in *Inferno* 2 and *Purgatorio* 30 and 31. See *Dante's Idea of Friendship*, especially chapters 3, 6, and 7.

66 *Convivio* 4.1.3: "Onde io, fatto amico di questa donna di sopra nella verace esposizione nominata, cominciai ad amare e odiare secondo l'amore e l'odio suo. Cominciai adunque ad amare li seguitatori della veritade e odiare li seguitatori dello errore e della falsitade, com'ella face" [Thus having become the friend of this lady who was mentioned above in the true explanation, I began to love and hate in accordance with her love and hatred. I therefore began to love the followers of truth and to hate the followers of error and falsehood, as did she].

67 On the tensions of friendship among the early humanists, see the discussion in the epilogue. The intricate workings of later humanist friendships are beyond the scope of the current project, and my understanding of the topic has been informed primarily by the following sources: Fenzi, "Petrarca e la scrittura dell'amicizia," 549–89; Houston, "Boccaccio on Friendship," 81–97; James and Kent, "Renaissance Friendships," 111–64; Kent, *Friendship, Love, and Trust*; Kircher, *Living Well*, 187–94; Kirkham, "The Classic Bond of Friendship," 223–35; Langer, *Perfect Friendship*; McLean, *The Art of the Network*; Sherberg, *The Governance of Friendship*; Wojciehowski, "Petrarch and His Friends"; Wojciehowski, "Petrarch: First Modern Friend"; Zak, "Soft Hearts," 125–36.

68 On the association of *locutio* with *mores et habitus* see Tavoni's note to 2.1.5 (1371).

69 *De vulgari eloquentia* 1.17.3.

70 Compare Ascoli's point that because *De vulgari* inextricably ties language to individual will, it "risks duplicating the uncommunicative isolation which punished the presumption of those who built Babel. Thus, if he is to assert himself as author, it is only through the oblique device of making himself, in objectified, third-person form, into the humble exemplar and representative of a language that is radically impersonal" (*Dante and the Making*, 154).

71 *De vulgari eloquentia* 1.3.1. On the Babel story and the figure of Nimrod as allegory of lay civic society in the Trecento *comune*, see Corti, "Dante e la Torre di Babele," 250–6. See also Ascoli, *Dante and the Making*, 157.

72 Barolini has discussed the similarly competitive metaphor of the goldsmith in Dante da Maiano's *Per pruova di saper com vale o quanto*: the goldsmith tests the worth of his own works in the fire as a representation of the fiery poetic agora, where his rivals would judge the worth of his lyrics. See Barolini, "A Young Man," 53–5.

73 On the civic turn of *De vulgari eloquentia*, see Tavoni, "Introduzione," 1069: "Il tradizionale abbinamento della 'rettorica' all'arte di 'reggere' la cosa pubblica, tipico della civiltà comunale, e in nessun altro Comune più vivo che a Firenze e a Bologna, era qualcosa di troppo prosaico, pragmatico, inferiore ed estraneo rispetto alla poesia aristocratica di un Cavalcanti, del giovane Dante suo allievo, nonché del Dante allievo di Arnaut Daniel delle canzoni petrose" [The traditional coupling of "rhetoric" with the art of "governing" public affairs, typical of communal culture – and in no other Commune more alive than in Florence and in Bologna – was something too prosaic, pragmatic, base and alien to the aristocratic poetry of someone like a Cavalcanti, or of the young Dante his apprentice, not to mention

that Dante, disciple of Arnaut Daniel, who wrote the *petrose*]. Luzzi ("Literary History and Individuality," 170–1) sees this shift to a public orientation already present in the penultimate chapter of *Vita nova*; Durling ("The Audience(s)," 29) sees the conflict between an elitist rejection of a larger public and the desire to reach that public in the fact of the *Vita nova*'s publication.

74 See *De vulgari eloquentia* 1.18.5: "Quare falsum esset dicere curia carere Ytalos, quanquam principe careamus; quoniam curiam habemus, licet corporaliter sit dispersa" [So it would not be true to say that the Italians lack a tribunal altogether, even though we lack a monarch, because we do have one, but its physical components are scattered]. He further explains that the *curia dispersa* is an assembly whose members are united "gratioso lumine rationis" [by the gracious light of reason]. On the insertion of the individual poetic authority into the foundation of a literary-historical "common cultural heritage," see Luzzi, "Literary History and Individuality," 162–6 (citation 164).

75 *Vita nova* 16.10.

76 As Durling notes of Dante's highly literate audience, "Dante needs an audience of trained intellectuals for the *De vulgari eloquentia*: only they can gauge his claims for the new poetry, his theory of the history of language, his revisionist references to the Bible, his knowledge of literature in French and Provençal, his witty put-downs of the local dialects, his knowledge of the Latin rhetorical tradition, his references to modal grammar (if that is indeed what they are), his urbanity, his cosmopolitanism, his command of *dictamen* or the other refinements of his style, including the refinement of his implicit aggression against the *literati*" (30). In Durling's assessment, *Convivio* and *De vulgari* share the pedagogical goal of training a national audience that does not yet exist. See Durling, "The Audience(s)," 29–34.

77 *De vulgari eloquentia* 2.4.1.

78 *De vulgari eloquentia* 2.4.1.

79 On the inherent contradictions of *De vulgari*'s attempt to train others in the art of a natural, ungrammatical language, see Shapiro, *Dante's Book of Exile*, 175–96.

80 *De vulgari eloquentia* 2.4.10–11. See also Luzzi, "Literary History and Individuality," 176.

81 In his note to 1.15.6 (1318), Tavoni points out that *discretio* "è posta come scopo educativo del trattato fin dalle sue primissime parole" [is positioned as the educational goal of the treatise from its very first words], noting that the term arises in 1.1.1, and then frequently in Book 2, at 2.4.5, 2.4.6, 2.4.10, 2.6.3, 2.6.4, 2.7.2, 2.7.7, 2.13.9, 2.14.2. We can attribute the higher frequency in Book 2 to the treatise's explicit turn to its educational purposes. The verb *habituare* appears in 2.2.2, a clear nod to the Aristotelian idea of *habitus*, a stable disposition of character towards a particular vice or virtue, acquired or earned through repeated practice. In the passage cited above, Dante uses the expression "habitu fieri," to be built by habit, again alluding to the repeated practice necessary to acquire virtue.

82 On intimacy and the use of pronouns, see Barolini, "Semantics of Friendship," especially 53–65.

83 Ascoli, *Dante and the Making*, 136–7 and 149–69 (citation 137). See also Luzzi, "Literary History and Individuality," 172.

84 Brunetto Latini, *La Rettorica* 1.10. See also 28.1, 32.6, 33.3, and 76.2.

85 See, for example, *La Rettorica* 33.3 and 76.2.

86 As I noted earlier, much is uncertain about Dante's itinerant trajectory in the early years of his exile: he appears to have spent the early months in Arezzo with his fellow exiles, followed by time in Casentino with the Conti Guidi and a diplomatic mission to (and possible stay of some ten months at) the court of Bartolomeo della Scala. In his biography, Marco Santagata evokes vividly the physical dangers of exile and the necessity of one's networks for sanctuary: "Dante had been banished and was under sentence of death, and this meant he no longer enjoyed the protection of Florence. He could be killed legitimately, and therefore with impunity, by anyone. A banished person living under constant threat of death had to carefully consider every movement and, so far as possible, travel under the protection of friends." See Santagata, *Dante*, 156–73 (citation 163).

87 See, for example, Dante's second epistle, where he laments his poverty and his inability to return to the Casentino for the funeral of the uncle of Oberto and Guido di Romena. Santagata reads the letter as an expression of loyalty to and intimacy with the Guidi brothers, newly made lords of Romena, in an effort to solicit their patronage (*Dante*, 169–70).

88 *Convivio* 1.3.4–5.

89 *Convivio* 1.3.5.

90 *Convivio* 1.4.13.

91 On the "maggiore autoritade" invoked in this passage from *Convivio* and its relationship to Dante's process of self-authorization, see Ascoli, *Dante and the Making*, 85–97.

92 On Cino's role as Dante's "guarantor" in university circles, see Santagata, *Dante*, 186.

93 Accounts of Cino's political affiliation (White or Black Guelph) and, thus, the precise dates of his exile vary. For the dates given above, see Carrai and Maffei, "Sinibuldi, Cino"; Inglese, *Vita di Dante*, 85; Livraghi, "Dante (e Cino)," 64–5. But compare the discussion in Ferrara, "Il distacco di Dante da Cino," 100–1, n. 6.

94 Carrai and Maffei, "Sinibuldi, Cino." See also Inglese, *Vita di Dante*, 84–5; Santagata, *Dante*, 185. Among Zaccagnini's figures is a miniature of Cino da Pistoia lecturing in the Studium; see *La vita dei maestri*, tavola vi.

95 Zaccagnini's 1925 collection of Cino's *Rime* includes fourteen sonnets Cino undoubtedly addressed to Bolognese poets. In addition, Zaccagnini records exchanges with anonymous friends (called only "amico" or "amico saggio") whom Cino may have encountered in Bologna, as well as poems composed to friends like Ser Mula de' Muli, who was Cino's Pistoian compatriot but was, like Cino, residing in Bologna as a student when they exchanged their lyrics. See Zaccagnini, *Rime di Cino da Pistoia*.

96 Zaccagnini, *Rime di Cino*, 101.

97 Kleinhenz, *The Early Italian Sonnet*, 148.

98 On Onesto's own ability to traffic freely among the various communal literary networks of the day, see Antonelli, "Nuove su Onesto da Bologna," 9–20.

99 In discussing Cino's connection to Onesto, Tavoni remarks, "In questo rapporto del vecchio maestro con Cino, che coinvolgeva nominativamente anche lui Dante, e che era ben noto alla società letteraria bolognese, Dante, che si presenta ostentatamente come l'amico di Cino, vede un varco per il proprio inserimento in quella società" [In this relationship between the old maestro and Cino, who Dante also includes by name, and who was well known to Bolognese literary society, Dante, who presents himself ostentatiously as Cino's friend, sees an opening for his admission into that society] (note to *De vulgari eloquentia* 1.15.6, p. 1321).

100 The texts of Onesto's sonnets are taken from *Le Rime di Onesto da Bologna*, ed. Orlando. The ten sonnets I refer to in the exchange include those directly exchanged between Cino and Onesto; Orlando and other editors also include a brief interlude in the exchange in which the two poets turn to Bernardo da Bologna for what Orlando calls "mediazione" [mediation] in the debate. I exclude the two sonnets addressed to Bernardo from the count.

101 See the final tercet of Onesto's *Siete voi, messer Cin, se ben v'adocchio*, where Onesto accuses Cino of having been excessive in his "folli'" [mania], which "né ciò mai vi mostrò Guido né Dante" [neither Guido nor Dante have shown to you]. "Guido" here is typically understood to be Cavalcanti, but in his edition of Onesto's lyrics Orlando raises another possibility: "perché non Guinizzelli (caposcuola degli stilnovisti e, come tale, 'istigatore' di Cino?" [why not Guinizzelli (head of the stilnovists and, as such, Cino's "instigator")?]. See *Le Rime di Onesto da Bologna*, 52 n. 14.

102 *Convivio* 1.4.13.

103 See Ascoli, *Dante and the Making*, especially 149–69. Citations appear on 149 and 154, respectively.

104 Kleinhenz, *The Early Italian Sonnet*, 206. Emphasis in original.

105 That the *consensio* projected from *De vulgari* extends outward to include many more than just the two masters of Italian vernacular excellence contrasts with the restrictive view of who *De vulgari* sees as authorized to use the *vulgare illustre*: "as groups rise above the mere local dialects and approach the ideal of the *vulgare illustre*, they become smaller and smaller, until the elite fully capable of using the *vulgare illustre*, and authorized to do so, is the smallest of all, perhaps consisting of only *Cynus et amicus eius*" (Durling, "The Audience(s)," 32).

106 Barolini, "Semantics of Friendship," 58.

107 Ascoli, *Dante and the Making*, 154. As De Robertis initially indicated ("Cino e i poeti bolognesi"), Cino's correspondence poems with several Bolognese poets in the 1290s marked his "entrée" into literary society (275). By the time Dante was writing *De vulgari*, Cino had engaged in an extensive and provocative exchange with Onesto degli Onesti on *stilnovismo* in particular, where the two poets clash in debate over the

"vecchia e nuova cultura" [old and new culture] (279). Because of Cino's deep ties to the network of Bolognese poets, Dante selects him as the named representative of the new poetics, seeing in this collaboration what Tavoni calls his "varco per il proprio inserimento" [opening for his admission] into Bolognese literary society (note to *De vulgari eloquentia* 1.15.6, p. 1321).

108 Livraghi, "Dante (e Cino)," 63.

109 See the discussion in the epilogue below, as well as note 67 above.

110 *De vulgari eloquentia* 2.8.8. Here I have given my own translation in lieu of Botterill's "single theme."

3 Hierarchy: The Court

1 On the issue of inequality in medieval friendship, see Mews and Chiavaroli, "The Latin West," 98–100.

2 Philip Jones, *The Italian City-State*, 636.

3 Verona, the city that will be the setting for this chapter, seems to have been particularly disposed to the dissolution of its communal structures in favour of a single *signore*: Silvana Anna Bianchi suggests that, unlike the Tuscan populations, "l'*élite* Veronese non avesse mai davvero assorbito l'idea della piena partecipazione democratica e fosse pronta a un regime signorile" (101). See the discussion in Bianchi, "Il Comune e le Signorie," 93–148.

4 Larner, *Italy in the Age of Dante and Petrarch*, 128.

5 Jones, *The Italian City-State*, 621–50.

6 Jones, *The Italian City-State*, 625–50. Interestingly, Jones points out that even Ezzelino was honored and revered by his immediate contemporaries; public opinion turned against him after extravagances in his later years, and hostile propaganda would permanently damage his good name (*The Italian City-State*, 632–3). On the language of "amicitia" to designate political allies, see Collodo, "Padova e gli Scaligeri," 46. For specific references to the term "amico" applied to a courtier, see Jones, *The Italian City-State*, 536–7, 541, 619, 624, 627, and 635.

7 Jones, *The Italian City-State*, 641–4. While many poets and other writers of the period decried *signori* as despots, others portrayed this same despotism as the guardian of liberty, the antidote to the fractious chaos of communal life. On the "normalization" of attitudes towards signorial governments, especially among the nobility, see Larner, *Italy in the Age of Dante and Petrarch*, 146–7. On constructions of *cortesia* in the literature of the period, see Olson, *Courtesy Lost.*

8 Zorzi, *Le signorie cittadine*, 133–4. On patronage and other means of circulating texts in medieval Italy, see Moore, "General Aspects of Literary Patronage," 386–7. On patronage and other forms of sponsorship in medieval Europe, see Holzknecht, *Literary Patronage.* Holzknecht's study primarily focuses on English literature and patronage, with a few notes about patronage across Western Europe.

9 See, for example, *Ethica Nicomachea* 8.14 [1163a24ff.].

10 See especially Kent, *Friendship, Love and Trust*; McLean, *The Art of the Network*. See also the examples listed in Holzknecht, *Literary Patronage*, 136–9, as well as Holzknecht's comment about the "shamelessness" of Renaissance Italians in their expectations of reward for dedication (*Literary Patronage*, 141).

11 Wojciehowski, "Petrarch: First Modern Friend," 283–5. Wojciehowski cautions, "it would be a stretch to call [Giovanni Colonna] Petrarch's friend, precisely because he was his patron" (283). Wojciehowski's caution here is, I would contend, unwarranted for the period, when many writers embraced Aristotle's wider definition of friendship, which could include utilitarian and instrumental forms.

12 McLean, *The Art of the Network*, 108–9.

13 McLean, *The Art of the Network*, 93, 99–101. The tradition of speaking of patrons as friends endures even now in such expressions as "Friends of the Arts" or "Friends of the Museum," in which donors are no longer treated as friends of the artists themselves, but of the institutions that rely on their support.

14 As discussed in the introduction, McLean contends that the language of friendship constituted "the loosest and most ambiguous frame Florentines had at their disposal" (*The Art of the Network*, 15).

15 On the use of the terms of friendship among twelfth-century *dictatores*, see Hartmann, "L'*amicitia* nei primi comuni italiani," 44–55. See also Hartmann, "Eloquence and Friendship," 67–86.

16 See, for example, Bene Florentini, *Candelabrum* 6.17, 6.18, 6.19; Bichilino da Spello, *Il Pomerium rethorice* 2.11; Guidonis Fabe, *Summa dictaminis* 2.10, 2.25, 2.26, 2.35, 2.45, 2.48, 2.50, 2.55, 2.57, 2.60.

17 Murphy, *Rhetoric in the Middle Ages*, 196.

18 *Il Pomerium rethorice* 2.11.5. Text cited from *Il Pomerium rethorice di Bichilino da Spello*, ed. Licitra, 33. See also Mews and Chiavaroli, "The Latin West," 100.

19 Mews and Chiavaroli, "The Latin West," 98. See Aristotle, *Ethica Nicomachea* 8.7 [1158b27ff] and 8.8. [1159b1]; Cicero, *De amicitia* 32 and 69–73; Aquinas, *Sententia libri ethicorum*, l. 8, lectio 7 [1630], and lectio 8 [1649]. See also *Convivio* 3.1.7–8 (discussed below).

20 *Summa dictaminis* 26: "Si autem dominabilibus amicus fuerit, ita scribes: 'Precordiali domino et amico' vel 'speciali tamquam domino et amico P. honestate morum fulgenti' vel 'multa sapientia decorato I. salutem, et quicquid dilectionis et servitii potest' vel 'salutem et votiva continua perfrui sospitate' vel 'salutem et illesam omni tempore amicitiam conservare'" [But if you were friend to powerful men, you will write, "To the beloved lord and friend" or "to my special lord and friend P. illustrious for his virtuous character" or "to I., decorated for his great wisdom, greetings, and whatever love and services he can render" or "that he enjoy health and promised and continued wellbeing" or "that he preserve health and keep friendship unharmed at all times"]. Text cited from Guidonis Fabe, *Summa dictaminis*, 287–338. See also Mews and Chiavaroli, "The Latin West," 99.

21 Mews and Chiavaroli, "The Latin West," 98–9.

22 Mews and Chiavaroli, "The Latin West," 98.

23 For the most complete bibliography of the debate, see Azzetta, "Nota introduttiva," 273–324, especially 273. Azzetta's edition also includes a thorough discussion of the indirect transmission of the document in the centuries leading up to the discovery of the complete text in the second half of the sixteenth century. See "Appendice: La tradizione indiretta dell'*Epistola a Cangrande*," in Baglio et al., ed., *Epistole, Egloghe, Questio*, 418–87. The most significant contribution to the debate in recent decades comes also from Azzetta, who detected a reference to a letter from Dante to Cangrande in Andrea Lancia's 1340s commentary on the *Commedia*. Azzetta, "Le chiose alla *Commedia*," 5–76. See also Ascoli, "Access to Authority," especially 340–1 n. 10; Robert Hollander, *Dante's Epistle to Cangrande*; and the bibliography in Kelly, "Epistle to Cangrande Updated."

24 See the overview in Azzetta, "Nota introduttiva," 273–5.

25 Bruno Nardi, *Il punto sull'epistola*. Nardi and Peter Dronke saw in the Latin of the first four paragraphs stylistic markers – specifically the use of the *cursus* – that bear strong resemblance to the corpus of Dante's Latin works. See Dronke, *Dante and Medieval Latin Traditions*, 103–11.

26 The most recent of these is Kelly, "Epistle to Cangrande Updated." Kelly notes, "if one believes that Dante's hand is only in the Dedication, as I do, one must try to judge when and how the other parts were added." As to the remainder of the Epistle, Kelly argues that attribution to Dante is impossible.

27 Brugnoli, *Epistola XIII*, 602. Both Brugnoli's and, more recently, Azzetta's (2016) commentaries indicate points of comparison with the Aristotelian theory of friendship, but neither discusses the Epistle's departures from or contributions to this theory.

28 Teodolinda Barolini makes the strong case that the burden of proof lies with the detractors. See her discussion of the attribution debate and its bearing on the exegesis of the *Commedia* in *The Undivine Comedy*, 3–20, especially 10.

29 Bourdieu, *Outline of a Theory of Practice*, 12, 191–2.

30 Bourdieu, *Outline of a Theory of Practice*, 13.

31 For Cangrade's biography, especially his military and political career, see Varanini, "Della Scala, Cangrande," with relevant biography. For biographical and historical data on Cangrande, the Scaligeri lords, and Verona, see Bianchi, "Il Comune e le Signorie," 93–148; Dean, "The Rise of the *Signori*," 104–24; Marini, et al., *Cangrande della Scala*; Varanini, *Gli Scaligeri 1277–1387*; and Zorzi, *Le signorie cittadine*.

32 Bianchi, "Il Comune e le Signorie," 114; Jones, *The Italian City-State*, 621–2. Bianchi (100) points out that Mastino had also been *podestà del comune* under Ezzelino in 1258 but was not politically damaged by his connection to the infamous despot.

33 Alberto secured the title of *capitaneus generalis*, a significant expansion of power from his previous title as *capitaneus populi*, in 1277, when he was granted "plenam, generalem et liberam auctoritatem et potestam in omnibus et per omnia regendi" [full, general, and free authority and power to reign in and through all things]. The title was granted in perpetuity. See Jones, *The Italian City-State*, 622–3.

34 Varanini, "Della Scala, Cangrande."
35 Varanini, "Della Scala, Cangrande."
36 Dean, "Rise of the *Signori*," 112.
37 Fornaciari, et al., "A Medieval Case of *Digitalis* Poisoning," 162–7. On accounts of the lord's death following the conquest of Treviso, including legendary predictions and astronomical events, see Di Salvo, "Percezioni e elaborazioni," 67–75 and 83–4. See also Varanini, "La morte di Cangrande della Scala," 11–21.
38 Castagnetti, "Formazione e vicende," 5.
39 Bianchi, "Il Comune e le Signorie," 114.
40 Jones, *The Italian City-State*, 635.
41 On the early formation of the Scaligera *signoria* in Verona, see especially Castagnetti, "Formazione e vicende," 5–14. On the family's rise in and control of Vicenza, see Varanini, "Sul dominio scaligero," 35–40. On the strategic celebrations of the victories of the della Scala lords among the intellectual class of Verona, see Di Salvo, "Celebrazioni politiche d'occasione," 287–310.
42 Varanini, "Gli Scaligeri, il ceto dirigente veronese," 113–24.
43 On the civic restoration attributed to the Scaligeri lords, see Brugnoli, "Donna e regina," 215–24.
44 On the transmutation of symbolic capital into economic capital, see Bourdieu, *Outline of a Theory of Practice*, 171–83, especially 180–1.
45 Rigoli cautions that the splendors of Cangrande's court should be understood as more military than courtly, arguing that contemporary and subsequent legends have obscured the reality of Cangrande's Verona. On the ways that chroniclers constructed the image of Cangrande's court, see Rigoli, "L'esibizione del potere," 149–56.
46 Vergani, "Dante e Verona," 35.
47 See, for example, the studies by Paola Frattaroli, Ina Vanden Berghe and Jan Wouters, Márta Járó, Lisa Monnas, David Jacoby and Doretta Davanzo Poli on Cangrande's fabric collection in "Le Stoffe di Cangrande: Nuove Ricerche," the third part of the extensive investigation of Cangrande's tomb in Marini et al., *Cangrande della Scala*, 83–163.
48 Placidi, "Dante and Cangrande"; Vergani, "Dante e Verona," 35. On the name "Cangrande" and the dispute over its meaning ("Khan," in the tradition of the Tartar lords, or "Cane," more appropriate to all the heraldic symbolism of the Scaligera court), see Höfler, *Cangrande di Verona.*
49 On contemporary accounts of Cangrande's person and court, see Di Salvo, "Percezioni e rielaborazioni," 36–87; Di Salvo, "Celebrazioni politiche," 287–310; Marchi, "Valore e cortesia," 485–96. See also the collection of texts in Cipolla and Pellegrini, "Poesie minori," 7–206.
50 "Suas enim variis hominum generibus habitationes assignatas, & affluentes victus impensas, pro hominum conditione factas, ac suos quibusque diverso cultu ministros datos fuisse meminit. Proprios etiam titulos singulis diversoriorum

januis praescriptos, veluti triumphos victoribus, bonam spem exulibus, Musarum umbracula Poëtis, Artificibus Mercurium, religiosis Concionatoribus Paradisum, aliaque cuique hominum generi congrua pro hospitiis depicta fuisse memorat. Musici concentus, festivique sanniones, & jocundi moriones alterna varietate coenationes circumibant; cubicula quoque splendissima instructa aulaeis, quae instabilis fortunae argumenta continebant, & picturis mirifice exornabantur" [Indeed he remembered that lodgings and abundant provisions were issued to the different sorts of men there, rendered according to his condition, and each was given his own servants to attend to his private care. He also remembered that special figures were carved on each door of the guest quarters, like triumphs for the victorious, good hope for exiles, the groves of the Muses for Poets, Mercury for Artists, Paradise for the religious Preachers, and other things appropriate to each sort of man were depicted, for the sake of hospitality. Choirs of musicians, merry jesters, and jovial fools moved through the dining rooms in various turns; the glorious bedrooms were also adorned with tapestries, wonderfully decorated with images, which involved the theme of capricious Fortune]. Guido Panciroli, cited by Ludovico Antonio Muratori in his preface to Sagacius and Petrus de Gazata Regienses, *Chronicon Regiense*, in *Rerum italicarum scriptores*, ed. Ludovico Antonio Muratori, vol. 18, 1–98. The citation appears on p. 2, and the translation is mine.

51 Petrarca, *Rerum memorandarum libri* II. 83, 98–9.

52 On Immanuel Romano's Jewish identity and his relationship to Cangrande, see Alfie, "Nonsense and Noise," 127–39.

53 Alfie, "Nonsense and Noise," 130.

54 Immanuel Romano, *Bisbidìs*, vv. 205–12. Text and translation cited from Alfie, "Nonsense and Noise," 136–7.

55 Immanuel Romano, *Bisbidìs*, v. 175.

56 On Mussato's civic poetry, and in particular his opposition to Cangrande, see Lummus, *The City of Poetry*, 22–62. See also Gianola, "Tra Padova e Verona," 51–60.

57 Cited in Cipolla and Pellegrini, "Poesie minori," 19. The epigram concludes with a reflection on the assistance of Sigonfredo Ganzera in the enterprise, using precisely the term "amicus" to describe his welcome intervention, which delivered the people of Vicenza to Cangrande's rule: "quem [Sigonfredo] Deus hoc longo vexit super equora cursu,/ ut tempestivam feret amicus opem" [whom God bore by long passage across the seas, so that this friend may bring his timely aid]. See also Di Salvo, "Celebrazioni politiche d'occasione," 293–6.

58 See Cipolla and Pellegrini, "Poesie minori," 19–20.

59 Cipolla and Pellegrini, "Poesie minori," 48.

60 The condemnation is uttered by Rolando della Piazzola in *De gestis Henrici VII*, 415–18, cited in Di Salvo, "Percezioni e rielaborazioni," 45.

61 Mussato scathingly describes Cangrande thus: "Ab infantia … habilem Canem Grandem Vicentiae vicarium, iuvenem insolentem, in tyrannide natum, educatumque, nunc adultum eorum adipe saturandum, incrassandum" [From

childhood … Can Grande, proper vicar of Vicenza, insolent youth, born and educated under the rule of despots, now fully grown, stuffing and fattening himself with their grease]. Albertino Mussato, *De gestis Henrici VII*, 545B, cited in Di Salvo, "Percezioni e rielaborazioni," 45 (my translation).

62 Di Salvo, "Percezioni e rielaborazioni," 53.

63 On Cangrande's role in the publication and distribution of the *Paradiso*, see Placidi, "Dante and Cangrande."

64 Cited from Cudini, *Poesia italiana del Trecento*, 8. My translation.

65 On servitude as one of the most common keywords in later (fifteenth-century) patronage letters, see McLean, *Art of the Network*, 108–9.

66 See the discussions of the "game of honour" in Bourdieu, *Outline of a Theory of Practice*, 1–30 (citation 12); Bourdieu, *The Logic of Practice*, 52–134 (citation 100).

67 On the use of Cangrande's titles to the dating of the letter, see Azzetta, *Epistola XIII*, 327; Brugnoli, "Introduzione," in *Epistola XIII*, 516–19, and *Epistola XIII*, 598.

68 On Dante's use of the term "devotissimus" and its relationship to the Epistle's claim to friendship, see Ferrara, "Devotissimus et amicus," 191–210.

69 On the transition from "exul immeritus" to "florentinus natione non moribus," see Ferrara, "Devotissimus et amicus," 193–4.

70 *Epistula* 13.1. The text of the Epistle is cited from the edition by Claudia Villa, in Dante Alighieri, *Opere. Volume secondo: Convivio, Monarchia, Epistole, Egloge*, eds. Fioravanti et al. Translations are my own. I have also consulted the editions by Azzetta and Brugnoli, cited above.

71 On the relationship between these four terms, my discussion is informed by Ferrara, "Devotissimus et amicus," 199–210.

72 Ferrara, "Devotissimus et amicus," 199–201.

73 *Epistula* 13.2.

74 Bourdieu, *Outline of a Theory of Practice*, 12; Bourdieu, *The Logic of Practice*, 100.

75 See Bourdieu, *Outline of a Theory of Practice*, 10–22, especially 18–19.

76 Bourdieu, *Outline of a Theory of Practice*, 13.

77 *Epistula* 13.2.5.

78 Azzetta points out, following Brugnoli, that the passage echoes *Convivio* 1.11.8 – itself an echo of Boethius, but with the Dantean addition of the term "discrezione." The Epistle's author reprises the phrase with his "sine discretione," but also adds the term "iudicium," a term that was not present in the *Convivio* passage but that does appear in Boethius. For both Azzetta and Brugnoli, the paired references to "discretione" and "iudicium" support attribution of this part of the letter to Dante, as it is unlikely that a falsifier would have both plagiarized the passage from *Convivio* and amended its citation from *Consolatione philosophiae*. See Azzetta, *Epistola XIII*, 334–5, and Brugnoli, *Epistola XIII*, 603.

79 Ferrara, "Devotissimus et amicus," 206–7.

80 Bourdieu, *Outline of a Theory of Practice*, 14.

81 Bourdieu, *Outline of a Theory of Practice*, 13.

82 See *Ethica Nicomachea* 8. 2 [1156a1–5].

83 *Convivio* 3.11.8. The Italian text is cited from Dante Alighieri, *Convivio*, ed. Fioravanti. The English translations are those of Lansing.

84 On *Convivio*'s arguments for the necessity of reciprocated benevolence in friendship, see Falzone, "Il *Convivio* e l'amicizia," 70–5.

85 *Convivio* 3.1.7–8.

86 Indeed, the commentaries of Brugnoli (601–2) and Azzetta (337) cite the *Convivio* passages as correlatives of the Epistle's way of thinking.

87 *Epistula* 13.3.

88 Bourdieu, *The Logic of Practice*, 105–6. My emphasis.

89 "In every society it may be observed that, if it is not to constitute an insult, the counter-gift must be deferred and different, because the immediate return of an exactly identical object clearly amounts to a refusal … To betray one's haste to be free of an obligation one has incurred, and thus to reveal too overtly one's desire to pay off services rendered or gifts received, to be quits, is to denounce the initial gift retrospectively as motivated by the intention of obliging one." Bourdieu, *The Logic of Practice*, 105.

90 *Epistula* 13.3.9. The term "thesaurum" has scriptural resonance, and the Epistle associates the use of the term here with an earlier citation from the Book of Wisdom: "infinitus thesaurus est hominibus; quo qui usi sunt, participes facti sunt amicitie Dei" [it is for men an infinite treasure; those who use it become participants in the friendship with God] (*Epistula* 13.2). But the term's nakedly economic meaning in the context of patronage exchange cannot be overlooked.

91 On the Thomist resonance of terms such as "adequari" and "analogo," see the notes in the editions of Azzetta, *Epistola XIII*, 338, and Brugnoli, *Epistola XIII*, 606.

92 "Only this kind of acquired mastery, functioning with the automatic reliability of an instinct, can make it possible to respond instantaneously to all the uncertain and ambiguous situations of practice." Bourdieu, *The Logic of Practice*, 104.

93 Bourdieu comments, "In the case where the offender [giver] is clearly superior to the offended [recipient], only the fact of avoiding the challenge is held to be blameworthy, and the offended party is not required to triumph over the offender in order to be rehabilitated in the eyes of public opinion: the defeated man who has done his duty incurs no blame" (*Outline of a Theory of Practice*, 13). The author of the Epistle reveals that his intentions transcend mere rehabilitation of his reputation in the public eye: beyond the praises of the lord he submits in his poem, he wishes, through his dedication, to equalize himself with the lord, his superior in fortune but his equal in honor.

94 On equilibrium in friendship, see Sharp, "Friendship as Gift Exchange," in *Friendship and Literature*, 82–117, especially 89.

95 Azzetta, *Epistola XIII*, 340.

96 *Epistula* 13.4.12.

97 *Epistula* 13.4.12.

98 As elsewhere throughout this book, I cite here Grosseteste's translation of *Ethica Nicomachea* 9. 7 [1168a20–2]. Translations of Grosseteste's Latin are my own.

99 Bourdieu, *The Logic of Practice*, 105.

100 On dedications in medieval literary patronage, see Holzknecht, *Literary Patronage*, 124–55.

101 Bourdieu, *The Logic of Practice*, 106. See also Bourdieu, *Outline of a Theory of Practice*, 195.

102 This release, in turn, opens the door for a new act of patronage, making the *petitio* at the end of the Epistle all the more likely to succeed.

103 Bourdieu, *Outline of a Theory of Practice*, 192.

104 Bourdieu, *Outline of a Theory of Practice*, 192–3.

4 Difference: The Afterlife

1 *Inferno* 2.61.

2 *De amicitia* 80.

3 *De amicitia* 81. I have slightly amended the translation here in favor of a more literal one.

4 See, for example, Emilio Pasquini's comment that *Purgatorio* is the "cantica dell'amicizia," or Piero Boitani's similar remark, that it is the "*cantica* of friendship." Sebastio calls friendship "la 'tematica' centrale del *Purgatorio*." Boitani, *Dante's Poetry of the Donati*, 19; Pasquini, *Enciclopedia dantesca*, s.v. "amistà"; Sebastio, "Un tema dantesco: L'amicizia," 357.

5 Modesto, *Dante's Idea of Friendship*. On Beatrice's love as disinterested Ciceronian friendship, see also De Robertis, *Il libro della "Vita nuova."*

6 Mazzaro, "From *Fin Amour* to Friendship," 121–37. Compare Martha Nussbaum, who argues the opposite: that with the disappearance of Virgil we see also the replacement of pagan *philia*, deemed inadequate for Christian salvation, with a love that is "more volatile, more erotic, more vulnerable." See Nussbaum, "Beatrice's 'Dante,'" 165.

7 Ciabattoni, "Dante's Rhetoric of Friendship," 97.

8 Masciandaro, *The Stranger as Friend*, 28.

9 Raffa, "A Beautiful Friendship," S72 and S73.

10 See Boitani, *Dante's Poetry of the Donati*; Gragnolati, "Nostalgia in Heaven," 117–37; Masciandaro, *The Stranger as Friend*, especially 57–96. On individual friendly encounters in the second canticle (especially that between the pilgrim and Forese Donati), see, for example, Borsellino, "Dante e Forese," 135–49; Bufano, "Forese Donati," 219–37; Della Terza, "Dante e Forese," 101–11; Mazzei, *Gli amici di Dante*; Russo, "*Pg* XXIII," 113–36; Savarese, *Una proposta per Forese*, 27–56.

11 Modesto, *Dante's Idea of Friendship*, 90–2 (citation 91).

12 *Purgatorio* 22.10, 15, and 16, respectively.

13 *Purgatorio* 22.19–21.

14 Admittedly, "amico" (both a noun and an adjective in Dante's vernacular) appears elsewhere in the poem as a broad-based affective expression. We might think of the "dolci amici" [sweet friends] missed by the traveling sailors in *Purgatorio* 8.3 or of the "accoglienza amica" [friendly greetings] of the lustful in *Purgatorio* 26.37. "Amico" can describe interspecies affections, where snakes (*Inferno* 25.4), rivers (*Purgatorio* 33.114), and truth (*Paradiso* 17.118) can be presented with affinity and kindness. The term "amico" likewise appears, in a different register, as meaning "lover," as we see in *Inferno* 30.39 (Mirra as "amica" of her father) and *Purgatorio* 9.3 (Tithonus as "amico" of Aurora). Nevertheless, it is striking to find the term uniquely applied in only these two instances of naming – *Inferno* 2 and *Purgatorio* 22 – and only once applied to the pilgrim himself, in Beatrice's reported speech.

15 *Paradiso* 14.61–6. On the resurrection of the body, see especially Gragnolati, "Nostalgia in Heaven," 134–7; Gragnolati, *Experiencing the Afterlife*, especially 109–37; Jacoff, "Our Bodies, Our Selves," 119–38; Muresu, "La 'gloria della carne': Disfacimento e trasfigurazione (*Paradiso* XIV), in *I ladri di malebolge*, 153–75. I will return to these verses below.

16 On the "outsider" status of Hell's inhabitants, see Honess, *From Florence to the Heavenly City*, especially 71–106.

17 On *Purgatorio* as "*cantica* of friendship," see Boitani, *Dante's Poetry of the Donati*, 19; Pasquini, *Enciclopedia dantesca*, s.v. "amistà"; Sebastio, "Un tema dantesca: L'amicizia," 357.

18 *Convivio* 4.25 adapts the phrase: "noi non potemo perfetta vita avere sanza amici" [we cannot have a perfect life without friends].

19 See the discussion of crowds and isolation in Honess, *Poetry of Citizenship*, 56–7, citing Usher, "Crowd Control in the *Commedia*," especially 57–8.

20 *Inferno* 3.112–17.

21 See Harrison, *The Dominion of the Dead*, 125–36, especially 131–2.

22 On the distinction between elective and natural friendship, see *Convivio* 3.11: "onde non diciamo Gianni amico di Martino, intendendo solamente la naturale amistade significare per la quale tutti a tutti semo amici, ma l'amistà sopra la naturale generata, che è propria e distinta in singulari persone" [Consequently when we speak of John as a friend of Martin, we do not intend to signify simply the natural friendship by which everyone is a friend to everyone but the friendship which is engendered over and above that which is natural, and which is proper and characteristic of individual persons].

23 Elena Lombardi, for one, sees in the pairing of Paolo and Francesca a transfigurative reciprocity, which "transforms the two lovers by changing one into the other, by melding the two subjectivities into one transformative and shifting 'us.'" See especially her chapter on "Love," in *The Wings of the Doves,* 132–74 (citation 171).

24 Masciandaro, *The Stranger as Friend*, 36.

25 *Inferno* 5.126. See Masciandaro's comments on the pilgrim's "mimetic response" to the figure of Paolo: *The Stranger as Friend*, 37. See also Honess's brief remarks on Francesca's individualism in *Poetry of Citizenship*, 56.

26 *Inferno* 5.91.

27 On the "tenuous presence of ethos" in this verse, see Masciandaro, *The Stranger as Friend*, 33.

28 See Dante's response to Saint James, on the rewards hoped for by God's friends: *Paradiso* 25.88–96 (citation v. 90). Dante employs the notion of preferential friendship with God once more in *Paradiso* (12.132), where he refers to the conversion of two of Francis's earliest followers, who, taking up the cord, "a Dio si fero amici" [make themselves friends of God] (I have slightly amended Durling's translation here). In order to take part in God's friendship, one must make oneself into a mirror of divine will; in their adoption of Francis's rule, Agostino and Illuminato submit to divine mandate, adopting God's desires as their own and thus assuring themselves places within the circle of God's friendship. Conversion and conformity to the rule of Francis bring Agostino and Illuminato into the circle of God's particular friendship, here treated as an "in-group" into which an individual is conscripted. On "insiders" and "outsiders" in the *Commedia*, see Honess, *The Poetry of Citizenship*, 14–36.

29 *Purgatorio* 1.88–9; *Inferno* 2.92.

30 Nietzsche famously quipped that Dante was wrong when he maintained that love created hell, suggesting instead that hate created heaven. On Nietzsche's accusation and the difficulty of identifying *odio* in the *Commedia*, see my essay "Eternal Hate Created Me As Well," 153–70. Much of the discussion of Ugolino that follows hews closely to my conclusions there.

31 Honess contrasts Ugolino and Ruggieri's "embrace" with that of Sordello and Virgil in *Purgatorio* 6, remarking that the contrast highlights Purgatory's "ideal of citizenship," which one might well call, following Aristotle, *politikē philia* or civic friendship. See Honess, *The Poetry of Citizenship*, 61. On Aristotle's notion of civic friendship, see Schwarzenbach, "On Civic Friendship," 97–128.

32 *Inferno* 33.15. On the "political tragedy" of the canto, where the presence of the other is perceived as a threat to be combatted with violence, see Freccero, "Bestial Sign and Bread of Angels," in *Dante: The Poetics of Conversion*, 152–66, especially 153–5.

33 *Inferno* 10.36. On Farinata's "perversion of authentic friendship" in his disengagement from his fellow-citizen, see Masciandaro, *The Stranger as Friend*, 42–56.

34 See *Purgatorio* 18.22–6: "Vostra apprensiva da esser verace / tragge intenzione, e dentro a voi la spiega, / sì che l'animo ad essa volger face; / e se rivolto inver' di lei si piega, / quel piegare è amor" [Your power of apprehension takes from some real thing an intention and unfolds it within you, so that it causes the mind to turn toward it; and if, having turned, the mind bends toward it, that bending is love]. On Ugolino's cannibalism as inversion of the banquet of love, see Herzman, "Cannibalism and Communion," 53–78.

35 *Inferno* 32.134. The additional preposition "ti" in the verse is an ethical dative: as Singleton notes (*Inferno*: Commentary, 603), the ethical dative is "untranslatable" in

English, and implies an emotional stake on the part of the agent. Thus it emphasizes Ugolino's passionate participation in the construction and execution of Ruggieri's additional punishment.

36 Herzman claims that "the sons of Ugolino are linked to their father with pathetic tenderness to show how cannibalism inverts the strongest ties of paternal love" ("Cannibalism and Communion," 61). On Ugolino's sin as a violent rejection of *civitas*, see Honess, *Poetry of Citizenship*, 75.

37 See, for example, his comments in *Vita nova* 13: "nulla sia sì intima amistade come da buon padre a bon figliuolo e da bon figliuolo a bon padre" [no friendship is so intimate as that of a good father towards a good son or daughter and of a good son or daughter towards a good father].

38 Freccero, *Dante: The Poetics of Conversion*, 152–66; Herzman, "Cannibalism and Communion."

39 Hollander, "Ugolino's Importunity," 549–55.

40 *Inferno* 33.56–7.

41 *Inferno* 33.49–50.

42 Piero Boitani also remarks on the "mirror-like opposition" that these verses indicate. See his *Lectura Dantis* on "*Inferno* XXXIII," 70–89 (citation 81). On the possibility of communion inherent in the sons' self-sacrifice, see Freccero, *Dante: The Poetics of Conversion*, 157.

43 *Inferno* 33.70–5.

44 See Freccero, *Dante: The Poetics of Conversion*, 163: "the 'savage repast,' 'fiero pasto,' has its counterpart in the sacred feast, the *agape*."

45 *Purgatorio* 15.55–60.

46 Freccero, *Dante: The Poetics of Conversion*, 163.

47 *Inferno* 33.1.

48 In his commentary on *Purgatorio* 13.40, which outlines the relationship between virtue and vice in Purgatory, Jacopo della Lana likewise uses medical metaphors: "contraria vuole essere la medicina del morbo, com'è detto."

49 On liturgical performance as site of interaction between humanity and divinity, see Phillips-Robins, *Liturgical Song and Practice*.

50 On music and healing, see Ciabattoni, *Dante's Journey to Polyphony*, 109–37. See also Phillips-Robins, *Liturgical Song and Practice*, especially 45–52 and chapter 3, "The Shared Voice of Liturgical Prayer."

51 On *civitas* and civic friendship across Dante's works, see Elisa Brilli, "*Civitas*/Community," 353–67; Honess, *Poetry of Citizenship*; Keen, *Dante and the City*; Lummus, *The City of Poetry*, 63–111.

52 The quoted terms come from Bourdieu, *Outline of a Theory of Practice*, especially 10–15. On the "embodiment" of souls in *Purgatorio* see Gragnolati, *Experiencing the Afterlife*, especially 109–37; Jacoff, "Our Bodies, Our Selves," 119–38, especially 128–31; Webb, *Dante's Persons*, especially chapter 2, "Gestural Persons," 34–82.

53 Bourdieu, *Outline of a Theory of Practice*, 15.

54 See *Purgatorio* 15.46–78 (citations from verses 65 and 61–2, respectively).
55 *Purgatorio* 15.50.
56 Webb, "Postures of Penitence," 219–36. See also Webb, *Dante's Persons*, 34–82.
57 Webb, "Postures of Penitence," 229–31.
58 See also the discussion in Webb, *Dante's Persons*, 114–18.
59 Barolini raises a similar question in her commentary on the virtue corrected in *Purgatorio* 13; see Barolini, "*Purgatorio* 13: Eyes Sewn Shut."
60 *Purgatorio* 13.39 and 27.
61 See, for example, Guittone's sonnet *Amistade d'envidia è medicina* and Brunetto's *Rettorica* 2.2, both discussed above in chapter 1.
62 Much as Dante juxtaposes envy and "amor," Albertano da Brescia's 1268 treatise *De amore et dilectione Dei et proximi* positions "dilectione Dei et proximi" against *invidia* as its opposite. See Liber III, *De amore et dilectione aliarum rerum corporalium*, caput V, "De invidia," in *De amore et dilectione Dei*, ed. Hiltz.
63 Cited from the commentaries to *Purgatorio* 13 by Jacopo della Lana, Pietro Alighieri, the Ottimo Commento, and Benvenuto da Imola (retrieved from *Dante Lab*, http://dantelab.dartmouth.edu). Albertano da Brescia's treatise on "amor proximi" nails down the relationship with a bit more specificity, claiming that "amor" is the sentiment the good Christian should cultivate for all, and "amicitia" the sentiment that "amor" becomes when one adds trust, conviviality, conversation and dialogue, and services both given and received. See "Unde oriatur amor et qualiter," caput 1 of Albertano's Liber secundus (*De amore proximi et dilectione liber*) in *De amore et dilectione Dei*, 42–3.
64 *Purgatorio* 13.36.
65 See the discussion of *amicitia caritatis* below.
66 *Purgatorio* 13.32.
67 The figure of Orestes puzzled the earliest commentators, who touched on it briefly, only mentioning that Orestes murdered his mother to avenge his father (Benvenuto, for one, cites this as an example of his "pietate erga patrum" [piety towards his father]). The earliest to discover the Ciceronian resonance and mention Pylades appears to have been Pietro Alighieri, who recounts the legend in his third redaction of the commentary on *Purgatorio* (1359–64). Although Pietro insists that the virtue described here is "virtutem karitatis et amoris proximi" or "delictionem proximi," he also notes that the Orestes-Pylades example demonstrates vividly how "ita se amicabiliter ardenter amabant" [they so loved one another ardently and in a friendly manner]. Commentators have been divided on whether to identify the exemplar as Orestes or Pylades. In his commentary to *Purgatorio* 13.31–3, Robert Hollander dismisses as "ungainly" the view that both are represented, but it is the ungainly view I defend here: the exemplar isn't one individual or the other, but the kind of self-sacrificing love that would make the two men indistinguishable from one another.
68 See *Paradiso* 9.73–81. On the two directions of paradisiacal love embodied by these terms, see Took, "'S'io m'intuassi,'" 402–13. On the mutual indwelling of the

one and the other, see also Janet Martin Soskice's reading of Martin Buber in *The Kindness of God,* 169–77.

69 *Purgatorio* 13.94–5. On the verse and its relationship to civic identity, see Brilli, "*Civitas*/Community," 361. On the contrast between Sapia's communal sense of citizenship and Sordello's "campanilismo," see Barański, "*Purgatorio* VI," 80–97, especially 90.

70 On pronouns as performative markers of intimacy and friendship, see Barolini, "Semantics of Friendship," 56–60. See also the essay accompanying *Guido, i' vorrei* in *Dante's Lyric Poetry*, 113–21.

71 In his discussion of the rise of mendicant orders in the thirteenth and fourteenth centuries, Luigi Pellegrini discusses the new socio-cultural organization that arose with the new orders, as well as in the incorporation of professional guilds, in the lay confraternities, and in the organization of the *Comune* itself. Of *fraternitas*, the key term for the new mendicant orders, Pellegrini notes, "Il legame, come abbiamo già avuto occasione di accennare, non sarà dunque quello del sangue e neppure quello dell'amicizia, ma quello del giuramento, inteso non tanto come promessa di fedeltà a una persona, riconosciuta come superiore in gerarchia e alla quale si deve 'omaggio' (come avveniva in ambiente feudale), quanto come impegno personale nei confronti di un gruppo di pari, che hanno obiettivi comuni da perseguire e comuni interessi da difendere" [The bond, as we have already had occasion to mention, will not then be that of blood, nor even that of friendship, but that of the oath, understood not so much as the promise of loyalty to a person, recognized as superior in the hierarchy and to whom one owes "homage" (as happened in the feudal environment), but instead as a personal commitment to a group of peers, who have common goals to pursue and common interests to defend]. See Pellegrini, *L'incontro tra due "invenzioni" medievali*, 95.

72 Webb (*Dante's Persons*, 116–17) suggests that an "ethics of gratitude" replaces the "ethics of reciprocity" in this canto.

73 The terms "pena" and "sollazzo" [occur in Forese Donati's description of the mountain's training procedure] in *Purgatorio* 23.72: "io dico pena, e dovria dir sollazzo" [I say pain, and I should say solace]. See also Webb, "Postures of Penitence," 230.

74 John Took, "'S'io m'intuassi," 403.

75 On the solitary and collective aspects of the purgatorial pilgrimage, see the brief but insightful discussion in Took, "S'io m'intuassi," 402–3.

76 *Purgatorio* 2.120–1. On the song and Cato's rebuke of it, see Ciabattoni, *Dante's Journey to Polyphony*, 99–109; Freccero, "Casella's Song: *Purgatorio* II, 112," in *Dante: The Poetics of Conversion*, 186–94; Hollander, "*Purgatorio* II," 348–63; Iannucci, "Casella's Song," 27–46; Masciandaro, *The Stranger as Friend*, 62–6. Martha Nussbaum offers an innovating reading of the dove metaphor as critiquing a certain kind of overindulgent passivity. See Nussbaum, "Beatrice's 'Dante,'" 16–70.

77 The poem in full reads: "Guido, i' vorrei che tu e Lapo ed io / fossimo presi per incantamento, / e messi in un vasel ch'ad ogni vento / per mare andasse al voler

vostro e mio; / sì che fortuna od altro tempo rio / non ci potesse dare impedimento, / anzi, vivendo sempre in un talento, / di star insieme crescesse il disio. / E monna Vanna e monna Lagia poi / con quella ch'è sul numer de le trenta / con noi ponesse il buono incantatore: / e quivi ragionar sempre d'amore, / e ciascuna di lor fosse contenta / sì come credo che sarémo noi." The text cited is from Barolini, *Dante's Lyric Poetry*. For Lansing's English translation, I refer the reader to chapter 1.

78 *Purgatorio* 2.41. David Bowe likewise draws a parallel between the metaphor of the ship in *Guido, i' vorrei* and the opening cantos of *Purgatorio*; Bowe reads the opening reference to the "navicella" of *Purgatorio* 1 as an "intertextual performance" that recasts the metaphor from the earlier lyric in light of the poetics ushered in by the *Commedia*. See Bowe, *Poetry in Dialogue*, 137–42 (citation 140).

79 Barolini, *Dante's Lyric Poetry*, 116. See also Barolini's introductory note to the sonnet in the Italian edition of Dante's *Rime giovanili*, 181–91 and especially 185.

80 *Purgatorio* 15.55–7.

81 *Purgatorio* 2.117.

82 Many commentators have read the encounter as a palinode, referring back to a *tenzone* the two young poets participated in, but the authenticity of the *tenzone* has been challenged. On the episode as a palinode, see, for example, Alfie, *Dante's Tenzone*, especially chapter 4, "The Terrace of the *Tenzone*: *Purgatorio* XXIII and XXIV," 82–99; Boitani, *Dante's Poetry of the Donati*, 21–4; Cudini, "La tenzone tra Dante e Forese," 1–25; Russo, "*Pg* XXIII," 113–36; Zaccarello, "L'uovo o la gallina," 5–26. I do not intend to address the content of the *tenzone* nor the attribution debates around it, as these lie outside the scope of my concerns here.

83 On recognition as a method for consciously reframing the past, see Boitani, "Recognition and Poetry: Forese," in *Dante's Poetry of the Donati*, 16–26.

84 On the political dimensions of the dialogue, see Pertile, "Canto XXIV," 262–76. Honess argues that the choice of female citizens as the objects of criticism here and elsewhere indicates that the critique is directed at moral, not political, behaviors; see Honess, *Poetry of Citizenship*, 45–51. On the predicted interdict alluded to in Forese's speech, see Cassell, "Mostrando con le poppe il petto," 75–81.

85 On Dante's enigmatic "traviamento" alluded to here, see, among others, Marti, "Sulla genesi del realismo dantesco," 1–32; Muresu, "Forese e la gola," 5–30; Saverese, "Una proposta per Forese. Dante e il "memorar presente" and "Qual fosti meco e qual io teco fui," in *Una proposta per Forese*, 27–50 and 51–6; Zaccarello, "L'uovo o la gallina," 5–26.

86 Purgatorio 24.1–3.

87 For an alternative reading of the ship as a reference to Ulysses, see Giovannuzzi, "Brunetto e Francesca in *Purgatorio*," 172.

88 See Bourdieu, *Outline of a Theory of Practice*, 18 (emphasis in original).

89 On selfhood ("persona") as an "achievement word" in *Purgatorio*, see Webb, *Dante's Persons*, especially 24–7. In calling "person" an "achievement word," Webb follows Avishai Margalit, *The Ethics of Memory*, 46. Masciandaro, likewise, sees the purgatorial

journey as the gradual revelation of the self through its mirroring in the other. See his chapter on "Friendship, Private and Political, in *Purgatorio*," in *The Stranger as Friend*, 57–96.

90 Soskice, *The Kindness of God*, 167.
91 Soskice, *The Kindness of God*, 176.
92 *Purgatorio* 15.65 and 61–2.
93 *Purgatorio* 15.50.
94 This is the central argument of Webb's discussion of *Paradiso*, in particular. See especially her chapter "Transhuman Faces," in *Dante's Persons*, 164–205. See also Grangolati's chapter "Now, Then, and Beyond: Air, Flesh, and Fullness in the *Comedy*," in *Experiencing the Afterlife*, 139–78.
95 On the concord of wills in divine and human friendships, see Schwartz Porzecanski, "Aquinas on Concord," 25–42.
96 See Hollander's suggestive remark, made in passing, that the bonds of Paradise are "post-personal" (commentary to *Paradiso* 3.43–5).
97 On vulnerability in individual attachment, see Nussbaum, "Beatrice's 'Dante,'" 175–6.
98 Three excellent recent studies highlight the centrality of the pilgrim's encounter with Piccarda to questions of gender, violence, freedom, and volition in the *Paradiso*: see Ingallinella, "The Canonization of Piccarda Donati," 463–84; Pegoretti, "La suora mancata: Piccarda," 19–36; Pierson, "Piccarda's Weakness," 68–93. On the two encounters, see the brief note in Pertile, "Canto XXIV," 262–76, especially 263–4. See also the three essays on the Donati family by Boitani, *Dante's Poetry of the Donati*.
99 *Paradiso* 3.43–45.
100 *Summa Theologiae* 2a2ae. 23.1.
101 On the divergence between Aquinas's theological theory of friendship expounded in the *Summa* and the theory he lays out in his *Sententia libri ethicorum*, which more closely follows Aristotle, see Fuchs, "*Philia* and *Caritas*," 203–19.
102 On the "impasse" between Aristotle's emphasis on reciprocity in friendship and Aquinas's insistence on the fusion of friendship with charity (such that it extends even to one's enemies), see Liuzzo Scorpo, *Friendship in Medieval Iberia*, 19–20. On this and other contradictions between Aristotle's and Aquinas's theories of friendship, see Fuchs, "*Philia* and *Caritas*," especially 207–18.
103 *Summa Theologiae* 2a2ae. 23.5.
104 *Purgatorio* 15. 67–75.
105 *Paradiso* 5.105. One might also read the reciprocal reduplication of joy in *Paradiso* 8.31–48, where the souls in the heaven of Venus assent to the pilgrim's pleasures as a redoubling of their own, in the same light: as mirrors that intensify love through reciprocal reflection.
106 For Webb's reading of the passage, see *Dante's Persons*, 150–1. On possible sources for Dante's mirror imagery here and elsewhere in the *Commedia*, see Gilson, "Light Reflection," 241–52.

107 *Paradiso* 3.64–6.

108 Took, "'S'io m'intuassi,'" 407.

109 *Paradiso* 3.70–8.

110 See *Summa Theologiae* 2a2ae. 24.1: "caritas, cuius objectum est finis ultimis, magis debet dici esse in voluntate quam in libero arbitrio" [it is more accurate to say that, since its object is the ultimate end, charity is in the will rather than in the free-will].

111 On the fixed standard of the "voler di colui che qui ne cerne," see Schwartz Porzecanski, "Aquinas on Concord," 29.

112 Pierson, "Piccarda's Weakness," 85.

113 See the extended discussion of concord as conformity of will in friendship with God in Schwartz, *Aquinas on Friendship*, 42–68.

114 *Inferno* 5.101, 104.

115 *Paradiso* 3.79–81.

116 On unity and multiplicity in *Paradiso*, see Barolini's chapter "Problems in Paradise: The Mimesis of Time and the Paradox of *Più e Meno*," in *The Undivine Comedy*, 166–93.

117 On imitation as participation in and conformity to the divine will in Aquinas, see Schwartz Porzecanski, "Aquinas on Concord," 29n17. See also Masciandaro's remarks on the perfection of friendship in charity: *The Stranger as Friend*, 114.

118 See chapter 1, above.

119 On possible sources for *Vita nova*'s notion of the "gradi dell'amistade," see Gorni, "*Vita nova*, libro delle 'amistadi' e della 'prima etade,'" in *Dante prima della* Commedia, 133–47, especially 138–9. As I discussed above in chapter 1, Dante uses the term "gradi" differently than do most of the sources Gorni lists; while most theologians describe the "gradus charitatis" as "stages" of intimacy within a particular relationship between two individuals, Dante (like John Cassian) appears more interested in a hierarchical ordering of "degrees" of love.

120 Barolini, *The Undivine Comedy*, 182.

121 *Paradiso* 3.82–5.

122 For Aquinas's discussions of *amicitia caritatis*, see *Summa Theologiae* 2a2ae. 23–46.

123 On the conformity (not unity) of the human will to the divine, see Schwartz Porzecanski, "Aquinas on Concord," 28–30. See also Schwartz, *Aquinas on Friendship*, 42–68.

124 On the surprising lack of predecessors for this view, that the blessed souls in Paradise would retain earthly attachments, see Gragnolati, "Nostalgia in Heaven," 135.

125 On the role of diversity in bringing about earthly beatitude and celestial harmony, see Peters, "Human Diversity," 51–70.

126 *Paradiso* 8.56–7. Carlo had not lived long enough to allow their friendship to see its fullest fruits. Masciandaro suggests that the verse points to the "essence of true friendship, namely, that it is not finite and quantifiable, but infinite and immeasurable" (*The Stranger as Friend*, 100). I would suggest, rather, that the verse

affirms the plenitude of human friendship, the fullness with which its delights can be enjoyed in the natural order, but that such delights have a finitude that will only be transmuted in the paradisiacal bonds of charity.

127 It is of note here that the fruits of Carlo's affections for the pilgrim, had they been permitted to flourish, would have provided both moral and material goods. Durling and Martinez (*Paradiso* 8.55–7) note that "Dante was already able, from their initial encounters, to foresee that Carlo Martello would express his growing affection for him by liberal support (material or moral or both)." In her notes to Stanley Lombardo's translation of *Paradiso*, Alison Cornish comments that "the relationship alluded to here as the 'fruit' of their budding friendship would have been that of sovereign and courtier, a position of protection and honor Dante might have enjoyed had Charles Martel lived longer" (374). Their friendship, in other words, was directed at both virtuous and instrumental ends, without the perception of any apparent contradiction between the two.

128 On hypostasis as "realization," see Pierson, "Piccarda's Weakness," 86–7.

129 On the twinned loves of Paradise as "co-presence" (the cooperative composition of the body of the Church) and "co-immanence" (the ecstatic "indwelling" of each within each, as the bounds of personhood are exceeded), see Took, "Se io m'intuassi," with reference to *Paradiso* 9.73–81.

130 *Paradiso* 9.7–9.

131 *Paradiso* 3.45.

132 Nussbaum is especially eloquent on the particular love between Dante and Beatrice, as well as on the limitations of reading that love as emblematic of a broader Christian doctrine of individual love. See Nussbaum, "Beatrice's 'Dante,'" 161–78.

133 See Harrison, "Community Among the Saintly Dead," 191–204. Of Bernard's writings, Harrison comments, "we can trace a tension between 'special friendships' in the eternity of heaven and the dissolution of the will into the comprehensive love of Christ" (200).

134 *Paradiso* 14.61–6.

135 Harrison's survey of how Bernard of Clairvaux treats community among the saints sheds contrasting light on the strangeness of Dante's addition: "despite [Bernard's] charged preoccupation with his brother's love for him, despite his broader interest in friends and friendship, despite his attention to the common life and to the relationship between self and other, Bernard thinks little about interaction when he thinks about the dead" ("Community Among the Saintly Dead," 191).

136 Muresu, *I ladri di malebolge*, 158.

137 Gragnolati, *Experiencing the Afterlife*, 154–61.

138 Gragnolati, *Experiencing the Afterlife*, 159.

139 Gragnolati, "Nostalgia in Heaven," 137. See also Barolini, *The Undivine Comedy*, 138; Nussbaum, "Beatrice's 'Dante,'" 168–74; Webb, *Dante's Persons*, 155–7. Later in her book Webb argues that the saints' exclamation here expresses a desire to see

"consortually" into the Godhead, to "look together into and with the divine light" (*Dante's Persons*, 191–2).

140 Jacoff, "Our Bodies, Our Selves," 132, emphasis added.

141 *Paradiso* 10.49–50.

142 *Paradiso* 10.52–54.

143 *Paradiso* 10.55–60.

144 Bernard, too, struggled to articulate the value of special friendships in the light of God's love, particularly in relationship to his cherished brother Gerard. Dismissing the forgetfulness of the saints, Bernard claims that the love of the saints is not "diminished but only changed" (Sermon Twenty-Six, quoted in Harrison, "Community Among the Saintly Dead, 198). In a sermon on the Feast of Saint Victor, Bernard would clarify, claiming that Heaven "is not a land of oblivion … Brothers, the breadth of heaven dilates, not contracts the heart; it delights, not estranges (*alienat*), the mind; it enlarges, not tightens (*contrahit*) the affections (*affectiones*). In the light of God, memory is made clear not obscured; in the light of God, that which is unknown is learned, that which is known is not unlearned" (quoted in Harrison, "Community Among the Saintly Dead," 199). For Bernard, particular relationships do not diminish or distract from affections for God but enhance and focus them.

145 Webb's account of "conjoined vision" in the Empyrean makes clear that the eclipse of Beatrice here is not an either/or: "Fundamentally, what happens to Dante in the final cantos of *Paradiso* is not that he learns to turn away from Beatrice and towards God, but rather that he transitions from an earthly logic of binary facing to the heavenly mode in which he conjoins his vision to Beatrice's so that he may come to see her in God" (199). See *Dante's Persons*, 192–205.

146 *Paradiso* 10.61–3.

147 On conjoined will as conjoined vision, see Webb, *Dante's Persons*, 192–205.

148 *Paradiso* 33.91.

149 See the discussion of human freedom and its struggle against the inclinations of the heavens in *Purgatorio* 16.73–78: "Lo cielo i vostri movimenti inizia; / non dico tutti, ma, posto ch'i' 'l dica, / lume v'è dato a bene e a malizia, / e libero voler, che, se fatica / ne le prime battaglie col ciel dura, / poi vince tutto, se ben si notrica" [The heavens begin your motions; I do not say all of them, but, supposing I say it, a light is given to you to know good and evil, and free will, which if it lasts out the labor of its first battles with the heavens, afterwards overcomes all things, if nourished well].

Epilogue: Friendship's Afterlife in Early Humanism

1 On friendship in Boccaccio's works, see, among others, Houston, "Boccaccio on Friendship," 81–97; Kirkham, "The Classic Bond of Friendship," 223–35; Langer, *Perfect Friendship*; Masciandaro, *The Stranger as Friend*; Sherberg, *The Governance of Friendship*. On Petrarch and friendship, see Fenzi, "Petrarca e la

scrittura dell'amicizia," 549–89; Wojciehowski, "Petrarch and His Friends," 26–35; Wojciehowski, "Petrarch: First Modern Friend," 269–98; Zak "Soft Hearts," 125–36.

2 On the "loose and ambiguous frame" that friendship provided Renaissance Florentine writers, see McLean, *The Art of the Network*, 15.

3 See, for example, Langer, *Perfect Friendship*, 23–6; Wojciehowski, "Petrarch and His Friends," especially 28–30.

4 McLean, *The Art of the Network*, 29.

5 From the light of the twelfth-century "renaissance" of monastic *vera amicitia* McGuire reconstructs in his influential tome, early humanist notions of friendship appear pessimistic, sceptical, or anxious. See the epilogue, "Ends and Beginnings in Community and Friendship," in McGuire, *Friendship and Community*, 407–27, especially 415–18.

6 Research by historians of medieval friendship, chiefly Julian Haseldine, has challenged this limited view of monastic friendship. See especially Haseldine, "Friendship Networks in Medieval Europe," 69–88; Haseldine, "Friends or *amici*?," 43–58. Additional bibliography on specific letter collections is provided in the introduction.

7 James and Kent, "Renaissance Friendships," 115.

8 James and Kent, "Renaissance Friendships," 115.

9 Houston, "Boccaccio on Friendship," 84.

10 On the *Certame*, see, for example, Kent, *Friendship, Love, and Trust*, 17–32; Kircher, *Living Well*, 187–94.

11 On debates over the value of friendship in the realm of *Realpolitik*, see Kircher, *Living Well*, 187–94; Langer, *Perfect Friendship*, 189–211. On Boccaccio's disappointment at his treatment by a friend and would-be patron, see Houston, "Boccaccio on Friendship," especially 85–93. On manliness and compassion as the defining features of Petrarch's community of friends (with discussions of Boccaccio's interventions), see Zak, "Soft Hearts."

12 On friendship in Boccaccio's *novelle*, see, most importantly, Kirkham, "The Classic Bond of Friendship"; Masciandaro, *The Stranger as Friend*, 117–45; Sherberg, *The Governance of Friendship*.

13 Houston, "Boccaccio on Friendship," 85.

14 Wojciehowski notes that Petrarch "sometimes fell short of his own friendship ideals, but he nevertheless articulated them clearly" ("Petrarch and His Friends," 34). Zak's recent essay complicates somewhat this clarity: Zak has identified a tension in Petrarch's conception of friendship, between masculinist and elitist ideals of "virtue" and the compassionate expression of human "vulnerability." See Zak, "Soft Hearts" 125–36.

15 Wojciehowski, "Petrarch: First Modern Friend," 283–5.

Bibliography

Primary Sources

Albertano da Brescia. *De amore et dilectione Dei et proximi.* In Sharon Lynne Hiltz, ed. "De amore et dilectione Dei et proximi et aliarum rerum et de forma vite: An Edition (Latin Text)." PhD diss., University of Pennsylvania, 1980.

Alighieri, Dante. *Dante's Lyric Poetry: Poems of Youth and the Vita Nuova (1283–1292).* Edited by Teodolinda Barolini. Translated by Richard H. Lansing and Andrew Frisardi. Toronto: University of Toronto Press, 2014.

– *De vulgari eloquentia.* Translated by Steven Botterill. Cambridge: Cambridge University Press, 1996.

– Epistola XIII. Edited by Giorgio Brugnoli. In *Opere minori.* Vol. 2. Edited by Pier Vincenzo Mengaldo, Bruno Nardi, Arsenio Frugoni, Giorgio Brugnoli, Enzo Cecchini, and Francesco Mazzoni. Milan: Ricciardi, 1979. 598–643.

– *Epistola XIII.* Edited by Luca Azzetta. In *Nuova Edizione commentata delle Opere di Dante.* Edited by Marco Baglio, Luca Azzetta, Marco Petoletti, and Michele Rinaldi. Introduction by Andrea Mazzucchi. Vol. 5: *Epistole, Egloghe, Questio de aqua et terra.* Rome: Salerno, 2016. 271–487.

– *Il Convivio* (*The Banquet*). Translated by Richard Lansing. New York: Garland, 1990.

– *Opere. Volume primo: Rime, Vita Nova, De vulgari eloquentia.* Edited by Claudio Giunta, Guglielmo Gorni, and Mirko Tavoni. Milan: Mondadori, 2011.

– *Opere. Volume secondo: Convivio, Monarchia, Epistole, Egloge.* Edited by Gianfranco Fioravanti, Claudio Giunta, Diego Quaglioni, Claudia Villa, and Gabriella Albanese. Milan: Mondadori, 2014.

– *Paradiso.* Edited by Robert Hollander. New York: Doubleday/Anchor, 2007. Retrieved from *Dante Lab*, http://dantelab.dartmouth.edu. Last accessed 3 October 2021.

– *Paradiso.* Translated by Stanley Lombardo. Notes by Alison Cornish. Indianapolis and Cambridge: Hackett Publishing Company, 2017.

– *Purgatorio.* Edited by Robert Hollander. New York: Doubleday/Anchor, 2003. Retrieved from *Dante Lab*, http://dantelab.dartmouth.edu. Last accessed 3 October 2021.

– *Rime giovanili e della* Vita Nuova. Edited by Teodolinda Barolini, with notes by Manuele Gragnolati. Milan: BUR, 2009.

– *The Divine Comedy.* Translated with a commentary by Charles S. Singleton. Princeton: Princeton University Press, 1970–5.

– *The Divine Comedy of Dante Alighieri.* Edited and translated by Robert M. Durling. Notes by Ronald L. Martinez and Robert M. Durling. 3 vols. Oxford: Oxford University Press, 1996.

– *Vita Nova.* Translated by Andrew Frisardi. Evanston, Ill.: Northwestern University Press, 2012.

Alighieri, Pietro. *Comentum super poema Comedie Dantis: A Critical Edition of the Third and Final Draft of Pietro Alighieri's "Commentary on Dante's 'Divine Comedy,'"* ed. Massimiliano Chiamenti. Tempe, AZ: Arizona Center for Medieval and Renaissance Studies, 2002. Retrieved from *Dante Lab*, http://dantelab.dartmouth.edu. Last accessed 3 October 2021.

Andrea, Monte. *Le Rime.* Edited by Francesco Filippo Minetti. Florence: Accademia della Crusca, 1979.

Aquinas, Thomas. *Commentary on Aristotle's* Nicomachean Ethics. Translated by C.I. Litzinger. Notre Dame: Dumb Ox Books, 1993.

– *Sententia Libri Ethicorum.* Library of Latin Texts: Series A. Turnhout: Brepols, 1969. Retrieved from *Library of Latin Texts* (LLT), http://clt.brepolis.net/LLTA/pages/TextSearch.aspx?key=MTHAQCTC__. Last accessed 1 October 2021.

– *Summa Theologiae. Vol. 34. Charity (2a2ae. 23–33).* Translated by R.J. Batten. Cambridge: Blackfriars, 1975.

Aristotle. *Ethica Nicomachea, traslatio Roberti Grosseteste Lincolniensis sive "Liber Ethicorum."* Edited by Renatus Antonius Gauthier. Leiden: E.J. Brill, 1972.

– *Nicomachean Ethics.* Edited by Roger Crisp. Revised ed. Cambridge: Cambridge University Press, 2013.

Benvenuto da Imola. *Comentum super Dantis Aldigherij Comoediam, nunc primum integre in lucem editum sumptibus Guilielmi Warren Vernon.* Edited by Jacobo Philippo Lacaita Florence: G. Barbèra, 1887. Retrieved from *Dante Lab*, http://dantelab.dartmouth.edu. Last accessed 3 October 2021.

Bichilino da Spello. *Il Pomerium Rethorice di Bichilino da Spello.* Edited by Vincenzo Licitra. Florence: La Nuova Italia, 1979.

Boncompagno da Signa. *Amicitia and De Malo Senectutis et Senii.* Edited and translated Michael W. Dunne. Dallas Medieval Texts and Translations. Paris and Walpole, MA: Peeters, 2012.

– *Amicitia di Maestro Boncompagno da Signa.* Edited by Sarina Nathan. Roma: Società filologica romana, 1909.

Cassian, John. *The Conferences.* Translated by Boniface Ramsey. New York and Mahwah, NJ: Paulist Press, 1997.

– *Opera Omnia.* Edited by J.-P. Migne. Paris: apud Garnier fratres, 1846.

Cicero. *On Old Age, On Friendship, On Divination.* Translated by W.A. Falconer. Loeb Classical Library 154. Cambridge, Mass: Harvard University Press, 1923.

– *How to be a Friend: An Ancient Guide to True Friendship*. Translated by Philip Freeman. Princeton and Oxford: Princeton University Press, 2018.

Cino da Pistoia. *Le Rime di Cino da Pistoia*. Edited by Guido Zaccagnini. Geneva: Olschki, 1925.

Fabe, Guidonis. *Summa dictaminis*. Edited by Augusto Gaudenzi. *Il Propugnatore* 3, no. 1 (1890): 287–338.

Guittone d'Arezzo. *Le Rime*. Edited by Francesco Egidi. Bari: Laterza, 1940.

Jacopo della Lana. *Comedia di Dante degli Allaghieri col Commento di Jacopo della Lana bolognese*. Edited by Luciano Scarabelli. Bologna: Tipografia Regia, 1866–7. Retrieved from *Dante Lab*, http://dantelab.dartmouth.edu. Last accessed 3 October 2021.

Latini, Brunetto. *The Book of the Treasure* (*Li Livres Dou Tresor*). Translated by Paul Barrette and Spurgeon W. Baldwin. New York: Garland, 1993.

– *Li Livres dou Tresor*. Edited by Spurgeon W. Baldwin and Paul Barrette. Medieval and Renaissance Texts and Studies. Tempe, Ariz: Arizona Center for Medieval and Renaissance Studies, 2003.

– *La Rettorica di Brunetto Latini*. Edited by Francesco Maggini. Florence: Galletti e Cocci, 1915.

Onesto da Bologna. *Le rime di Onesto da Bologna*. Edited by Sandro Orlando. Florence: G.C. Sansoni, 1974.

The Ottimo Commento della Divina Commedia. Edited by Alessandro Torri. Pisa: N. Capurro, 1827–9. Retrieved from *Dante Lab*, http://dantelab.dartmouth.edu. Last accessed 3 October 2021.

Panciroli, Guido. *Chronicon Regiense*. In *Rerum italicarum scriptores*. Edited by Ludovico Antonio Muratori. Vol. 18. Milan: Ex typographia Societatis palatinae in regia curia, 1731. 1–98.

Peraldi, Guilelmus. "De Vera Amicitia." In *Summa virtutum ac vitiorum*. Lyon: apud Gulielmus Rovillium, 1585. 271–4.

Petrarca, Francesco. *Rerum memorandarum libri*. In *Edizione nazionale delle opere di Francesco Petrarca*. Edited by Giuseppe Billanovich. Vol. 2. Florence: G.C. Sansoni, 1945. 98–9.

Secondary Sources

Ahern, John. "The New Life of the Book: The Implied Reader of the *Vita Nuova*." *Dante Studies*, no. 110 (1992): 1–16.

– "The Reader on the Piazza: Verbal Duels in Dante's *Vita Nuova*." *Texas Studies in Literature and Language* 32, no. 1 (1990): 18–39.

Alfie, Fabian. *Dante's Tenzone with Forese Donati: The Reprehension of Vice*. Toronto: University of Toronto Press, 2011.

– "Nonsense and Noise: The Audial Poetics of Immanuel Romano's Bisbidis." *International Studies Humor 5* 1 (2016): 127–39.

– "Politics, and Not Poetics: A Reading of Guido Cavalcanti's Sonnet 'Una figura della donna mia.'" *Italica* 93, no. 2 (2016): 209–24.

Anselmi, Gian Mario, and Stefano Scioli. "Literary Culture in Bologna from the Duecento to the Cinquecento." In *A Companion to Medieval and Renaissance Bologna*. Edited by Sarah Rubin Blanshei. Leiden and Boston: Brill, 2018. 499–529.

Anselmi, Gian Mario, Angela De Benedictis, and Nicholas Terpstra, eds. *Bologna. Cultural Crossroads from the Medieval to the Baroque: Recent Anglo-American Scholarship*. Bologna: Bononia University Press, 2013.

Antonelli, Armando. "Nuove su Onesto da Bologna." *I quaderni del m.æ.s*, no. 10 (2007): 9–20.

Ardizzone, Maria Luisa. *Guido Cavalcanti: The Other Middle Ages*. Toronto: University of Toronto Press, 1992.

– *Guido Cavalcanti tra i suoi lettori*. Fiesole: Cadmo, 2003.

Arendt, Hannah. "Philosophy and Politics." *Social Research* 57, no. 1 (1990): 73–103.

Armour, Peter. "Friends and Patrons." In *Dante in Oxford: The Paget Toynbee Lectures*. Edited by Tristan Kay, M.L. McLaughlin, and Michelangelo Zaccarello. London: Legenda, 2011. 102–30.

Arqués, Rossend, and Silvia Tranfaglia. *Cino da Pistoia nella storia della poesia italiana*. Florence: Franco Cesati, 2016.

Ascoli, Albert Russell. "Access to Authority: Dante in the Epistle to Cangrande." In *Seminario Dantesco Internazionale*. Edited by Zygmunt G. Barański. Florence: Le Lettere, 1997. 309–52.

– *Dante and the Making of a Modern Author*. Cambridge: Cambridge University Press, 2008.

Asor Rosa, Alberto. *Letteratura italiana. Gli autori. Dizionario bio-bibliografico e indici*. Vol. 8.2. Turin: Einaudi, 1991.

Azzetta, Luca. "Le chiose alla *Commedia* di Andrea Lancia, L'*Epistola a Cangrande*, e altre questioni dantesche." *L'Alighieri* 21 (2003): 5–76.

– "Nota introduttiva" to *Epistola a Cangrande*. Edited by Luca Azzetta. In *Epistole, Egloge, Questio de aqua et terra*. Vol. 5 of *Nuova Edizione Commentata delle Opere di Dante*, edited by Marco Baglio, Luca Azzetta, Marco Petoletti, and Michele Rinaldi, 273–324. Rome: Salerno, 2016.[EC14].

Baker, Steve. "Ad Comunis Epystole Lectionem: Pan-Italian Familiarties and Petrarch's Community of Friends." In *Friendship and Sociability in Premodern Europe: Contexts, Concepts, and Expressions*. Edited by Amyrose McCue Gill and Sarah Rolfe Prodan. Toronto: Centre for Reformation and Renaissance Studies, 2014. 125–52.

Barański, Zygmunt G. "*Purgatorio* VI." *Lectura Dantis*, no. 12 (Spring 1993): 80–97.

Barolini, Teodolinda. "'Amicus eius': Dante and the Semantics of Friendship." *Dante Studies*, no. 133 (2015): 46–69.

– *Dante's Poets: Textuality and Truth in the* Comedy. Princeton, NJ: Princeton University Press, 1984.

– "Purgatorio 13: Eyes Sewn Shut." *Commento Baroliniano*, Digital Dante. New York: Columbia University Libraries, 2014. https://digitaldante.columbia.edu/dante/divine-comedy/purgatorio/purgatorio-13/. Last accessed 3 October 2021.

– "Sociology of the Brigata: Gendered Groups in Dante, Forese, Folgore, Boccaccio – From 'Guido, i' vorrei' to Griselda." *Italian Studies* 67, no. 1 (March 2012): 4–22.

– "The Poetic Exchanges Between Dante and His Amico Dante da Maiano: A Young Man Takes His Place in the World." In *Legato Con Amore in Un Volume. Essays in Honour of John A. Scott.* Florence: Olschki, 2013. 39–61.

– *The Undivine Comedy: Detheologizing Dante.* Princeton: Princeton University Press, 1992.

Bianchi, Anna. "Il Comune e le Signorie." In *Storia di Verona: Caratteri, aspetti, momenti.* Edited by Giovanni Zalin. Vicenza: Neri Pozza, 2001. 93–148.

Boitani, Piero. *Dante's Poetry of the Donati.* Leeds: Maney Publishing, 2007.

– "*Inferno* XXXIII." In *Cambridge Readings in Dante's* Comedy. Edited by Kenelm Foster and Patrick Boyde. Cambridge: Cambridge University Press, 1981. 70–89.

Borsellino, Nino. "Dante e Forese. Autobiografia di un'amicizia." In *Lectura Dantis Interamnensis: Purgatorio: Catone, Sordello, Marco Lombardo, Forese, Matelda.* Edited by Giancarlo Rati. Rome: Bulzoni, 2009. 135–49.

Bourdieu, Pierre. *The Logic of Practice.* Translated by Richard Nice. Stanford: Stanford University Press, 1990.

– *Outline of a Theory of Practice.* Translated by Richard Nice. Cambridge: Cambridge University Press, 1977.

– "Séminaires sur le concept de champ, 1972–1975: Introduction de Patrick Champagne." *Actes de la recherche en sciences sociales* 200, no. 5 (2013): 4–37.

Bowe, David. *Poetry in Dialogue in the Duecento and Dante.* Oxford: Oxford University Press, 2020.

Brilli, Elisa. "Civitas/Community." In *The Oxford Handbook of Dante.* Edited by Manuele Gragnolati, Elena Lombardi, and Francesca Southerden. Oxford: Oxford University Press, 2021. 353–67.

Brugnolo, Furio. "Cino (e Onesto) dentro e fuori la *Commedia*." In *Omaggio a Gianfranco Folena.* Padua: Editoriale Programma, 1993. 369–86.

Brugnoli, Giorgio. "Introduzione all'*Epistola a Cangrande*." In *Opere minori.* Vol. 2. Edited by Pier Vincenzo Mengaldo, Bruno Nardi, Arsenio Frugoni, Giorgio Brugnoli, Enzo Cecchini, and Francesco Mazzoni. Milan: Ricciardi, 1979. 512–21.

Brugnoli, Pierpaolo. " 'Donna e regina de le terre italice': realtà e immagine di Verona scaligera." In *Gli Scaligeri, 1277–1387.* Edited by Gian Maria Varanini. Verona: Mondadori, 1988. 215–24.

Bufano, Antonietta. "Forese Donati nel canto XXIII del Purgatorio: La forza dell'amicizia." *Italianistica: Rivista di letteratura italiana* 15, no. 2–3 (1986): 219–37.

– "Pugnare." In *Enciclopedia Dantesca.* Rome: Treccani, 1970. https://www.treccani.it/enciclopedia/pugnare_(Enciclopedia-Dantesca). Last accessed 3 October 2021.

Caine, Barbara, ed. *Friendship: A History.* London: Equinox, 2009.

Carrai, Stefano, and Paolo Maffei. "Sinibuldi, Cino." In *Dizionario biografico degli italiani.* Vol. 92. Treccani, 2018. https://www.treccani.it/enciclopedia/cino-sinibuldi_(Dizionario-Biografico). Last accessed 3 October 2021.

Cassell, Anthony K. "'Mostrando con le poppe il petto' (*Purg.* XXIII.102)." *Dante Studies*, no. 96 (1978): 75–81.

Cassidy, Eoin G. "He Who Has Friends Can Have No Friend: Classical and Christian Perspectives on the Limits to Friendship." In *Friendship in Medieval Europe.* Edited by Julian Haseldine. Stroud, UK: Sutton, 1999. 45–67.

Castagnetti, Andrea. "Formazione e vicende della signoria Scaligera." In *Gli Scaligeri, 1277–1387.* Edited by Gian Maria Varanini. Verona: Mondadori, 1988. 5–14.

Ciabattoni, Francesco. *Dante's Journey to Polyphony.* Toronto: University of Toronto Press, 2010.

– "Dante's Rhetoric of Friendship from the *Convivio* to the *Commedia.*" In *Friendship and Sociability in Premodern Europe: Contexts, Concepts, and Expressions*, edited by Amyrose McCue Gill and Sarah Rolfe Prodan. Toronto: Centre for Reformation and Renaissance Studies, 2014. 97–123.

Cipolla, Carlo, and Flaminio Pellegrini. "Poesie minori riguardanti gli Scaligeri." In *Bollettino dell'Istituto storico italiano* 24 (1902): 7–206.

Classen, Albrecht and Marilyn Sandidge, eds. *Friendship in the Middle Ages and Early Modern Age: Explorations of a Fundamental Ethical Discourse.* Berlin and New York: Walter de Gruyter, 2010.

Coggeshall, Elizabeth. "'Eternal Hate Created Me as Well': In Search of Hate in Dante's *Commedia.*" In *Dante's Volume from Alpha to Omega.* Edited by Carol Chiodo and Christiana Purdy Moudarres. Tempe, AZ: Arizona Center for Medieval and Renaissance Studies, 2021. 153–70.

– "Jousting with Verse: The Poetics of Friendship in Duecento *Comuni.*" *Italian Culture* 38.2 (2020): 99–118.

Collodo, Silvana. "Padova e gli Scaligeri." In *Gli Scaligeri, 1277–1387.* Edited by Gian Maria Varanini. Verona: Mondadori, 1988. 41–50.

Contini, Gianfranco. *Poeti Del Duecento.* 2 vols. Milan: Ricciardi, 1960.

Copeland, Rita, and Ineke Sluiter, eds. *Medieval Grammar and Rhetoric: Language Arts and Literary Theory, AD 300–1475.* Oxford: Oxford University Press, 2010.

Corti, Maria. "Dante e la Torre di Babele: una *allegoria in factis.*" In *Il viaggio testuale: Le ideologie e le strutture semiotiche.* Turin: Einaudi, 1978. 243–56.

Cox, Virginia. "Ciceronian Rhetoric in Italy, 1260–1350." *Rhetorica* 17, no. 3 (1999): 239–88.

– "Ciceronian Rhetoric in Late Medieval Italy." In *The Rhetoric of Cicero in Its Medieval and Early Renaissance Commentary Tradition.* Leiden and Boston: Brill, 2006. 109–43.

Cox, Virginia, and John O Ward, eds. *The Rhetoric of Cicero in Its Medieval and Early Renaissance Commentary Tradition.* Leiden and Boston: Brill, 2006.

Cudini, Piero. "La tenzone tra Dante e Forese e la 'Commedia' (*Inf.* XXX; *Purg.* XXIII–XXIV)." *Giornale storico della letteratura italiana* 159 (1982): 1–25.

– ed. *Poesia Italiana Del Trecento.* Milan: Garzanti, 1978.

De Robertis, Domenico. "Cino e i poeti bolognesi." *Giornale storico della letteratura italiana* 128 (1951): 273–312.

– "Cino e le 'imitazioni' dalle rime di Dante." *Studi Danteschi* 29 (1950): 103–77.

– *Il Libro della 'Vita Nuova.'* Florence: G.C. Sansoni, 1961.

Dean, Trevor. "The Rise of the Signori." In *Italy in the Central Middle Ages: 1000–1300.* Edited by David Abulafia. *Short Oxford History of Italy.* Oxford: Oxford University Press, 2004. 104–24.

Della Terza, Dante. "Dante e Forese: L'incontro in Purgatorio." *Dante: Rivista internazionale di studi su Dante Alighieri* 1 (2004): 101–11.

Delle Donne, Fulvio. "Amicus amico: L'amicizia nella pratica epistolare del XIII secolo." In *Parole e realtà dell'amicizia medievale: Atti del convegno di studio svoltosi in occasione della XXII edizione del Premio internazionale Ascoli Piceno (Ascoli Piceno, Palazzo Dei Capitani, 2–4 Dicembre 2010).* Edited by Isa Lori Sanfilippo and Antonio Rigon. Rome: Istituto storico italiano per il Medio Evo, 2012. 107–26.

Di Salvo, Andrea. "'Celebrazioni politiche d'occasione': Il caso dei primi Scaligeri." In *Le forme della propaganda politica nel Due e Trecento. Relazioni tenute al convegno internazionale di Trieste (2–5 marzo 1993).* Edited by Paolo Cammarosano. Rome: École française de Rome, 1994. 287–310.

– "Il signore della Scala: Percezioni e rielaborazioni della figura di Cangrande I nelle testimonianze del secolo XIV." *Rivista storica italiana* 108, no. 1 (1996): 36–87.

Dronke, Peter. *Dante and Medieval Latin Traditions.* Cambridge: Cambridge University Press, 1986.

Dunne, Michael. "Good Friends or Bad Friends? The *Amicitia* of Boncompagno Da Signa." In *Amor Amicitiae: On the Love That Is Friendship, Essays in Medieval Thought and Beyond in Honor of the Rev. Professor James McEvoy.* Edited by Thomas A. F Kelly and Philipp Rosemann. Leuven and Paris: Peeters, 2004. 147–66.

Durling, Robert M. "The Audience(s) of the *De vulgari eloquentia* and the *Petrose.*" *Dante Studies,* no. 110 (1992): 25–35.

Falzone, Paolo. "Il *Convivio* e l'amicizia secondo i filosofi." *Annali dell'Istituto italiano per gli studi storici* 17 (2000): 55–101.

Feng, Aileen A. "Desiring Subjects: Mimetic Desire and Female *Invidia* in Gaspara Stampa's *Rime.*" In *Rethinking Gaspara Stampa in the Canon of Renaissance Poetry.* Edited by Unn Falkeid and Aileen A Feng. London: Routledge, 2015. 75–91.

Fenzi, Enrico. "Petrarca e la scrittura dell'amicizia (con un'ipotesi sul Libro VIII delle *Familiari*)." In *Motivi e Forme delle* Familiari *di Francesco Petrarca.* Edited by Claudia Berra. Milan: Cisalpino, 2003. 549–89.

Ferrara, Sabrina. "Devotissimus et amicus: L'amitié possible entre le poète et le seigneur dans l'épître XIII de Dante." *Arzanà* 13: *Écritures et pratiques de l'amitié dans l'Italie médiévale* (2010): 191–210.

– "Io mi credea del tutto esser partito. Il distacco di Dante da Cino." In *Cino da Pistoia nella storia della poesia italiana.* Edited by Rossend Arqués and Silvia Tranfaglia. Florence: Franco Cesati, 2006. 99–111.

Fontes Baratto, Anna. "En guise d'avant-propos: L'amitié en questions." *Arzanà* 13: *Écritures et pratiques de l'amitié dans l'Italie médiévale* (2010): 9–28.

Fornaciari, Gino, et al. "A Medieval Case of *Digitalis* Poisoning: The Sudden Death of Cangrande della Scala, Lord of Verona (1291–1329)." *Journal of Archaeological Science* 54 (February 2015): 162–7. Retrieved from https://doi.org/10.1016/j.jas.2014.12.005. Last accessed 4 October 2021.

Freccero, John. *Dante: The Poetics of Conversion.* Edited by Rachel Jacoff. Cambridge, Mass: Harvard University Press, 1986.

Fuchs, Marko. "*Philia* and *Caritas*: Some Aspects of Aquinas's Reception of Aristotle's Theory of Friendship." In *Aquinas and the Nicomachean Ethics.* Edited by Tobias Hoffmann, Jörn Müller, and Matthias Perkams. Cambridge: Cambridge University Press, 2015. 203–19.

Ghetti, Noemi. *L'ombra di Cavalcanti e Dante.* Rome: L'asino d'oro Edizioni, 2010.

Gianola, Giovanna Maria. "Tra Padova e Verona: il Cangrande di Mussato (e quello di Dante)." In *Gli Scaligeri, 1277–1387.* Edited by Gian Maria Varanini. Verona: Mondadori, 1988. 51–60.

Gilson, Simon A. "Light Reflection, Mirror Metaphors, and Optical Framing in Dante's *Comedy*: Precedents and Transformations." *Neophilologus* 83 (1999): 241–52.

Giovannuzzi, Stefano. "Brunetto e Francesca in *Purgatorio* (sul Canto XXIV)." *Filologia e Critica* 22 (1997): 161–85.

Giunta, Claudio. *Due saggi sulla tenzone.* Rome and Padua: Antenore, 2002.

– *Versi a un destinatario: Saggio sulla poesia italiana del Medioevo.* Bologna: Il Mulino, 2002.

Gorni, Guglielmo. *Dante prima della Commedia.* Florence: Cadmo, 2001.

Gragnolati, Manuele. *Experiencing the Afterlife: Soul and Body in Dante in Medieval Culture.* Notre Dame: University of Notre Dame Press, 2008.

– "Nostalgia in Heaven: Embraces, Affection and Identity in the *Commedia*." In *Dante and the Human Body: Eight Essays.* Edited by John C. Barnes and Jennifer Petrie. Dublin: Four Courts Press, 2007. 117–37.

Hainsworth, Peter. "Cavalcanti in the 'Vita Nuova.'" *The Modern Language Review* 83, no. 3 (July 1988): 586–90.

Harrison, Anna. "Community Among the Saintly Dead: Bernard of Clairvaux's Sermons for the Feast of All Saints." In *Last Things: Death and the Apocalypse in the Middle Ages.* Edited by Caroline Walker Bynum and Paul Freedman. Philadelphia: University of Pennsylvania Press, 2000. 191–204.

Harrison, Robert Pogue. *The Body of Beatrice.* Baltimore and London: Johns Hopkins University Press, 1988.

– *The Dominion of the Dead.* Chicago: University of Chicago Press, 2003.

Hartmann, Florian. "Eloquence and Friendship: Letter-Writing Manuals and the Importance of Being Somebody's Friend." In *Networks of Learning: Perspectives on Scholars in Byzantine East and Latin West, c. 1000–1200.* Edited by Sita Steckel, Niels Gaul, and Michael Grünbart. Zurich: LIT, 2014. 67–86.

– "L'*amicitia* nei primi comuni italiani: Un sondaggio nelle artes dictandi alla luce dei recenti orientamenti della storiografia tedesca sull'amicizia medievale." In *Parole e realtà dell'amicizia medievale: Atti del convegno di studio svoltosi in occasione della XXII edizione del*

Premio internazionale Ascoli Piceno (Ascoli Piceno, Palazzo Dei Capitani, 2–4 Dicembre 2010). Edited by Isa Lori Sanfilippo and Antonio Rigon. Rome: Istituto storico italiano per il Medio Evo, 2012. 32–55.

Haseldine, Julian P. "Friends or Amici? Amicitia and Monsatic Letter-Writing in the Twelfth Century." In *Varieties of Friendship: Interdisciplinary Perspectives on Social Relationships*, edited by Bernadette Descharmes, Eric Anton Heuser, Caroline Krüger, and Thomas Loy, 43–58. Freunde, Gönner, Getreue. Göttingen: V&R Unipress, 2011.

– "Friends, Friendship and Networks in the Letters of Bernard of Clairvaux." *Cîteaux: Commentarii Cistercienses* 42 (2006): 243–80.

– ed. *Friendship in Medieval Europe.* Stroud, UK: Sutton, 1999.

– "Friendship, Intimacy and Corporate Networking in the Twelfth Century: The Politics of Friendship in the Letters of Peter the Venerable." *The English Historical Review* CXXVI, no. 519 (1 April 2011): 251–80.

– "Friendship Networks in Medieval Europe: New Models of a Political Relationship." *Amity: The Journal of Friendship Studies* 1 (2013): 69–88.

– "Monastic Friendship in Theory and Action in the Twelfth Century." In *Friendship in the Middle Ages and Early Modern Age: Explorations of a Fundamental Ethical Discourse.* Edited by Albrecht Classen and Marilyn Sandidge. Berlin and New York: Walter de Gruyter, 2010. 349–93.

– "Understanding the Language of Amicitia: The Friendship Circle of Peter of Celle (c. 1115–1183)." *Journal of Medieval History* 20, no. 3 (1 January 1994): 237–60.

Herzman, Ronald B. "Cannibalism and Communion in *Inferno* XXXIII." *Dante Studies* 98 (1980): 53–78.

Höfler, Otto. *Cangrande di Verona e il simbolo del cane presso i longobardi.* Translated by Roberto Pasini. Introduction by Marcello Meli. Verona: Cierre Edizioni, 1988.

Hollander, Robert. "Dante and Cino da Pistoia." *Dante Studies* 110 (1992): 201–31.

– *Dante's Epistle to Cangrande.* Ann Arbor: University of Michigan Press, 1993.

– "*Inferno* XXXIII, 37–74: Ugolino's Importunity." *Speculum* 59, no. 3 (July 1984): 549–55.

– "*Purgatorio* II: Cato's Rebuke and Dante's *Scoglio.*" *Italica* 52, no. 3 (1975): 348–63.

Holzknecht, Karl Julius. *Literary Patronage in the Middle Ages.* New York: Octagon, 1966.

Honess, Claire E. *From Florence to the Heavenly City: The Poetry of Citizenship in Dante.* Oxford: Legenda, 2006.

Houston, Jason. "Boccaccio on Friendship (Theory and Practice)." In *Reconsidering Boccaccio: Medieval Contexts and Global Intertexts.* Edited by Olivia Holmes and Dana E Stewart. Toronto: University of Toronto Press, 2018. 81–97.

Hyatte, Reginald. "Complementary Humanistic Models of Marriage and Male *Amicitia* in Fifteenth-Century Literature." In *Friendship in Medieval Europe.* Edited by Julian Haseldine. Stroud, UK: Sutton, 1999. 251–61.

– *The Arts of Friendship: The Idealization of Friendship in Medieval and Early Renaissance Literature.* Brill's Studies in Intellectual History, v. 50. Leiden and New York: Brill, 1994.

Iannucci, Amilcare A. "Casella's Song and the Tuning of the Soul." *Thought* 65, no. 1 (1990): 27–46.

Ingallinella, Laura. "The Canonization of Piccarda Donati." *Forum Italicum* 55, no. 2 (2021): 463–84.

Inglese, Giorgio. *Vita di Dante: una biografia possibile.* Roma: Carocci, 2015.

Jacoff, Rachel. "'Our Bodies, Our Selves': The Body in the *Commedia.*" In *Sparks and Seeds: Medieval Literature and Its Afterlife: Essays in Honor of John Freccero (Binghamton Medieval and Early Modern Studies 2).* Edited by Dana E. Stewart and Alison Cornish, Turnhout: Brepols, 2000. 119–38.

Jaeger, C. Stephen. *Ennobling Love: In Search of a Lost Sensibility.* University of Pennsylvania Press, 1999.

– "Friendship of Mutual Perfecting in Augustine's *Confessions* and the Failure of Classical *Amicitia.*" In *Friendship in the Middle Ages and Early Modern Age Explorations of a Fundamental Ethical Discourse.* Edited by Albrecht Classen and Marilyn Sandidge. Berlin and New York: Walter de Gruyter, 2011. 185–200.

James, Carolyn, and Bill Kent. "Renaissance Friendship: Traditional Truths, New and Dissenting Voices." In *Friendship: A History.* Edited by Barbara Caine. London: Equinox, 2009. 111–64.

Jones, Philip. *The Italian City State: From Commune to Signoria.* Oxford and New York: Clarendon Press, 1997.

Karras, Ruth Mazo. *From Boys to Men: Formations of Masculinity in Late Medieval Europe.* Philadelphia: University of Pennsylvania Press, 2003.

Keen, Catherine. *Dante and the City.* Stroud, UK: Tempus, 2003.

Kelly, Henry Angsar. "Epistle to Cangrande Updated." In *Dante Notes*, 28 September 2018. https://www.dantesociety.org/node/131. Last accessed 4 October 2021.

Kent, Dale. *Friendship, Love, and Trust in Renaissance Florence.* Cambridge, Mass: Harvard University Press, 2009.

Kircher, Timothy. *Living Well in Renaissance Italy: The Virtues of Humanism and the Irony of Leon Battista Alberti.* Tempe: Arizona Center for Medieval and Renaissance Studies, 2012.

Kirkham, Victoria. "The Classic Bond of Friendship in Boccaccio's Tito and Gisippo (*Decameron* 10.8)." In *The Classics in the Middle Ages.* Edited by Aldo S. Bernardo and Saul Levin. Binghamton: Medieval and Renaissance Texts and Studies, 1990. 223–35.

Kleinhenz, Christopher. "Adventures in Textuality: Lyric Poetry, the *Tenzone*, and Cino da Pistoia." In *Textual Cultures of Medieval Italy.* Edited by William Randolph Robins. Toronto: University of Toronto Press, 2011. 81–111.

– *The Early Italian Sonnet: The First Century (1220–1321).* Lecce: Milella, 1986.

– "Reading the *Divine Comedy*: A Textual Approach." In *Approaches to Teaching Dante's* Divine Comedy. Edited by Carole Slade. New York: Modern Language Association, 1982. 72–8.

Kumar, Akash. "'Cotale gioco mai non fue veduto': Reading *Tenzoni* in a Ludic Key." Paper presented at Modern Language Association Annual Meeting, New York, 4–7 January 2018.

Langer, Ullrich. *Perfect Friendship: Studies in Literature and Moral Philosophy from Boccaccio to Corneille.* Geneva: Droz, 1994.

Larner, John. *Italy in the Age of Dante and Petrarch, 1216–1380.* London and New York: Longman, 1980.

Le Goff, Jacques. *Intellectuals in the Middle Ages.* Translated by Teresa Lavender Fagan. Cambridge, Mass.: Blackwell, 1993.

Leach, Eleanor Winsor. "Absence and Desire in Cicero's 'De Amicitia.'" *The Classical World* 87, no. 2 (1993): 3–20.

Lefler, Nathan. *Theologizing Friendship: How* Amicitia *in the Thought of Aelred and Aquinas Inscribes the Scholastic Turn.* Cambridge: James Clarke & Co., 2015.

Leushuis, Reinier. *Le mariage et l'"amitié courtoise" dans le dialogue et le récit bref de la Renaissance.* Florence: Olschki, 2003.

Lewis, C.S. *Four Loves.* New York: Harcourt, 1960.

Liuzzo Scorpo, Antonella. *Friendship in Medieval Iberia: Historical, Legal and Literary Perspectives.* Farnham: Ashgate, 2014.

Livraghi, Leyla M.G. "Dante (e Cino) 1302–1306." *Tenzone* 13 (2012): 49–92.

Lombardi, Elena. *The Wings of the Doves: Love and Desire in Dante and Medieval Culture.* Montreal and Kingston: McGill-Queen's University Press, 2012.

Lummus, David. *The City of Poetry: Imagining the Civic Role of the Poet in Fourteenth-Century Italy.* Cambridge: Cambridge University Press, 2020.

Luzzi, Joseph. "Literary History and Individuality in the *De vulgari eloquentia.*" *Dante Studies* 116 (1998): 161–88.

Malato, Enrico. *Dante e Guido Cavalcanti: Il dissidio per la «Vita Nuova» e il "disdegno" di Guido.* Rome: Salerno, 1997.

Maldina, Nicolò. "A Classicising Friar in Dante's Florence: Servasanto Da Faenza, Dante and the Ethics of Friendship." In *Ethics, Politics and Justice in Dante.* Edited by Giulia Gaimari and Catherine Keen. London: University College London Press, 2019. 30–45.

Marchi, Gian Paolo. "'Valore e cortesia': l'immagine di Verona e della corte scaligera nella letteratura e nella memoria storica." In *Gli Scaligeri, 1277–1387.* Edited by Gian Maria Varanini. Verona: Mondadori, 1988. 485–96.

Margalit, Avishai. *The Ethics of Memory.* Cambridge, MA: Harvard University Press, 2002.

Margueron, Claude. "La notion d'amitié chez Guittone d'Arezzo et ses sources classiques." *Lettere Italiane* 11, no. 4 (1959): 411–31.

Marini, Paola, Ettore Napione, and Gian Maria Varanini, eds. *Cangrande della Scala: La morte e il corredo di un principe nel medioevo europeo.* Venice: Marsilio, 2004.

Marrani, Giuseppe. "Ai margini della «Vita Nova»: Ancora per Cino 'imitatore' di Dante." In *La Lirica Romanza Del Medioevo: Storia, Tradizione, Interpretazioni.* Edited by Furio Brugnolo and Francesca Gambino. Padua: Unipress, 2009. 757–76.

Marti, Mario. *Poeti del Dolce stil nuovo.* Florence: Le Monnier, 1969.

– "Stil Nuovo." In *Enciclopedia Dantesca.* Rome: Treccani, 1970. https://www.treccani.it/enciclopedia/stil-nuovo_(Enciclopedia-Dantesca)/. Last accessed 4 October 2021.

– "Sulla genesi del realismo dantesco." In *Realismo dantesco e altri studi.* Milan and Naples: Ricciardi, 1961. 1–32.

Martinez, Ronald L. "Guido Cavalcanti's 'Una figura della donna mia' and the Specter of Idolatry Haunting the Stilnovo." *Exemplaria* 15, no. 2 (2003): 297–324.

Masciandaro, Franco. *The Stranger as Friend: The Poetics of Friendship in Homer, Dante, and Boccaccio.* Florence: Firenze University Press, 2013.

Mazzaro, Jerome. "From Fin Amour to Friendship: Dante's Transformation." In *The Olde Daunce: Love, Friendship, Sex, and Marriage in The Medieval World.* Edited by Robert R. Edwards and Stephen Spector. Albany: State University of New York Press, 1991. 121–37.

Mazzei, Vincenzo. *Gli amici di Dante nella* Divina Commedia. Milan: Editrice Nuovi Autori, 1987.

Mazzotta, Giuseppe. "The Language of Poetry in the *Vita Nuova*." *Rivista di studi italiani* 1 (1983): 1–16.

McCue Gill, Amyrose, and Sarah Rolfe Prodan, eds. *Friendship and Sociability in Premodern Europe: Contexts, Concepts, and Expressions.* Toronto: Centre for Reformation and Renaissance Studies, 2014.

McEvoy, James. "Notes on the Prologue of St. Aelred of Rievaulx's 'De Spirituali Amicitia,' with a Translation." *Traditio* 37 (1981): 396–411.

– "The Theory of Friendship in the Latin Middle Ages: Hermeneutics, Contextualisation and the Transmission and Reception of Ancient Texts and Ideas, from c. AD 350 to c. 1500." In *Friendship in Medieval Europe.* Edited by Julian Haseldine. Stroud, UK: Sutton, 1999. 3–44.

McGuire, Brian Patrick. *Friendship & Community: The Monastic Experience, 350–1250.* 2nd ed. Ithaca: Cornell University Press, 1988.

McLean, Paul D. *The Art of the Network: Strategic Interaction and Patronage in Renaissance Florence.* Durham, NC: Duke University Press, 2007.

McLoughlin, John. "*Amicitia* in Practice: John of Salisbury (c. 1120–1180) and His Circle." In *England in the Twelfth Century: Proceedings of the 1988 Harlaxton Symposium.* Edited by Daniel Williams. Woodbridge, UK: Boydell, 1990. 165–81.

Mews, Constant J. "Cicero and the Boundaries of Friendship in the Twelfth Century." *Viator – Medieval and Renaissance Studies* 38, no. 2 (2007): 369–84.

Mews, Constant J., and Neville Chiavaroli. "The Latin West." In *Friendship: A History.* Edited by Barbara Caine. London: Equinox, 2009. 73–110.

Milani, Giuliano. *Bologna.* Spoleto: Fondazione Centro italiano di studi sull'alto Medioevo, 2012.

Milner, Stephen J. "Communication, Consensus and Conflict: Rhetorical Precepts, the *Ars concionandi*, and Social Ordering in Late Medieval Italy." In *The Rhetoric of Cicero in Its Medieval and Early Renaissance Commentary Tradition.* Edited by Virginia Cox and John O Ward. Leiden and Boston: Brill, 2011. 365–401.

– "Exile, Rhetoric, and the Limits of Civic Republican Discourse." In *At the Margins: Minority Groups in Pre-Modern Italy.* Edited by Stephen J. Milner. Minneapolis: University of Minnesota Press, 2005. 162–91.

Modesto, Filippa. *Dante's Idea of Friendship: The Transformation of a Classical Concept.* Toronto: University of Toronto Press, 2015.

Moore, Samuel. "General Aspects of Literary Patronage in the Middle Ages." *The Library* 4, no. 16, 3rd series (1913): 369–92.

Mullett, Margaret. "Power, Relations and Networks in Medieval Europe: Introduction." *Revue Belge de Philologie et d'Histoire* 83, no. 2 (2005): 255–9.

Muresu, Gabriele. "Forese e la gola (*Purg.* XXIII)." *L'Alighieri: Rassegna bibliografica dantesca* 29 (2007): 5–30.

– *I ladri di malebolge: Saggi di semantica dantesca.* Rome: Bulzoni, 1990.

Murphy, James Jerome. *Rhetoric in the Middle Ages: A History of the Rhetorical Theory from Saint Augustine to the Renaissance.* Berkeley: University of California Press, 1974.

Najemy, John M. *Between Friends: Discourses of Power and Desire in the Machiavelli-Vettori Letters of 1513–1515.* Princeton: Princeton University Press, 1993.

Nardi, Bruno. *Il punto sull'epistola a Cangrande.* Florence: Le Monnier, 1960.

Nederman, Cary J. "Friendship in Public Life during the Twelfth Century: Theory and Practice in the Writings of John of Salisbury." *Viator* 38, no. 2 (1 January 2007): 385–97.

Nehamas, Alexander. *On Friendship.* New York: Basic Books, 2016.

– "The Good of Friendship." *Proceedings of the Aristotelian Society* 110 (2010): 267–94.

Nussbaum, Martha C. "Beatrice's 'Dante': Loving the Individual?" *Apeiron: A Journal for Ancient Philosophy and Science* 26, no. 3–4 (1993): 161–78.

Pangle, Lorraine Smith. *Aristotle and the Philosophy of Friendship.* Cambridge: Cambridge University Press, 2002.

Pasquini, Emilio. "Amica." In *Enciclopedia Dantesca.* Rome: Treccani, 1970. https://www.treccani.it/enciclopedia/amica_(Enciclopedia-Dantesca)/. Last accessed 4 October 2021.

– "Amicizia." In *Enciclopedia Dantesca.* Rome: Treccani, 1970. https://www.treccani.it/enciclopedia/amicizia_(Enciclopedia-Dantesca)/. Last accessed 4 October 2021.

– "Amico." In *Enciclopedia Dantesca.* Rome: Treccani, 1970. https://www.treccani.it/enciclopedia/amico_(Enciclopedia-Dantesca)/. Last accessed 4 October 2021.

– "Amistà." In *Enciclopedia Dantesca.* Rome: Treccani, 1970. https://www.treccani.it/enciclopedia/amista_(Enciclopedia-Dantesca)/. Last accessed 4 October 2021.

– "Amistanza." In *Enciclopedia Dantesca.* Rome: Treccani, 1970. https://www.treccani.it/enciclopedia/amistanza_(Enciclopedia-Dantesca)/. Last accessed 4 October 2021.

– "Concezione e lessico dell'amicizia fra Stilnovo e 'Commedia.'" In *Parole e realtà dell'amicizia medievale: Atti del convegno di studio svoltosi in occasione della XXII edizione del Premio internazionale Ascoli Piceno (Ascoli Piceno, Palazzo Dei Capitani, 2–4 Dicembre 2010).* Edited by Isa Lori Sanfilippo and Antonio Rigon, 145–54. Rome: Istituto storico italiano per il Medio Evo, 2012.

– "Dante e Bologna." *Strenna storica bolognese*, no. 30 (1980): 277–96.

– "Dante e lo Studio." In *Storia illustrata di Bologna* 4/VI. San Marino: AIEP, 1988. 61–80.

Pegoretti, Anna. "La suora mancata: Piccarda." In *Nel Duecento di Dante: I personaggi.* Edited by Franco Suitner. Florence: Le Lettere, 2020. 19–36.

Pellegrini, Luigi. *L' incontro tra due invenzioni medievali: università e ordini mendicanti.* Naples: Liguori Editore, 2003.

Pertile, Lino. "Canto XXIV: Of Poetry and Politics." In *Lectura Dantis: Purgatorio.* Edited by Allen Mandelbaum, Anthony Oldcorn, and Charles Ross. Berkeley and Los Angeles: University of California Press, 2008. 262–76.

Peters, Edward. "Human Diversity and Civil Society in Paradiso VIII." *Dante Studies* 109 (1991): 51–70.

Petrocchi, Giorgio. *Vita di Dante.* Rome and Bari: Laterza, 1984.

Phillips-Robins, Helena. *Liturgical Song and Practice in Dante's* Commedia. Notre Dame: University of Notre Dame Press, 2021.

Picone, Michelangelo. "Dante e Cino: Una lunga amicizia. Prima parte: I tempi della 'Vita Nova'." *Dante: Rivista internazionale di studi su Dante Alighieri* 1 (2004): 39–53.

Pierson, Inga. "Piccarda's Weakness: Reflections on Freedom, Force, and Femininity in Dante's Paradiso." *Speculum* 94, no. 1 (2019): 68–95.

Placidi, Andrea. "Dante and Cangrade." In *Dante Notes.* 25 November 2017. https://www.dantesociety.org/publicationsdante-notes/dante-and-cangrade. Last accessed 4 October 2021.

Raffa, Guy P. "A Beautiful Friendship: Dante and Vergil in the Commedia." *MLN* 127, no. 1 (2012): S72–80.

Rigoli, Paolo. "L'esibizione del potere. Curie e feste scaligere nelle fonti cronistiche." In *Gli Scaligeri, 1277–1387.* Edited by Gian Maria Varanini. Verona: Mondadori, 1988. 149–56.

Rosier-Catach, Irène. "'Solo all'uomo fu dato di parlare': Dante, gli angeli e gli animali." *Rivista di filosofia neo-scolastica* 98, no. 3 (2006): 435–65.

Russo, Vittorio. "*Pg* XXIII: Forese, o la maschera del discorso." *MLN* 94, no. 1 (1979): 113–36.

Sanfilippo, Isa Lori, and Antonio Rigon, eds. In *Parole e realtà dell'amicizia medievale: Atti del convegno di studio svoltosi in occasione della XXII edizione del Premio internazionale Ascoli Piceno (Ascoli Piceno, Palazzo Dei Capitani, 2–4 Dicembre 2010).* Rome: Istituto storico italiano per il Medio Evo, 2012.

Santagata, Marco. *Dante: The Story of His Life.* Translated by Richard Dixon. Cambridge, Mass.: The Belknap Press of Harvard University Press, 2016.

Santangelo, Salvatore. *Le tenzioni poetiche nella letteratura italiana degli origini.* Florence: Olschki, 1928.

Savarese, Gennaro. *Una proposta per Forese, e altri studi su Dante.* Rome: Bulzoni, 1992.

Schwartz, Daniel. *Aquinas on Friendship.* Oxford: Oxford University Press, 2007.

Schawrtz Porzecanski, Daniel. "Aquinas on Concord: 'Concord Is a Union of Wills, Not of Opinions.'" *The Review of Metaphysics* 57, no. 1 (2003): 25–42.

Schwarzenbach, Sibyl A. "On Civic Friendship." *Ethics* 107, no. 1 (1996): 97–128.

Scott, John. "Cino da Pistoia and Dante." In *Flinders Dante Conferences (2002, 2004).* Edited by Margaret Anne Baker, Flavia Coassin, and Diana Glenn. Adelaide: Lythrum Press, 2005. 26–37.

Sebastio, Leonardo. "Da 'Guido i' vorrei' alla *Commedia.* Un tema dantesco: L'amicizia." *Critica Letteraria* 23 (1995): 347–63.

Sère, Bénédicte. *Penser l'amitié au Moyen Âge: Étude historique des commentaires sur les Livres VIII et IX de l'Éthique à Nicomaque (XIIIe-XVe siècle).* Turnhout: Brepols, 2007.

Shapiro, Marianne. *De Vulgari Eloquentia, Dante's Book of Exile.* Lincoln: University of Nebraska Press, 1990.

Sharp, Ronald A. *Friendship and Literature: Spirit and Form.* Durham, NC: Duke University Press, 1986.

Sherberg, Michael. *The Governance of Friendship: Law and Gender in the Decameron.* Columbus: The Ohio State University Press, 2011.

Singleton, Charles. *An Essay on the* Vita Nuova. Cambridge, Mass: Harvard University Press, 1949.

Soskice, Janet Martin. *The Kindness of God: Metaphor, Gender, and Religious Language.* Oxford: Oxford University Press, 2007.

Steinberg, Justin. *Accounting for Dante: Urban Readers and Writers in Late Medieval Italy.* Notre Dame: University of Notre Dame Press, 2007.

Stern-Gillet, Suzanne. *Aristotle's Philosophy of Friendship.* Albany: State University of New York Press, 1995.

Swartz, David. *Culture and Power: The Sociology of Pierre Bourdieu.* Chicago: University of Chicago Press, 1997.

Tanturli, Giuliano. "Guido Cavalcanti contro Dante." In *Le tradizioni del testo: Studi di letteratura italiana offerti a Domenico De Robertis.* Edited by Franco Gavazzeni and Guglielmo Gorni. Milan and Naples: Ricciardi, 1993. 3–13.

Tavoni, Mirko. Introduction to *De vulgari eloquentia.* Edited by Mirko Tavoni. In Dante Alighieri, *Opere. Volume primo: Rime, Vita Nova, De vulgari eloquentia.* Edited by Claudio Giunta, Guglielmo Gorni, and Mirko Tavoni, 1067–116. Milano: Mondadori, 2011.

Took, John. "'S'io m'intuassi, come tu t'inmii' (*Par.*, IX. 81): Patterns of Collective Being in Dante." *The Modern Language Review* 101, no. 2 (2006): 402–13.

Usher, Jonathan. "'Più di mille': Crowd Control in the *Commedia.*" In *Word and Drama in Dante.* Edited by John C. Barnes and Jennifer Petrie. Dublin: Academic Press, 1993. 55–71.

Varanini, Gian Maria. "Della Scala, Cangrande." In *Dizionario Biografico degli italiani.* Rome: Treccani, 2010. https://www.treccani.it/enciclopedia/cangrande-della-scala_(Dizionario-Biografico).– ed. *Gli Scaligeri, 1277–1387.* Verona: Mondadori, 1988.

– "Gli Scaligeri, il ceto dirigente veronese, l'*élite* internazionale." In *Gli Scaligeri, 1277–1387.* Edited by Gian Maria Varanini. Verona: Mondadori, 1988. 113–24.

– "La morte di Cangrande della Scala. Strategie di comunicazione intorno al cadavere." In *Cangrande della Scala: La morte e il corredo di un principe nel medioevo europeo.* Edited by Paola Marini, Ettore Napione, and Gian Maria Varanini. Venice: Marsilio, 2004. 11–21.

– "Sul dominio scaligero a Vicenza (1312–1387)." In *Gli Scaligeri, 1277–1387.* Edited by Gian Maria Varanini. Verona: Mondadori, 1988. 35–40.

Vergani, Luisa. "Dante e Verona." *Italica* 43, no. 1 (1966): 32–7.

Webb, Heather. *Dante's Persons: An Ethics of the Transhuman.* Oxford: Oxford University Press, 2016.

– "Postures of Penitence in Dante's Purgatorio." *Dante Studies* 131 (2013): 219–36.

West, Simon. "A Short-Lived Enchantment: Some Observations on the Sonnet Exchange Between Dante and Cavalcanti." In *Flinders Dante Conferences 2002 & 2004.* Edited by Margaret Anne Baker, Flavia Coassin, and Diana Glenn. Adelaide: Lythrum Press, 2005. 17–25.

White, Carolinne. *Christian Friendship in the Fourth Century.* Cambridge: Cambridge University Press, 1992.

Wojciehowski, Hannah Chapelle. "Francis Petrarch: First Modern Friend." *Texas Studies in Literature and Language* 47, no. 4 (2005): 269–98.

– "Petrarch and His Friends." In *The Cambridge Companion to Petrarch.* Edited by Albert Russell Ascoli and Unn Falkeid. Cambridge: Cambridge University Press, 2015. 26–35.

Zaccagnini, Guido. *I rimatori pistoiesi dei secoli XIII e XIV.* Pistoia: Tipografia sinibuldiana, 1907.

– *La vita dei maestri e degli scolari nello Studio di Bologna nei secoli XIII e XIV.* Geneva: Olschki, 1926.

Zaccarello, Michelangelo. "L'uovo o la gallina? *Purg.* XXIII e la tenzone di Dante e Forese Donati." *L'Alighieri: Rassegna bibliografica dantesca* 44, no. 22 (2003): 5–26.

Zak, Gur. "'Soft Hearts': Virtue, Vulnerability, and Community in Petrarch's Letter-Collections." *Petrarchesca* 9 (2021): 125–36.

Ziolkowski, Jan M. "Twelfth-Century Understandings and Adaptations of Ancient Friendship." In *Mediaeval Antiquity.* Edited by Andries Welkenhuysen, Herman Braet, and Werner Verbeke. Leuven: Leuven University Press, 1995. 59–81.

Zorzi, Andrea. *Le signorie cittadine in Italia (secoli XII–XV).* Milan: Mondadori, 2010.

Index